The Americans in Brittany - 1944
THE BATTLE FOR BREST

by Jonathan Gawne

*This book is dedicated to First Lieutenant John O. Gawne
and his comrades of the 8th Infantry Division*

(National Archives)

Histoire & Collections

CONTENTS

PREFACE

"The siege of Brest probably never will receive the world-wide recognition it rightfully deserves. Tougher than Caen, it is said to have been one of the hardest battles fought by American infantry in Europe since 1918."

Yank Magazine, 1944

Growing up as the son of a Brittany veteran, I couldn't brag about my dad having been at D-Day, Bastogne, or Guadalcanal. Very few people even knew that any fighting had taken place in Brittany, let alone knew anything about it. Books on the subject were nonexistent (and just about still are). It was not until I was much older that I was able to look beyond the published books about WW2.

My father told me the occasional war story, but for the most part he had repressed his time spent in the Army and was unable to recall much of it. I've found this common among combat vets. A planned family trip to France proved a good excuse to visit the U.S. National Archives and Records Administration, in hopes of figuring out something about where my dad had served in the war as an infantry officer. With some documents from his regiment in hand, my father and I, more or less, traveled from his landing at Utah Beach on 4 July 1944, down the Cotentin Peninsula, across Brittany, into Brest, and down to the Crozon Peninsula. Poking about the farm of Joseph Lavanant we discovered the spot where my dad had been shot roughly 40 years before. As he stood there in the field he said, "This is where it happened. I don't really remember it too much, but I can feel it in my bones. This is the place."

In 1986 my father passed away; the cancer going undiagnosed until too late due to the scar tissue left on his liver by the bullets from the Crozon. I suppose I should have been glad for it, after all he did live a good long life after the war (even if he was missing half his liver - which by the way grew back - and most of the ribs on his left side).

I think it's important that I mention my connection to the campaign as some may feel it distorts my view of the battle. I grew up reading that the Brittany campaign was "a sideshow," "unnecessary," and "a waste of effort." It would be wrong not to consider I might want to change that for the sake of my father and his men. But, as a matter of fact, I started this book under the impression that it really wasn't an important event in the war and the small unit actions were of themselves the interesting part. I pride myself on reporting only what I am fairly sure of, so if it comes out of this book that Brittany played a more important role

than you may have thought, those are the facts speaking - not a son trying to reinvent his father's war. I don't have to do that. My father served in the Pacific as an enlisted man in the Infantry. In Europe he was an infantry platoon leader (the toughest job in the Army) and later company commander. He did his part, tried to get as many men home safely (both Americans and Germans I might add), and won two Bronze Stars for valor; no easy feat in that war. I don't have to rewrite history, it speaks for itself.

My search to understand my father's experience in WW2 led me down many strange paths, but none stranger than finding that people seemed to enjoy my writing. When the chance came to write on Brittany I grabbed it and this book is the result. With any luck other children of Brittany veterans will have a chance to read a little about what their fathers did in the great World War Two.

In talking to veterans of the 8th Infantry Division I discovered something especially interesting. The unit fought in Normandy before, and in the Hürtgen Forest after Brittany. When questioned as to what was the toughest battle most veterans immediately said the Hürtgen Forest. When asked why, the veterans said it was because of the extreme cold and bad weather they were subjected to. When pressed for what was the toughest fight, excluding weather conditions, the majority said Brittany. As one said, *"Those German paratroopers were darn good soldiers."*

A few notes about this book: after much thought it seemed the best way to organize it was not chronologically, but geographically and by unit. This way you can follow the path of the 6th Armored Division through Brittany without having to jump north to Task Force A, then south to Rennes, and back north again to Saint-Malo. The only place it gets confusing is when dealing with the Ranger battalions. They were shuttled between larger units and appear in a few different chapters. There are times in the text where it does not seem like much fighting is going on. Don't let that fool you. Every day where two armies are in contact something is happening. Patrols are sent out, snipers watch for targets, artillery and mortars shell positions, and men are wounded and killed. For space reasons I have had to focus on the major actions of the campaign. I apologize to soldiers involved in the smaller actions on the "quiet" days because their contributions were just as important as if they had fought at Hill 154, Ft. Montbarey, or at the city wall. Even the quietest day becomes important when someone is shooting at you.

For the notation of military units I have adopted a modern shorthand method of referring to them. Com-

pany A of the 116th Infantry Regiment is called A/116th. The First Battalion of the 38th Infantry Regiment is 1/38th. Company D of the 709th Tank Battalion is D/709th. If it's a letter to the left of the slash it is either a company, battery or troop; a number to the left indicates a battalion. The number to the right of the slash is the parent organization, either a battalion or regiment.

I have tried to use secondary sources only as clues to guide me to original unit records and published unit histories. Most of the records are available through various government sources. I have attempted to talk to as many veterans of Brittany as possible, but carefully also checked their testimony against the official records. One of the most interesting things I discovered on my many trips to the National Archives was a mysterious handwritten notation on one after action report. It read, "Place little faith in statements of generals and colonels as to specific actions." I am not exactly sure what it referred to, but they are wise words for any historian.

I had originally planned to write only about the American involvement in the fighting. I quickly found this was impossible without dealing with the French Resistance, or the opposing German forces. Both of these subjects deserve more attention, but my space is limited. Sadly, it has been difficult finding records of the German units in Brittany. Many of the German troops seem to have destroyed their files when capture was imminent.

The quest for photos of Brittany has been a tough one because the official coverage was very poor. Unless noted, all photographs in this book are from the various WW2 Army, Navy and Air Force collections in the National Archives. The majority of Signal Corps photos from Brittany consist of studies of ruined buildings taken after the fighting had ceased. Thus my grateful thanks go out to those veterans, families and collectors who supplied me with copies of their own personal photographs.

And finally, I know I am in for some complaints from WW2 vets when they see I did not cover their specific actions. It was a question of space and documentation. With such limited space I was only able to mention the main actions or events that were well-documented. The Brittany campaign covered hundreds of square miles and almost two months of time. My aim was not to document every single action, but to provide an overview of the fighting and attempt to give some idea of what it was like.

Jonathan Gawne
Massachusetts, 1999

Chapter 1

BRITTANY

The French province of Brittany sticks out into the Atlantic like a finger pointing to the west. Just under the tip is the port of Brest. During WW2 Brest was the largest naval facility and the second largest port in France.

It was no surprise that when the Germans occupied France in 1940 they took over the naval base at Brest and used it to support their own campaign in the Atlantic. The other ports of Brittany, Lorient, Saint-Nazaire and Saint-Malo were also put to good use by the occupying Germans. When drawing up plans to liberate France in 1944, these ports would be considered vital to the logistical support of the American Army and would bring the fighting deep into Brittany.

Brittany is a curious part of France. Surrounded by the sea on three sides, it was colonized by Celts fleeing Anglo-Saxon rule in Britain. The native language, Breton, bears a greater similarity to English than to French. For a great many years Brittany was a country with its own royalty, language, customs and culture. It became part of France in 1532 when the last Duchess, Anne of Brittany, gave the territory to the King of France. As the years passed, France attempted to stamp out the last vestiges of Breton nationality and language. The native Bretons were enlisted in the French Navy, and slowly the land joined the nation of France, in feeling as well as law.

Brittany has never quite become "just part of France." Fiercely proud of their heritage, the Bretons have always known they were something special. They continued to pass down the ancient words and customs even when it was forbidden. A part of the Bretons has always wanted to break free from France and once again rule their own land. This movement continues, although in a weaker form, to this day. However, it was in World War Two that Brittany would find itself drawn closest to the French nation.

Brest

The port of Brest is divided into two sections by the Penfeld River. To the east is the actual city of Brest, while across the Penfeld River to the west is the city of Recouvrance. A massive stone wall had been constructed around the main section of the old city and divided the old inner city from the newer construction outside. The Bay of Brest (Rade de Brest) was formed by the Crozon Peninsula branching up from the south. The narrow inlet to the bay was known as the Channel of Brest (Goulet de Brest).

The city of Brest had long been a military stronghold. All along the seaward approaches to Brest, both on the mainland and the Crozon,

"He is not the Duke of Brittany who is not the Lord of Brest"

Old French axiom

forts and strongpoints had been built up over the years. The basis for the modern forts had originally been constructed by Vauban in the 17th century. Never had an enemy force breached its defenses. In 1694 both the British and Dutch fleets were destroyed trying to take Brest. In 1794 the British badly damaged the French fleet off the Brittany coast, but were unable to capture the port.

Over the years the forts had been improved and modernized with more tunnels, electricity, modern bunkers and better guns. The series of small forts and strongpoints around the city had been constructed on the best possible terrain. In WW2 the entire area was a well-fortified complex with over 75 major defensive positions outside the city.

Brest in World War One

The Americans first came to Brittany in World War One. They needed Atlantic ports to land and supply their armies. The British were already using the French ports further up the coast, so it was decided to use the Brittany facilities to bring Uncle Sam into the fight. The Brittany ports were far from the front lines, and so had not been as heavily utilized as those further east. It was thought that bringing the green American troops onto the continent so far from the fighting would allow them a chance to recover from their ocean voyage, reorganize, and find training areas where they could brush up on the latest in trench warfare techniques.

The first American troops to land in France arrived at Saint-Nazaire on 16 June 1917. Eventually Saint-Nazaire would host a reception camp for 16,000 men. Over 3,000 American stevedores, mostly black, unloaded the ships that docked there. However, the larger city of Brest soon developed into the main port of debarkation for troops shipped to France on American ships. Many American soldiers were shipped to England on British ships during the manpower crisis of 1918, but they would return to the States through Brittany. Brest would also become the home port for over 30 American destroyers and a host of smaller vessels involved in protecting the convoys from German submarines. The American Army facilities in the Brest area were called "Base Section Number 5."

Pontanezen Barracks, to the north of Brest, had been constructed to house roughly 1,500 men during Napoleon's time. In the years 1917-1918 it would see a staggering number of American soldiers pass

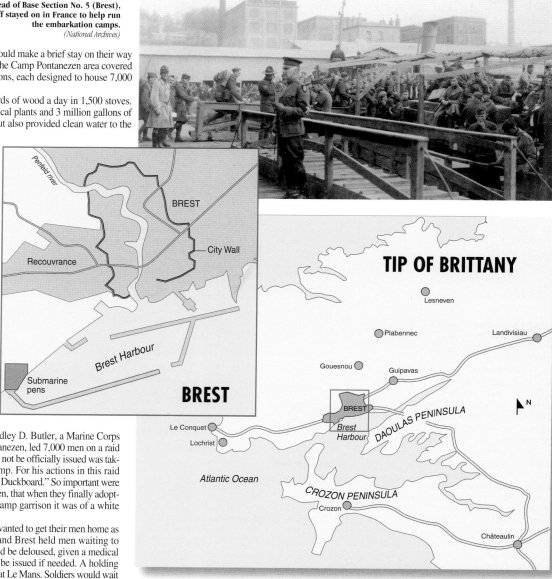

through it. In 1919 even more men would make a brief stay on their way back across the Atlantic. At its peak the Camp Pontanezen area covered 1,700 acres, divided up into 15 sections, each designed to house 7,000 men.

Camp Pontanezen burned 250 cords of wood a day in 1,500 stoves. Electricity was provided by 15 electrical plants and 3 million gallons of water supplied not only the troops, but also provided clean water to the civilian areas of Brest. 15,000 permanent troops, including 1,400 clerks, needed 900 trucks to keep the barracks functioning. Each camp section had 100 cooks. They were scheduled to feed their 7,000 man section in just one hour. To keep the food palatable the cooks at Pontanezen had a weekly contest to see which was the best cooking section in the camp. The winners got to fly a special banner to indicate their status and, more importantly, got a week's leave at Saint-Malo.

There were over 75 miles of boardwalk in the camp. These boards had an unusual history. The roads in the Pontanezen area had degraded to rivers of thick mud with the heavy military traffic. The quartermasters in Brest had an enormous store of duckboards, designed to be laid at the bottom of a trench to keep the men out of the mud, but they refused to issue any to the camp. Finally, Brigadier General Smedley D. Butler, a Marine Corps officer and commander of Camp Pontanezen, led 7,000 men on a raid against the quartermasters. What would not be officially issued was taken as the men stormed the supply dump. For his actions in this raid Smedley earned the nickname "General Duckboard." So important were the duckboards to the men at Pontanezen, that when they finally adopted a shoulder sleeve insignia for the camp garrison it was of a white duckboard on a red background.

After the Armistice the Americans wanted to get their men home as fast as possible. Both Saint-Nazaire and Brest held men waiting to embark for the States. There they would be deloused, given a medical inspection, and new equipment would be issued if needed. A holding camp for 250,000 men was constructed at Le Mans. Soldiers would wait in Le Mans until space became available for them at either of the two ports, then they would be fed into the line that would end with them boarding a ship for home. As a reminder of the Great War, the main square of Brest was renamed "Place President Woodrow Wilson" after the American president in charge during the war. In the post-WW1 years Camp Pon-

tanezen would slowly be dismantled and revert to its prewar size of a few large barracks buildings.

German Occupation

When the Americans finally departed Brittany, after WW1, they left behind many improved and modernized facilities. The French Navy was particularly pleased at the construction the Americans had put into the port and made Brest the largest naval base in France. During the 1940 invasion of France most of the heavy fighting took place further to the east, but there was some scattered fighting along the route the Germans took to the Atlantic. On 22 June 1940, the day France surrendered, a final battle was fought at Lorient. The armistice

agreement gave control of the coastal areas to the Germans. When the German occupiers moved into the Brittany region they were delighted with the French naval facilities and immediately began to move into their bases on the Atlantic.

The Germans wanted to use the Brittany ports as bases for their submarines. Before they had these Atlantic ports German subs were forced to make a long passage out of the Baltic and around England. The subs were very vulnerable during this voyage through the English Channel, so the Brittany ports were an invaluable boost to the German sub crews. It was only after they had started using the French ports that the German subs began to come close to controlling the Atlantic.

Some of the French facilities were usable as is, other construction was started from scratch. The French ports of Brest, Lorient, Saint-Nazaire, La Pallice (La Rochelle), and Bordeaux were selected to become the new home of the German submarine fleet. The construction of submarine facilities was given the highest priority. The Germans needed to control the Atlantic through submarine warfare if they were to destroy English supply lines and keep the US Army from crossing to Europe. These submarine bases were of the utmost importance to the overall German strategy and no effort was spared to construct modern, secure shelters. So important were the sub pens to the Germans, at the start of 1944 they ranked third in importance of construction priorities, behind only the Atlantic wall and the V-weapon launching sites.

Submarine pens served not only to protect the vessels from air attack, but also as a place to repair them around the clock. Many of the sub pens were constructed so that the water could be pumped out and the sub worked on in dry dock. Keeping the subs out of sight was also important, so their movements could not be spotted by local civilians or aerial reconnaissance. Once the sub was inside a slip, armored metal doors, or shutters, were used to shut off the seaward entrance.

The reinforced concrete roofs of the submarine bunkers were between 2.5 and 3.5 meters thick. In some special areas they could be up to 6 meters thick. They were cleverly engineered to withstand bomb blasts by using concrete castings on top to detonate the bombs, then had open cavities beneath to contain the explosion. In an effort to penetrate these defenses a British specialty bomb nicknamed "Tallboy" was developed. It was a 12,000 pound bomb designed to be dropped from a very high altitude. Originally the designer planned to drop them next to the bunkers and allow the resulting underground explosion to weaken the structure, but the British Air Force insisted upon trying to penetrate the bunkers with a direct hit. Three different times the specialty flyers of Squadron 617 ("The Dam Busters") dropped Tallboys on the Brest sub pens. Out of these three raids nine Tallboys actually hit the bunker roof. Only five of these penetrated the reinforced ceiling, but the result-

ing explosion beneath did not seem to cause as much damage as was hoped.

In Brest the Germans constructed a 15-berth sub pen, 10 of the berths being able to function as dry docks. So elaborate was the facility that three electrical generators were installed: each was capable of powering the base by itself. Brest would become home to both the 1st and 9th U-boat flotillas. On D-day there were 17 submarines at Brest. After the Americans had broken out of Normandy the order was given to shift the subs to new bases in Norway, to prevent their capture by the Allies. The last U-boat to leave Brest was the U-256 which finally left port on 3 Sept. 1944. It left behind the U-415 which had struck a mine and was not considered worth repairing. During the coming year the other German held Brittany ports would see

OPERATION HANDS UP

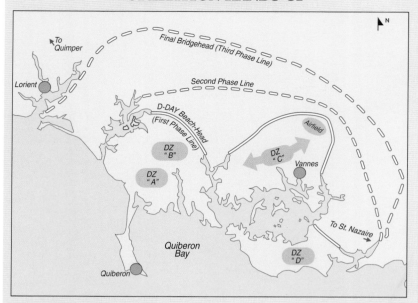

The Americans hoped that they would be able to attack directly across country to capture the Quiberon Bay region, but so vital was this area to their plans that nothing was to be left to chance. The Navy claimed that unless the area was captured by 1 Sept. 1944 the fall weather would make it impossible to tow the heavy port components from England. A combined air and sea operation was developed so that if the Americans were on a line roughly Saint-Malo-Rennes-Laval and still facing tough opposition, Quiberon Bay could be quickly captured and construction started.

The "Operation Hands Up" plan called for an air landing under Lt. General "Boy" Browning with the British 1st Airborne Division and 1st Polish Parachute Brigade, combined with a sea landing by the Special Service Brigade. This would be followed by bringing in the British 52nd Division by air. The force planned to hold out for 14 days, at which time the Third Army should have been able to link up with them. Once the Americans reached the area the British troops were to be sent back to their own sector.

Naval support for Hands Up would include H.M.S. Rodney, H.M.S. Roberts, three cruisers, three destroyers and two frigates. Their primary job was to neutralize shore batteries. There would also be eight antisubmarine escorts, along with various landing craft and transport ships.

At midnight, pathfinders of the 1st Para Division and 1st Polish Brigade were to land and mark the drop zones. The schedule would then be:
— 0100 hrs.- two parachute brigades of the 1st A/B Div. and 1st Polish Para Brigade were to be dropped

— 0600 hrs.- the naval convoy arrives offshore
— 0700 hrs.- the 1st glider echelon of the 1st Airlanding Brigade and advance HQ A/B troops land
— 1400 hrs. - The following units arrive by air:
2nd glider echelon and U.S. 878th Airborne Engineer Aviation Bn.
2nd glider lift of 1 A/B Div.
1st glider lift of Polish Para Brigade
Vannes Airfield Control Advance Party
The 878th Aviation Engineers were to put the airfield at Vannes into operation as soon as possible (hopefully D +2), and construct two additional strips in the area.

The German coastal artillery positions on Belle-île were to be captured by combined air/sea assault. Shortly after dawn a parachute landing by the 1st Para Regt. on the eastern half of the island would seize the high ground and cut the island in half. Then an amphibious assault by a regiment from the 28th U.S. Infantry Division on the beaches would capture the coastal artillery guns. Following up as reinforcements from the sea would be the American 80th Infantry Division.

Operation Hands Up was never put into action because the American forces passed through the Rennes region without meeting heavy German resistance. By the time the Americans had reached the Quiberon Bay area the decision was made to push for the northern channel port of Le Havre, which was much closer to the main fighting in Eastern France.

However, the fact that such an operation was seriously considered indicates how much the Allies had wanted Quiberon Bay.

The beaches in Brittany were mined and covered with obstacles just the same as those in Normandy. The Germans were always on the alert for a possible amphibious landing. Some Allied commanders considered landing in Brittany and using the region as the starting place for the liberation of France. *(National Archives)*

submarines no longer venturing forth to control the Atlantic, but quietly slipping in and out at night, making regular runs to keep them in contact with the Fatherland.

Saint-Nazaire

In March 1942 Saint-Nazaire was the site of a British Commando raid named Operation Chariot. This was an attempt to ram an explosive laden ship into the locks, thus denying the Germans the port facilities needed for larger ships to operate in the Atlantic. A handful of other commando raids ventured into Brittany before D-day, most were minor in nature to force the Germans to leave valuable troops guarding Brittany. In 1943 the American 29th Ranger Battalion raided a radar station on the small island of Ouessant. Their mission was to leave American equipment behind so the Germans would feel they had to move more men into Brittany to defend against the new American Ranger raids, or a possible full-scale landing.

The Allies periodically considered landing in Brittany and using the area as the first step for the liberation of France. Some generals felt that the province could be captured and securely defended while more troops poured in. Others felt that the Germans would be able to build impregnable defenses along the base of the peninsula sealing off the invading force. The Germans continually added to the defenses around the Brittany ports, making sure they could be defended from an attack by land as well as from the sea. In January 1944 the German high command designated all the ports along the Atlantic as fortresses, to be defended and held to the last man. With manpower losses in Russia, German soldiers were continuously transferred out of France. To replace them the Germans relied more and more on second-rate units or Russian POWs who had volunteered to help the Germans.

The FFI and Allied Special Units

No history of the war in Brittany would be complete without mention of the French Forces of the Interior (FFI), and the Allied organizations associated with the Resistance movement. A history of the FFI and the various factions involved in the Resistance would need an entire book just to scratch the surface. Some of the Resistance organizations were well organized, others were not. Communist groups tended to be better organized than many of the Nationalist French groups, but not trusted or supported as well by the Allies. The factions were loyal to different commanders, and many competed in trying to get assistance from the Allies. It was not uncommon for one Resistance group to light phony signal fires in an attempt to divert a supply drop destined for another unit.

Brittany was considered to be one of the better areas to develop a Resistance movement. The terrain was rough enough to allow groups of men to hide, and the local people were considered some of the more aggressive in their anti-German feelings. The Allies hoped that when the time was right the Breton people would rise against the Germans and assist in the liberation of their homeland. In the early years of the war the British Special Operations Executive (SOE) ran an intelligence circuit code named "Racketeer" in Brittany. Just before the Normandy Invasion two Special Intelligence teams, code named "Monkey" and "Giraffe," were sent into Brittany on PT boats to collect information.

In an attempt to focus the efforts of the various Resistance factions the Allies dropped teams of three men, known as Jedburgh teams, into France to help coordinate and train the Resistance groups. These teams were supposed to be composed of two officers and a radio operator; one French, one British and one American. It was not always possible to have all three nationalities in each team because of the numbers and types of men that were trained and ready when needed.

Ten Jedburgh teams were dropped in Brittany from early July 1944 right up to the beginning of August. The Jeds were specifically focused on organizing the resistance for the uprising, planned to take place when the Allied ground forces entered Brittany. By the time some Jed teams entered France the area they were responsible for was already being liberated by American armor. Once their region was fully in control by the Allies, and the local FFI organized and operating, the Jeds were supposed to return to England. A handful stayed on to assist in the mop up of the scattered Germans.

One example of a Jed team in Brittany was Team "Giles," under command of Captain Bernard Knox (a Greek scholar in civilian life). French Captain Paul Lebel and British radioman Sgt. Gordon Tack made up the rest of Team Giles. This team dropped into Brittany on 6 July and was able to organize and equip roughly 2,000 Frenchmen. Knowing that the Germans would pass through their area when moving reinforcements from Brest to Normandy, they arranged ambushes along the Brest-Rennes road. When elements of the 2nd Fallschirmjäger (FJ) Division attempted to move down the road, they were ambushed, delayed, and finally pulled back.

On 3 Aug. 1944 General Pierre Koenig, the FFI representative at Supreme Headquarters Allied Expeditionary Force (SHAEF), broadcast the following message, *"French people of Brittany, the hour of your liberation has come. The time has come for you to take part, with or without weapons, in the last battle. The whole of France will follow you in the national insurrection."* This was followed by a coded mes-

This photograph shows one of the guns outside Brest being inspected by German officers. Of special interest are the two Japanese officers, seen at lower right in peaked caps. It was not known until long after the war that the Americans acquired a lot of intelligence about German defenses in Europe because they had broken the Japanese diplomatic codes, and were able to read the Japanese reports on such trips as this sent back to their homeland.
(Courtesy Donald VanRoosen)

Below.
This photograph of a German soldier with an MP-40 was taken off a German prisoner, by Donald VanRoosen of the 29th Division at Brest. Probably a staged shot, this man carries the standard potato masher grenades on his belt and in both boots. The rectangular case on his chest is the anti-gas cape bag, normally attached to the gas mask canister strap.

sage on the BBC *"Is Napoleon's hat still in Perros-Guirrec?"* which told the various Resistance groups to start their operations against the Germans.

The commander of all Resistance groups in Brittany was Col. Albert M. Eon. His headquarters, the "Aloes" Mission, was given the task of unifying the various groups the Jed teams had organized. They jumped into Brittany on the night of 2/3 August 1944. However, Eon had been delayed in entering France as he had a bad leg and his superiors did not think he could make the parachute jump. He was exasperated that the Americans were already moving through Brittany, most of his unit had already landed in France and he was still in England. He demanded to be dropped no matter what happened to him. He was safely parachuted into Brittany on the night of 4/5 Aug. and took command of the FFI.

Along with the Jeds and the Aloes Mission, a number of French Special Air Service (SAS) troops were dropped into Brittany to assist the locals with their military actions. They would later come under criticism from the Jeds for starting their activities too soon. This drew the attention of the Germans to the areas where the Resistance groups were still organizing and forced the developing Resistance groups to move before they were fully ready. Much like the diverse Resistance units, the Allied special forces were not always reporting to the same commanders and at times seemed to be working towards conflicting goals.

There were two groups of French SAS troops sent into Brittany. The 4th SAS (also known as 2e Regiment de Chasseurs Parachutistes) was led by Commandant Bourgoin. He was known as "Le manchot" because Bourgoin had previously lost an arm. His unit would be later popularized as the Battalion of Heaven (Battalion du Ciel). The 4th SAS jumped in Brittany on the night of 5/6 June to support the main invasion. Their task was to disrupt German communications and slow the movement of reinforcements to Normandy. They then were to establish two operation bases in Brittany and help build the Resistance army.

Base "Samwest" was set up in the forest of Duault, and Base "Dingson" at Saint-Marcel. "Dingson" quickly became known to the Germans and was destroyed in an attack on the night of 18 June. "Samwest" Base scattered into the countryside to prevent the same occurrence. At the end of July, out of 400 SAS troops, roughly 260 remained in Brittany. They were centered on three bases; Base "Wash" near Guingamp with roughly 30 SAS men and 2,500 FFI, Base "Grog" near Pontivy with roughly 30 SAS troops and 4,500 FFI, and the remains of Base "Dingson" in the Morbihan with roughly 160 SAS troops and 4,000 FFI.

The 3rd SAS (also known as the 3e Régiment de Chasseurs Parachutistes) operation in Brittany was code named "Derry." Split into three groups, each had its own mission and jumped into Brittany on 5 Aug. "Derry I," composed of five planeloads of men, was commanded by Captain Sicaud who was in charge of all SAS operations in Finistère. "Derry I" was to make contact with the FFI in the Ploudaniel-Lesneven area and assist the U.S. Army's advance. "Derry II" was composed of Lt. Paul Quelen and nine men. They were dropped near Morlaix with the mission of securing the railway bridges there with the help of Jed Team Hilary and the local FFI. "Derry III" was composed of two planeloads of men, with the mission of protect-

ing the bridge at Plougastel. The first planeload missed their drop zone, but would eventually take part in the fight to liberate Daoulas. The second aircraft became lost and had turned back to England, but the team leader decided to jump into France blindly and landed by the northern coast where they did what they could to fight the Germans.

The American version of the SAS team was the OSS Operational Group (OG). These were units of 30 men, all speaking the local language, that were dropped into enemy occupied territory with a specific military objective. In Brittany the only such unit was OG "Donald." Due to a navigational error only one planeload, 11 men, from OG Donald jumped into Brittany. Their mission was to protect the railroad bridges along the northern coastal route. They would help rally the FFI along the route of Task Force A as it moved west into Brittany, and keep the Germans from blowing up the important bridges.

There will probably never be a complete study of the actual effects the Jeds, SAS, OSS and FFI had in the Brittany campaign. The records of the covert units remain incomplete. In most cases the reports of the American ground units do not mention the SAS and OSS units. In some cases this may be due to a lack of knowledge of who they actually were. The veil of secrecy was not lifted until long after the war because the Allies did not want to explain to the Russians how they operated in an occupied country during wartime. It was all too probable that the Allies would need to perform the same types of operations in Eastern Europe at some point in the future.

It is estimated that in the area around the city of Brest there were roughly 5,000 members of the FFI serving under Lt. Col. Baptiste "Louis" Faucher. Over 200 of them were inside the city itself and caused a number of casualties in the German ranks by sniping from buildings

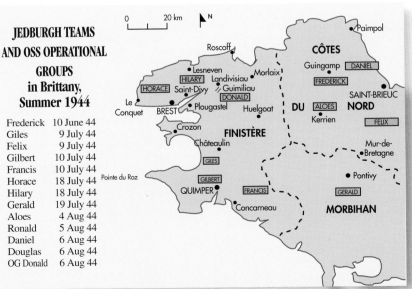

JEDBURGH TEAMS AND OSS OPERATIONAL GROUPS in Brittany, Summer 1944

Frederick	10 June 44
Giles	9 July 44
Felix	9 July 44
Gilbert	10 July 44
Francis	10 July 44
Horace	18 July 44
Hilary	18 July 44
Gerald	19 July 44
Aloes	4 Aug 44
Ronald	5 Aug 44
Daniel	6 Aug 44
Douglas	6 Aug 44
OG Donald	6 Aug 44

until the population was evacuated. In the Crozon area the FFI commander was Major Philippot. After the fall of Brest many of the FFI troops were formed into the 19th Breton Infantry Division and helped to contain Lorient until the end of the war.

The roles played by the local members of the FFI in Brittany varied tremendously. Many were extremely brave and capable men with service in the prewar French Army. In some cases individual Bretons attached themselves to American units and acted as guides or fought alongside them until killed. In a few rare instances some Frenchmen served with an American unit well into Germany. Many Breton FFI served honorably, performing their assigned tasks well (even if it was only to guard an area against a German attack that never came). It is sad that the true achievements of the FFI are distorted by the tales of those who were too late, or too scared, to actually take part in the fighting. The numbers of men (and women) who played active parts in the liberation are but a fraction compared to the numbers who claim to have fought the Germans.

One curious situation occurred in Brittany where a small group of GIs was given a local unit of FFI to help them guard the area. As nightfall came the Frenchmen started to wander off. When asked where they were going, they replied that they were farmers and if they did not go home there would be no one to milk the cows or take care of their farms. They assured the GIs that they would return in the morning after their chores had been finished. True to their word, they did come back the next day, but the Americans were not all that happy with the situation. All farmers will understand, while the war was important, the farm takes priority over everything.

Unfortunately, far too many remained silent until the fighting had passed, then picked up guns from the battlefield and asserted themselves a bit too loudly. It was not unheard of for an American unit to fight for a town, only to have a group of Frenchmen appear after the last shot was fired and attempt to claim credit for the victory. Other Frenchmen would attach themselves to an American unit and brag about their fighting skills, only to disappear when the first shot was fired. All too often these men would use the situation for their own benefit and take what they wanted or accuse old enemies of being collaborators. It will never be known how many Germans, or German sympathizers, were murdered by vigilante groups, often after the Germans surrendered peacefully.

The situation became so bad that German units generally refused to surrender to Frenchmen, and demanded assurances of the Americans that they would not be handed over to them. Some of the Frenchmen were justifiably seeking retribution for crimes committed by the German occupiers. Many of those crimes, however, were actually committed by the Russians serving in the German Army. Even the Germans claimed to be disgusted with the actions of some of the Russian volunteers. Curiously, once the Russians surrendered to the Allies, they were often welcomed to fight alongside the FFI.

There is a interesting part played by the FFI which sheds more light on the actions of George Patton in France. The FFI had liaison officers with the Americans at both army group and army headquarters, but not below at corps or division level. When Patton drove into France around the German Seventh Army he claimed to not be worried about his flanks. He publicly stated that the American tactical air force could keep an eye on that. What he did not say was that he had been assured by the FFI liaison to the Third Army HQ (Special Forces Detachment #11) that Resistance groups all along his flank had been called up, armed by Allied airdrops, and were ready to delay any German attack crossing the Loire River. 3,400 men were stationed along the line from Nantes to Angers. The lightly armed units would probably not have been able to delay the Germans for long, but

it would have given him some warning if the Germans did try to attack his exposed right flank. As the advance continued another 2,500 men were armed, extending the line to Tours, and then an additional 2,500 out to Bourges.

There is no record that Patton mentioned this to his corps or divisional commanders, and as they did not have an FFI liaison in their headquarters, there is no way they could have known. Curiously, Patton did mention that he had used the fighter-bombers of his tactical air force to watch his flanks. It may be that mention of the Resistance was left out to prevent the Germans, and later the Russians, from learning how the Allies operated.

The Vital Ports

An army without adequate logistical support can not fight. This was the underlying fact that drove the Allied plans for the liberation of France. Putting men and vehicles ashore was the easy part; it was keeping up a steady flow of food, gasoline, and ammunition that was difficult. The 1942 landing at Dieppe showed the Allies that a direct assault on a port by sea was not an option. The decision to land on the Normandy beaches could only have been made thanks to the development of a portable artificial harbor. Constructed in secret and towed across the Channel, the Mulberry harbors (one British, one American) were considered a temporary solution until actual port facilities could be captured. Once the Americans were ashore their first order of business was to capture the port of Cherbourg and get it back into operation.

The Allies thought they would have a long hard fight getting across France. The next objective on the continent after Cherbourg would be to break out of Normandy, specifically to capture the Brittany ports. With these large ports allowing a steady uninterrupted stream of replacements and supplies, only then did the American Army feel it would be able to attack across France and into Germany. Two operations to land troops directly at the ports, (operations "Swordhilt" at Brest and "Beneficiary" at Saint-Malo) were considered, but never put into effect.

For a while after the invasion the Americans could supply their troops over the Normandy beaches. A major storm on 20 July damaged the artificial harbor at Omaha Beach, but the efforts of the American Engineer Special Brigades enabled the Americans to bring more tonnage over the Normandy beaches than had been originally been planned for the artificial harbor. The problem was that not all the material the Army needed could be brought across a beach or landed in a small shallow water port. The majority of the Allied transport ships needed a deep water port to dock at. Locomotives and rolling stock needed to come in at a major port with rail connections. Ammunition and supplies could be shipped much more easily through the bulk cargo facilities at a major port than manhandled box by box from ship to shore. It was not just the docks and cranes that the Allies needed: a working port consists of other facilities such as warehouses, as well as a good road and railway system to move the supplies on.

However, the Germans also knew the Allies needed ports and were not about to hand them over that easily. In some ways, the capture of Cherbourg on 26 June 1944 was unexpected. The Americans had been able to advance much faster than expected, and the Germans were not able to fully man the defenses. General von Schlieben, the commander of "Fortress Cherbourg" had not fought to the last man, and the port facilities were not as badly damaged as they might have been. Even with the German demolition of the docks, Allied supply ships were docking 21 days after Schlieben surrendered. The gasoline and oil facilities at Cherbourg were captured nearly intact. This was tremendously important to the

Allies as the much vaunted Pipeline Under the Ocean (PLUTO) project proved a colossal failure. It is important to note, however, that the Allied port reconstruction units did miracles in bringing the destroyed areas of the port back into operation. Had these units been sent to Brest, it can only be assumed that they would have been able to bring that port at least partially back into operation within a reasonable amount of time.

It was too much to assume that the Germans would make the same mistake with the rest of the major ports in France. The Allies needed a plan that assumed the Germans would be adept at port defense and demolition. Colonel Harold Mack, in charge of the supply and transportation plans for the European invasion, had realized well before D-day that there was no way the ports and railroads the Allies expected they would capture in France could meet the supply demands of their large forces. Mack had noticed that one of the best railroads in France ran along the coast of the Bay of Biscay, which then turned east into France and Germany. The nearby sheltered beaches on the Quiberon Peninsula seemed ideal for landing supplies on. The senior commanders in both Washington and London, as well as General Eisenhower, approved Mack's plan to organize a landing site for supplies at Quiberon and it was given the codename "Chastity."

Operation Chastity then grew from that simple plan to include developing a semi-artificial harbor out of the natural protected area in Quiberon Bay. This region was already served by a good road and railway system and the bay allowed for anchorage of deep water ships. The Americans planned to tow elements of piers, such as used for the Mulberries, to Quiberon Bay and build a port where there was only empty shoreline.

So secret was this plan that documents about it were stamped "Top Secret Bigot," the same high classification system that protected the secret of where the D-day invasion itself would be. One of the reasons for the secrecy was that the Allies could not afford to plan on building a port in this area, only to find that the Germans had discovered their intention and mined and blockaded the area. Many histories of the Brittany campaign do not understand that the original goal of capturing Brest was not to hope the port would be captured intact, but to allow for the construction of the new port facility at Quiberon.

Quiberon Bay was expected to land 7,000 tons a day from deep water vessels one month after construction was started. The Navy felt that construction and operations would be able to proceed throughout the winter months when the Normandy beaches were forced to shut down. The only problem was that the Navy insisted the Quiberon Bay plan could not proceed if Brest was left in German hands. The Navy felt that towing the large pier structures around the Brittany Peninsula could not be done until the coastal artillery guns at Brest were eliminated. They worried that the German Navy would be able to sally forth and easily attack the slow convoys if they still held Brest. The sailors also wanted to be able to use Brest as a safe harbor for the large towed components in case of bad weather. For these reasons the Navy stated that if the Quiberon Bay port was to become a reality, construction could not start until Brest was captured. Therefore, to follow the overall plan to supply the American Army in France, Brest had to be taken even if no ships would ever dock there.

It was far more efficient to haul large quantities of supplies on trains rather than endless convoys of trucks. Trucks burn more fuel, and consume tires and spare parts on long hauls. Railroads had always been the best way to haul supplies up to the front, where they could then be transferred to trucks for distribution. Once the Allies broke out of Nor-

The large shells of one of the naval artillery guns are stacked inside the gun position for quick loading. These are probably antiaircraft shells. It was important during the air raids to fire the guns as fast as possible, to get as much flak in the air before the planes passed out of the area. One of the gunners wears a leather coat, possibly obtained from a friend in the U-boat service.
(Courtesy Donald Van Roosen)

Bottom.

The size and thickness of the Brest sub pen walls are vividly shown here in relation to the size of two GIs examining the structure after the surrender. Two submarines could dock next to one another inside each opening.
(National Archives)

The Breakout into France

After the Allied invasion of France on 6 June 1944 things bogged down. Vicious fighting in the hedgerows kept the American advance to a slow, bloody crawl. While the infantry was moving ahead a field at a time, more troops and supplies were pouring ashore over the beaches. There was not enough manpower to drive into Germany, but it was enough for the next step: a grab for Brittany.

On 25 July 1944 a massive air bombardment along the Périers-Saint-Lô road opened the path for the 4th, 9th and 30th Infantry Divisions to move forward. Assisted by fighter-bombers, the 2nd and 3rd Armored Divisions moved through the infantry and began to exploit the hole opened in the German defensive line. After three days it was clear that this was a major penetration and the German defenses in Normandy were on the verge of shattering. A week later the Americans had pushed south, through some of the best troops the Germans had, to the base of the Cotentin Peninsula. They were ready to break out into Brittany.

If the agreed upon plan was to be followed, three American corps would turn into Brittany to capture the ports. However, the breakthrough was so successful that the Allied generals decided to change their plans and make their main effort the surrounding of the German forces in France. Only one American corps, the VIIIth, would be sent into Brittany. The rest of the American Army would attempt to swing around the southern flank of the German Seventh Army and link up with the British forces in the north.

Once the breakout from Normandy occurred, it appears that the senior commanders in Europe forgot the continued need for Quiberon. As Patton's Third Army was suddenly in a position to surround the main German forces in France, the Chastity plans no longer seemed important. Middleton had previously expected to take his corps to the Rennes area, and so was probably not completely familiar with the details of Chastity. When General Wood of the 4th Armored Division was sent to the Quiberon area, there is no evidence that he understood, or was told, the rationale of his mission. No attempts seem to have been made to eliminate the German coastal artillery in the area. In fact, it was Patton's chief of staff, Hugh Gaffey, that had to order Wood back to the Quiberon area, which indicates a lack of knowledge about Chastity in Middleton's VIIIth Corps.

It was, of course, important for the Americans to grab the chance to surround and destroy the German Army in France. One of Napoleon's main rules of warfare was that it is more important to destroy an enemy army than to capture territory. However, in this case it is strange that Quiberon was suddenly forgotten. The plan certainly could have been put into action without detracting from the encirclement in France. A few minor excuses are found in the official histories, but none of them are acceptable. The claims that Quiberon was too far away from the fighting is negated by the excellent railway system that led from that area into the heart of France. Without much work the rail system would have allowed Quiberon to supply Patton's army, far easier than trucking supplies down from the ports on the northern coast.

The claims that Quiberon was no longer needed due to the capture of ports in Northern France is negated by the proven fact that those ports were not ready, and unable to land enough supplies to support the armies until far later in the war. It is true that the port of Le Havre was captured on 12 Sept. With the hard work of the Navy construction battalions and port reconstruction units the first supply ships docked on 19 Sept. Le Havre is often cited as the reason Quiberon was no longer needed. However, it was known by the quartermasters that Le Havre was simply not large enough, nor did it have the infrastructure, to supply the needs of the Allied armies in Europe. There is no good answer as to why Quiberon was abandoned. It certainly should not be forgotten that it was glamorous for generals to attack east, capture territory, and encircle the Germans, while there was no glamour or headlines for someone to move west and mop up an area already out of the fighting and prepare it to be a supply point. But it is too easy to blame the senior generals. A general's job is to lead their troops, not to be an expert on every aspect of running their armies. The blame more properly falls on the logistics staff that did not insist to their commanders that Quiberon had to be developed to sustain the Allied forces in Europe.

The original Chastity plan called for supplies to be landed on the bare beaches and rapidly moved to the railroads just inland. This plan could easily have been put into operation before Brest had fallen, but on the insistence of the Navy, Chastity could not be started until Brest had fallen. Once Brest had been taken, the Allies thought they would soon have the ports of Le Havre and Rouen (both, by the way, without an adequate rail or road system to support them as major ports), and then thought Chastity unnecessary.

The consequence of not implementing Chastity was that in the autumn of 1944 the Allied armies began to run out of all categories of supplies. Patton complained he was stopped due to a lack of gasoline, but in reality the supply shortage reached every category of material. If Quiberon Bay had operated as planned, it would have meant that Patton's Army would not have run out of supplies as he approached the German border. Eisenhower could have continued his plan to move against Germany on a broad front, not just attack in the north with the British while the rest of his forces held their positions in the south due to lack of supplies.

mandy, they planned to use the rail lines leading from Quiberon to supply the troops in central France.

One of the reasons that the Quiberon rail lines were so important was that they had not been damaged by the Allied Air Forces. All major railways and roads in Northern France had been devastated by air bombardment to prevent German reinforcements from reaching Normandy. The Normandy area, the only place the Allies had been landing supplies, had been isolated from the rest of Europe by their own pre-invasion bombing plans. Not only had bridges and rail lines been destroyed but so had the more difficult to replace support facilities such as marshalling yards and locomotive repair facilities. The railways leading from the Quiberon area into the heart of France, and to the German border, were in much better shape than their Normandy cousins and could be quickly put into action hauling the vitally needed supplies. That is, as soon as ports were available to land the materiel.

This need for ports was very real. By June the Allies were 30% behind in planned port capacity. In August 207 ships sat waiting to be unloaded, but there was nowhere for them to go. Cargo ships began to be used as floating warehouses until they could be unloaded. This caused a chain reaction across the Atlantic, as the ships could not be unloaded and sent back to the States for their next planned load of cargo. Every day that the ships could not keep to their timetable set things back even further. In the fall of 1944 American divisions arriving in France were forced to sit idle because there was no way to support them. Eventually, Le Havre and Antwerp would become the major ports in northern Europe, but it would take two months after Antwerp was captured for the Germans to be driven from the approaches and ships allowed to dock. In southern France the ports of Toulon and Marseille would later fall to the Allies, but in the late summer and fall of 1944 the need for ports was still quite desperate.

THE 4TH ARMORED DIVISION

Chapter 2

A few days after the breakthrough of Operation Cobra, the Americans were near the base of the Cotentin Peninsula ready to move into Brittany. General George Patton was in France waiting for the activation of his Third Army. Eventually, General Troy Middleton's VIIIth Corps would become part of the Third Army, but until that time General Bradley had Patton act as his deputy in overseeing the actions of the VIIIth Corps.

Bradley knew that Patton was just the kind of commander he needed for the type of mobile warfare he expected. Unfortunately, this put Middleton in the position of being directly responsible to two different commanders - both Patton and Bradley.

On the evening of 28 July the VIIIth Corps held Coutances, and it appeared that the Germans to their front were in total disarray. Middleton ordered his troops to move south to Avranches. The city of Avranches sits on the very base of the Cotentin Peninsula and was the key to the Americans breaking out into Brittany. Surrounded on three sides by water (it is situated between two rivers), Avranches is a major road junction that controlled traffic moving between Normandy and Brittany. The city is on high ground with a commanding view of the area. It was one of the most important objectives the Americans had and it was expected to be very heavily defended.

The 6th Armored found itself held up at the Sienne River, so Middleton ordered it to divert its attention from Avranches and clear the coastal town of Granville. The 4th Armored had been making excellent progress and was in a better position to take Avranches. Initially the 4th was also delayed at the Sienne River, but by the evening of 30 July it had crossed and was rolling into enemy territory.

To keep the 4th and 6th Armored Divisions supplied with ammunition the 665th Ammunition Company formed a mobile ammo supply point. Ten tank transporters, massive diesel trucks towing trailers designed to carry tanks, were each stocked with 50 tons of

ammunition. This group followed behind the armored divisions providing a close source of ammunition supply during the break out.

One of the columns from the 4th Armored CCB actually passed within a few hundred yards of the German 7th Army advance command post. The German commander, General Hausser, and his officers were forced to abandon the HQ and escape the area on foot. This temporarily disrupted the German chain of command at a time when they could least afford it.

The 4th Armored was a well-trained unit, which would generate some of the best tank commanders of the war. Creighton Abrams, who went on to command the American Army in Vietnam, was one of them. Commanding the 37th Tank Bn. Abrams pulled one tank from each company and gave them to his S-2, S-3, and liaison officers. This put his staff right up front where they could affect the action. Later in the war, when many junior officers became casualties, these experienced men were up front, able to assist the new green platoon leaders become accustomed to combat.

When the 4th Armored Division's CCB, commanded by General Holmes E. Dager, got to Avranches early that evening they were amazed to see the See River bridges outside the city still intact. A quick rush was made and the unit entered an undefended city. Word was sent back to the VIIIth Corps that CCB had taken Avranches. Although everything pointed to the fact that the Germans were very disorganized in the area, Middleton was amazed the Germans had allowed his men to just walk in and take the vital city.

If the Third Army was going to move into Brittany, the single main road south of Avranches leading to Pontaubault and the Sélune River crossing there was the next step. Middleton ordered more troops to Avranches to reinforce Dager's CCB, and told him to move on if at all possible. Middleton, however, was quite worried about the armored unit's ability to both hold Avranches and continue the advance. He feared it would be just like the Germans to pull back enough to draw in the Americans, then cut off the leading elements and destroy them.

About 2200 hours on 31 July a column of German vehicles approached Avranches from the north. The lead vehicles were marked with red crosses, so the American tankers assumed it was a medical unit evacuating German casualties. A sudden fire fight broke out

Top.
Tanks are what first come to mind when an armored division is mentioned, but there were three battalions of infantry, mounted in half-tracks, that were part of every armored division. Infantrymen, like this machine gunner of the 4th Armored, played an important role in protecting the tanks against Germans armed with panzerfausts and other antitank weapons.

and the Americans discovered that the trucks were filled with ammunition. The Germans in the convoy surrendered, but informed the Americans that a heavily armed force was following closely behind them. Two hours later another German convoy arrived, and in the initial shooting a shell struck an ammunition truck. The resulting fire illuminated the area and left the handful of tanks guarding the city approach good targets. Without any infantry protection, the armored commander ordered a withdrawal.

The retreating Germans were thus able to reenter Avranches from the north. In the early morning hours the Americans at the southern end of Avranches were surprised to find German troops moving in behind them. After two brutal assaults trying to pass through Avranches, the Germans finally gave up and several hundred surrendered. The fighting might have continued, except the Germans had been seeking to escape the American infantry to the north and were disheartened to have to fight through an unexpected line of American forces.

Once Avranches was again secure, the 4th Division CCA moved through it onto to the Sélune River crossing at Pontaubault. Splitting into four groups, the tanks of CCA swiftly captured a smaller bridge at Ducey and two dams that controlled the level of the Sélune. The fourth group arrived at the intact Pontaubault Bridge on the afternoon of 31 July. No sooner than they had taken up defensive positions, a German battalion sized unit from the already battered 77th Infantry

Division arrived with orders to hold the bridge. The Americans had arrived just in time and the Germans were driven away by tank and artillery fire. On the morning of 1 August General Middleton's VIIIth Corps held three bridges over the See River, four over the Sélune, and every natural defensive line at the edge of Brittany.

According to the plans made before D-day, once the Americans had broken out into Brittany the VIIIth Corps was to proceed to Rennes, the XVth Corps would take the shore route along the north coast of Brittany, and the VIIth Corps would take the southern flank of Brittany and proceed to Brest. The plans for the use of three full corps in Brittany were scrapped as it became apparent the entire German left flank had been broken open and the German Army in France was on the verge of collapse.

With General Hausser out of contact (due to his hasty evacuation of his command post), command of the German 7th Army was taken over by General Kluge, commander of the German Army Group West. He realized what would be lost if the Americans were to keep control of the Pontaubault bridges. He ordered the German XXVth Corps to move every available mobile unit in the Saint-Malo area to Pontaubault in a desperate effort to prevent the Americans from breaking into Brittany. From there he hoped to counterattack and recapture Avranches.

Now the Germans faced one of their main handicaps in Brittany. Although there were many navy and air force personnel in the area, as an army commander, Kluge was unable to give them orders. The separation of command by branch of service caused troops that might have played a vital role to sit idle. After the 77th Division attack on the Pontaubault Bridge was beaten back, there were few available combat ready German Army troops in the region, and the last chance to keep the Americans out of Brittany had been lost.

After dark on the 31st, when German reconnaissance planes were not active, both the 4th and 6th Armored Divisions moved down the narrow highway and over the Pontaubault bridges. Moving this many troops at night on one road was considered impossible. Middleton later remarked that if he had used this tactic as a solution to a problem at one of the Army's service schools they would have certainly given him an "F." He claimed they accomplished the feat by placing officers at critical points and just shoving the vehicles on through. What would become known as the Avranches bottleneck would become even more congested in the coming days, when three infantry divisions and many corps units would move along the single road and all the units would use it for their lines of communications.

The German situation in Brittany

At the end of July Hitler was faced with a military disaster in France. He ordered his fortress policy into effect. This meant that all troops in the port cities of Saint-Malo, Lorient, Saint-Nazaire, and Brest (as well as Dunkirk, Calais, Boulogne, and Le Havre) were to come under command of a special fortress commander who had sworn an oath to defend the port to the last man and last cartridge. Hitler felt that the static troops defending the ports would be more help to him by tying down Allied troops than retreating to the west.

They would also deny the Allies the ports they desperately needed for supply purposes. This was in opposition to his senior commanders who felt that this action would cause them to lose 180,000-280,000 men, and their equipment, which could be put to good use someplace else. Once in charge, the fortress commander was authorized to issue orders to all military forces in his city. He controlled not just the army, but navy, air force, labor troops, police - anyone in German service.

Hitler refused to evacuate the 319th Infantry Division on the Channel Islands. His army commanders had hoped this unit could be brought to the mainland and used to defend Brittany. The 319th would sit out the fight without being able to contribute much to the war effort. Hitler did finally agree to let the 2nd Fallschimjäger (FJ) Division withdraw from Brittany, but the decision was made too late and these paratroopers found themselves trapped in Brest. With matters more serious elsewhere on the Western front, Brittany was written off, and its defense was turned over to General Fahrmbacher and his XXVth Corps to hold out as long as they could.

Although he was in charge of all Brittany, General Fahrmbacher had few troops to command. Only one third of the 100,000 troops that had been based in Brittany in June were left. The rest had been sent to the Normandy front. He was left with the 2nd FJ Division, 343rd Infantry Division (static), the 266th Infantry Division (static) and elements of the 265th Infantry Division. In addition there were various coastal artillery, antiaircraft and navy troops. The remnants of the 77th Infantry Division had been sent to hold Pontaubault and the 91st Infantry Division was sent to Rennes.

Fahrmbacher set up his headquarters in Lorient. When he was later ordered to take command of Brest, he felt that moving there would accomplish nothing and remained where he was. He felt the officers in Brest were very competent and in no need of his supervision. Even though he was technically in command of all German forces in Brittany, there was nothing he could do to influence the battle for Saint-Malo, Brest, or Saint-Nazaire. On 10 Aug. the fortress commander of Lorient was injured and Fahrmbacher assumed direct command of the

GENERAL JOHN WOOD

John Wood was born in Arkansas and attended the University of Arkansas where he played football while earning a chemistry degree. After graduation he applied to West Point specifically to be able to play another year of football. He was slightly older than most cadets, and quickly earned the nickname "P" (short for professor) while tutoring them. Graduating in 1912, he entered the Army and in 1918 went to France as a staff officer in the 3rd Division. After attending the Allied staff officer school at Langres he was sent back to the States to help organize the 81st Division.

Always known to be very headstrong and independent, he was given a new nickname in WW2: "Tiger Jack." Supposedly this was because he was known to pace back and forth in front of his tent like a tiger in a cage. His strong personality clashed with his corps' commander, Manton Eddy, and in

General John S. Wood, commander of the 4th Armored Division. He was given the nickname "P" Wood (short for "Professor" Wood) while tutoring fellow cadets at West Point. He was considered one of the greatest American armored unit commanders in WW2, and some historians refer to him as "the American Rommel"
(National Archives)

December 1944 Eddy decided Wood was worn out and sent him back to the States for a rest. At Ft. Knox he was in charge of training tank crews. A far cry from commanding a division in combat, but he made sure that replacement tank crews met a high level of training before being shipped overseas. After the war he retired from the Army and took a position helping solve the refugee problem in Europe.

troops there. Fahrmbacher felt that he finally had something to do. Once overrun by the Americans, Brittany would become a series of unconnected battles for a few heavily defended positions.

Patton's 3rd Army activated

At noon on 1 August 1944 General Patton's Third Army was activated. General Bradley moved up to command the 12th Army Group (consisting of both the First and Third Armies) and General Courtney Hodges was promoted to lead the First Army. Changes in command structure such as this often result in temporary confusion, and the situation in Brittany was to be no exception. Previously Patton had been serving as a deputy to Bradley, only informally in command of Middleton's VIIIth Corps, and had developed his own theory of what to do in Brittany. Soon Patton's Third Army would expand to include the XVth, XXth, and XIIth Corps. However, until he got those troops Patton remained focused on the VIIIth Corps and wanted swift results from this unit. The command situation, coupled with the growing communication problems from corps to division as the troops moved further and further to Brest, was a recipe for disaster.

Between Patton and the three cavalry oriented commanders Grow (6th Armored Division), Wood (4th Armored Division) and Ernest (Task Force A) was General Middleton, a very experienced infantry officer who had been preparing to fight in the Rennes area for months. Bradley, another infantry officer, was very familiar with all the plans for the region. This included not only the military plans to liberate Brittany, but also the overall logistical picture for all of France which included the importance of the Brittany ports. Middleton later remarked in his biography that he was informed by Bradley that his principal objectives were to capture Saint-Malo and the Quiberon Bay area. Saint-Malo would guard the approaches to Brittany and Quiberon Bay would supply the army.

It is not clear if Patton was aware of, or fully understood, the plans for Quiberon Bay. His intelligence officer, Colonel Oscar Koch, remarked in his memoirs that while in England his job had been to plan for the Third Army's operations in Brittany. Patton, however, directed that the intelligence planning instead be focused on the area in Eastern France around Metz. This took place months before the landing in Normandy, so it was clear from the start that Patton had little interest in Brittany, which he perceived to be unimportant.

The Drive on Rennes

On 1 Aug. General Wood's 4th Armored Division moved southwest from Pontaubault towards Rennes 40 miles away. When planning for the expected Brittany campaign months before, the Allied generals had decided that the largest battle of the western front would probably take place at Rennes. The city is not only the capital of Brittany, but at the center of a major road network. It was considered a very valuable piece of real estate for both sides and it was expected the Germans would fight to hold onto it.

Middleton was worried about a German counterattack that was expected to take place at Rennes. This was not an imaginary fear. The Third Army's own intelligence reports indicated that the locations of four panzer divisions were then unknown. The report stated that *"Such*

a concentration would give the enemy a force capable of driving a wedge to the Channel between our north and south forces. Such a severance would rupture the jugular supply vein of our southern columns, rendering them logistically useless." This expected counterattack would in fact take place, but be directed at Mortain.

Middleton, concerned by Patton's own intelligence report, wanted the 4th Armored to occupy Rennes, then hold until an infantry force could move up. Apparently Patton expected the 4th to drive hard all the way to the coast, thereby cutting off Brittany. Middleton had ordered Wood to go no further than Rennes, but on hearing this Patton overruled the command. He told Wood to go ahead and seal off the entire Brittany Peninsula.

In the early evening of 1 Aug. the 4th Armored hit strong defensive positions on the outskirts of Rennes. Two Luftwaffe companies of Flak Battery Schmidt (88mm antiaircraft guns), protecting the Rennes airport, stopped CCA of the 4th and drove them back to regroup. Reports

This burned-out Sherman near Avranches probably comes from the 8th Tank Bn. The 8th was very concerned about vehicle camouflage and routinely added wire netting to garnish with vegetation, and painted out the white identification star. Gunners on both sides generally made it a point to continue shooting at tanks until they caught on fire, thus making the kill certain. A burnt-out tank could not be recovered and put back into action by maintenance troops.
(National Archives)

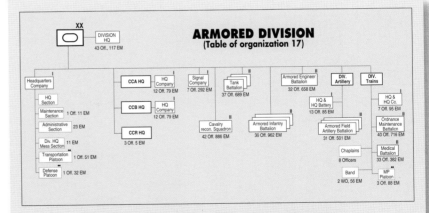

4th ARMORED DIVISION HISTORY

The 4th AD trained in England from January 1944 until it landed in France on 13 July 1944. Moving south from Normandy, it drove to Lorient and cut off the Brittany Peninsula. Moving north of the Loire it crossed the Moselle, passed Nancy, and captured Lunéville. Attacking again in November it crossed the Saar and fought a major engagement at Singling. Two days after the Germans attacked in the Ardennes, the 4th raced 150 miles in 19 hours to help relieve Bastogne. After regrouping, it attacked from Luxembourg to Trier and crossed the Rhine in March 1945; continuing across the Saar into Czechoslovakia when the war ended.

4th ARMORED DIVISION (OLYMPIC)

- 8th Tank Bn.
- 35th Tank Bn.
- 37th Tank Bn.

- 10th Armored Inf Bn.
- 51st Armored Inf Bn.
- 53d Armored Inf Bn.

Division Artillery
- 22d Armored Field Artillery Battalion
- 66th Armored Field Artillery Battalion
- 94th Armored Field Artillery Battalion

- 25th Cavalry Recon Squadron
- 46th Armored Medical Bn.
- 126th Maintenance Bn.
- 24th Armored Engineer Bn.
- 144th Armored Signal Co.

Attached: 489th AAA Bn.

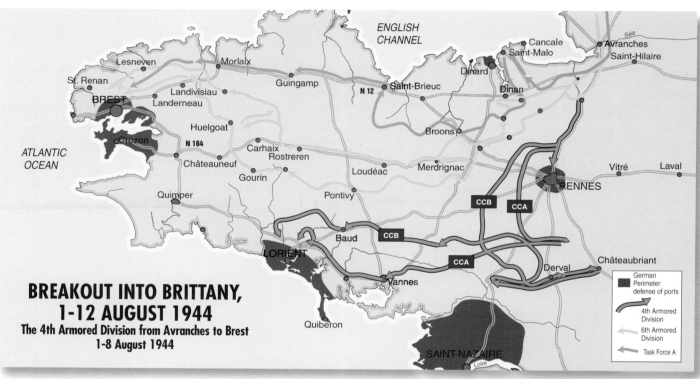

BREAKOUT INTO BRITTANY, 1-12 AUGUST 1944

The 4th Armored Division from Avranches to Brest 1-8 August 1944

German Perimeter defense of ports
4th Armored Division
6th Armored Division
Task Force A

Above.
This slightly blurred photo shows a jeep from the 2nd Armored Division racing through Velay, near Avranches. The white recognition star and yellow bridge marker (on the front grill) stand out against the drab colors of the vehicle and crew.
(Courtesy Frank Orville Gray)

Opposite, top.
Men from F/28th Infantry Regiment enjoy K rations and local cider. They wear the cotton HBT fatigue uniform with the gas flap at the neck closed. From left to right are Pvt. Phoenix, Sgt. Moss, Supply Sgt. Renz, and Pvt. Kavalier.
(Courtesy Frank Orville Gray)

Left.
Under an overcast sky Charlie Jenkins, from the 28th Infantry Regiment, is seen riding in the back of a jeep through Avranches. The rifleman walking in the street just behind him appears to have a condom over the muzzle of his rile to protect it against rain.
(Courtesy Frank Orville Gray)

COMBAT COMMAND HEADQUARTERS
(Table of organization 17-20-1)

Combat Command HQ
10 Officers

Headquarters Company

Company HQ

HQ Section	1 Off. 5 EM
Admin. Section	14 EM x 2
Maintenance Section	1 Off. 8 EM

Liaison Section
9 EM x 5

Tank Platoon
1 Off. 9 EM x 3

Staff Section
1 WO, 32 EM x 5
x 3
x 2

Attached Chaplain
2 Officers

Attached Medical
2 Off. 2 EM

LEGEND

- M5 Light tank
- Half-track
- 2 1/2 ton truck
- 1/4 ton truck
- Ammunition trailer
- M10 Ammo trailer
- 1/4 ton trailer

WO: Warrant Officer
EM: Enlisted Men
Note: table valid only for CCA and CCB, CCR is only 3 officers and 5 EM with no organic vehicles.

During WW2 a bold experiment was made to make the organization of the American armored divisions as flexible as possible. In every armored division (except the 2nd and 3rd Armored Divisions) elements were broken down into no larger than battalion size. Two special headquarters, known as combat commands were formed that could control flexible numbers and types of units.

The division commander could, as the situation warranted it, assign any combination of his men, splitting up battalions, companies, or platoons if need be to tailor the force to the specific mission.

On one day Combat Command A (CCA) might be given the majority of the artillery support, while the next day it might lose most of its tank units, but be given the Engineer Bn. It all depended upon what the situation was at the time. Each battalion had its own internal support structure and, in theory, could be moved about as needed without hampering its combat effectiveness.

The original theory of the combat command was that each armored division would have two main combat forces and a third headquarters, known as CCR (Combat Command Reserve), which would act as a reserve force controlling all combat units not currently assigned to the two main combat commands. In some armored units, such as General Grow's 6th Armored Division, this is how the combat command system was used.

Grow gave both CCA and CCB the resources he thought they needed, while CCR moved along behind whichever combat command was making the most progress, ready to reinforce it.

The combat command system was hard on the officers in the division. They never knew from one day to the next exactly whom they would be reporting to. One day a tank platoon leader might be filling his normal position in his battalion, yet the next day find his platoon pulled out and assigned as the only tank unit in Combat Command B. The American GI proved to be quite flexible and made the system work. Most divisions tended to develop a standard organization where certain tank, infantry, and artillery battalions were normally assigned to a specific combat command. The Engineer Bn. was split into three companies, one to each command, and the headquarters remained in CCR.

In practice most armored divisions ended up using CCR as a third combat unit. This put strain on the division as the actual components of CCR were no more than three officers and five men. Any vehicles or extra manpower needed to control the unit in combat had to be pulled from the division headquarters transportation platoon, or other subordinate units. This form of flexible organization makes it confusing to follow exactly which unit was present at specific engagements.

If records indicate that CCA attacked a certain town, there is no real way of knowing exactly which elements of the division were present unless a detailed listing of the combat command composition can be found for that specific day.

This officer from the 4th Armored Division wears the standard tank crew uniform of winter combat jacket and trousers. These were thickly lined garments that kept the crew warm while they were sitting in an unheated vehicle, or driving along exposed to the wind. His leather helmet was designed to protect the head from banging on the inside of the tank, and to hold the intercom headphones so he could hear the rest of the crew over the noise of battle.
The goggles are one of many patterns worn by vehicle crews to protect their eyes from the sun and dust. His boots are the same as worn throughout the army and he wears a pistol belt with first aid pouch, an ammo pouch for his pistol. The only way this man can be identified as an officer is the insignia barely visible on his shirt collar.
(Reconstruction by Militaria Magazine)

A column of the 4th Armored Division passes through the Avranches area. The first two vehicles are M-8 armored cars from the 4th Division's 25th Cavalry Reconnaissance Squadron. The driver and his assistant in both M-8's wear leather tank crew helmets, while the men in the turret wear the standard steel helmet. *(National Archives)*

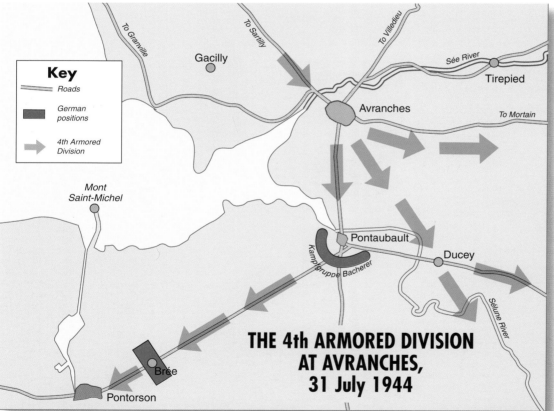

Key

Roads

German positions

4th Armored Division

THE 4th ARMORED DIVISION AT AVRANCHES, 31 July 1944

THE 4th ARMORED DIVISION
on 27 July 1944

CCA
● B/25 Cavalry Squadron (two companies)
● 10th Armored Infantry Bn.
● 94th Armored Field Artillery Bn.
● C/704th Tank Destroyer Bn.
● A/24th Armored Engineer Battalion.

Forward Division HQ
● one battery, 489th AAA Bn. (less 1 plt)
● 37 Tank Bn. (-)
● B/46th Medical Bn.
● A/126th Ordnance Bn.

CCB
● 8th Tank Bn.
● 53rd Armored Infantry Bn.
● B/70th Tank Destroyer Bn.
● B/24th Armored Engineer Battalion.
● 995th Engineer Bridge Co.
● B/126 Ordnance Bn.
● A/489th AAA Bn.
● B/46th Medical Bn.
● Division Artillery
● C&B/25th Cavalry Squadron.

indicate that 15 tanks and four half-tracks were knocked out and 20 Americans taken prisoner. Other than the flak units, the Germans claimed the northern approaches were guarded by only 100 men, eight machine guns, and three 40mm guns. The southern approaches to Rennes were guarded by only 100 men without any heavy weapons.

The remnants of the German 91st Infantry Division then arrived at Rennes and began to dig in. The importance of the city was apparent to the Germans and men from two replacement battalions arrived from Le Mans at 1800 hrs. to defend it. General Koenig, the commander of the 91st Division, also arrived that night with two assault guns, assumed command of Rennes, and set up a defensive perimeter all around the city. General Wood realized that with his armored division still spread out along the road from Pontaubault, he was in no position to storm Rennes. Tanks not being suited for city fighting, Wood radioed Middleton for immediate assistance from an infantry unit. The 13th Infantry Regiment (8th Infantry Division) was picked up by a few quartermaster

truck companies and sent off to help the 4th Armored.

Meanwhile, Wood was consolidating his position and examining his maps. He felt that he could make a greater impact if he could swing around Rennes and prepare to drive east into France, not west into Brittany as planned. He felt that Brittany was soon to become a backwater to the war, and if he could move fast to the east he could knife into the rear areas of the German Army. He started his troops moving around Rennes to the west. When the 13th Infantry arrived he planned to head southeast to seize Châteaubriant, and then possibly move to Angers on the Loire River.

Wood theorized that this maneuver would still seal off Brittany, only on a different line than had been planned. He did not take into account the logistical need for Quiberon Bay. He sent his plan to Middleton by messenger, stating that he strongly recommended that the 4th be allowed to push on to Angers. Wood felt so secure in his idea that he went ahead and gave his troops the orders to proceed. Just after

this message had left for Middleton, a different messenger arrived from corps HQ restating the original plan for the 4th to establish blocking positions from Rennes to Quiberon. Middleton had sent this, wanting to make sure that Wood was following the agreed upon plan. With these orders Wood, as a professional officer, had to rescind his own plan and again move on Quiberon.

When Middleton received word of Wood's idea, he sent a message that it was all right for Wood to make the drive around Rennes (as this would cut off the city), but to be sure Rennes was secured before moving further. When this new directive arrived Wood had already knifed through the countryside as far south as Derval. Although the powerful feeling of being able to drive deep into the heart of the enemy was just what the tankers wanted, Wood now had orders to block the retreat routes from Rennes. Wood recalled his columns and moved back to Rennes to take up positions outside the city. By this time Wood had traveled so far in front of the American lines that supplying his troops was becoming a real problem. It would have become much worse if they had left a major German stronghold behind them.

On 3 Aug. the 13th Infantry Regiment (now attached to the 4th Armored) arrived at Rennes and went directly into an attack. These men from the 8th Division began to move slowly into the city, but the Germans had had enough. Almost totally encircled by the 4th Armored and under heavy attack from the 13th Infantry, General Hausser (now back in control of his army) ordered that Rennes be abandoned at 2300 hrs. The German soldiers burned the supplies remaining in the city and then divided up into two groups- those that were motorized and those on foot. Both of these German groups, roughly 2,000 soldiers, safely made the five day journey to Saint-Nazaire without incident. At times they had brushed against columns from the 4th Armored, but both sides were all too willing to move away from a fight.

Once the German garrison had evacuated Rennes, the 13th Infantry returned to the control of the 8th Infantry Division. The rest of the 8th Division moved up and took up blocking positions around Rennes in case the Germans attempted to recapture this vital crossroads. Middleton now felt that this position was secure, but he was now in a predicament. He wanted to allow Wood to press on to the east, but he also had his orders to capture Quiberon Bay as soon as possible. He had indications that the breakthrough in Normandy was altering Allied strategy, but until his orders from Patton or Bradley were officially changed he needed to follow the approved plan.

Middleton decided to split the difference and ordered Wood to secure all crossings over the Vilaine River from Rennes to the coast. This would seal off Brittany and put Wood in a position to move on, either to Quiberon or east into the heart of France. Due to the communications difficulties encountered over such a distance this order never reached Wood.

Without receiving any new orders Wood was furious. He felt he was in a position to make a major contribution to the war, but was being held back. Wood sent word to Middleton to come immediately to the 4th Armored headquarters. Middleton figured a division commander would not ask his corps commander to travel such a long distance through unsecured roads unless there was good reason, so he took a small escort and drove down on 4 Aug. Middleton would later recall that when he got there he asked, "What's the matter John, you lost your division?" Wood replied, "Heck no. They are winning this war the wrong way, we ought to be going towards Paris." Middleton agreed to allow Wood to keep his positions facing east, but to also block the bridges on the Vilaine. When the VIIIth Corps' list of current objectives reached Patton's Third Army HQ, it set off another string of actions.

Patton's chief of staff, General Hugh Gaffey, noted that while they were still cutting off Brittany, the Third Army expected that the bulk of the 4th Armored would still be moving on Lorient, Vannes, and Quiberon. Gaffey sent out one of Patton's cavalry sections to clarify these orders to Wood immediately. But by now the 4th Armored was nearly out of gas. Many of their supply trucks had been stripped from the 4th and used to bring up the 13th Infantry to Rennes. Most of their supply and maintenance units were still north of Rennes. It was not until the afternoon of 4 Aug. that a direct supply line to the 4th was reestablished.

With the gas again flowing and the newly restated mission from Third Army overriding Middleton's last order, Wood pushed his forces west to Vannes. After a rapid seven hour drive the tanks of CCA, under Colonel Clarke, entered Vannes with the assistance of the local FFI battalion. Wood moved so quickly that the German garrison did not have time to prepare their demolitions and the city was taken before the installations could be destroyed.

Outside Vannes, S/Sgt. Howard Smith of C/37th Tank Bn. had five direct hits on his tank. First his gun was knocked out, then his periscope was destroyed. While exposed outside his hatch another round burst on his tank and blinded him in one eye. Smith continued to direct the

fire from the other tanks in his platoon and, without an operating gun, ran his tank over and crushed four German antitank gun positions. When the platoon leader was killed Smith took over command and continued to lead the platoon, refusing evacuation until the unit was taken out of the line. Smith was given a battlefield commission, but was later killed in action near Nancy.

CCA then moved north to make contact with CCB at Lorient. At one point outside Lorient the Germans tried to run a train of two locomotives and 14 cars through the 4th Armored lines. With two shots from a Sherman both steam engines were put out of commission, and a platoon of tanks and armored cars raked the disembarking German troops with machine gun fire. Two more German trains were knocked out by the 4th Armored near Queven on the Quimperlé to Lorient rail line.

CCB had taken a more northern route to the coast. Reaching Lorient on 7 Aug. the tankers had run into strong opposition from the German defenses. CCB was subjected to heavy shelling just south of Saint-Truchard where the unit had bivouacked in an open field. Unknown to them, the Germans had an observation post only 800 yards away that called in a massive barrage from the guns at Lorient. The 4th took more casualties in this one incident than at any other time since they had entered combat. The local French population told the Americans that the Germans were well dug in at Lorient with a plentiful supply of food and ammo. CCB probed the outskirts but did not want to get stuck fighting in a well-defended city. Middleton agreed with this and told Wood to take up a secure position and see what developed. One reason that Middleton wanted to be cautious at this time was that the German attack at Mortain had started, and he felt it best to wait and see exactly what the Germans would do before proceeding further into enemy territory.

After the war the German commander of Brittany, General Fahrmbacher, stated that Lorient was in such a poor state of preparedness at that time, that had the tankers pushed into the city they would have had a good chance of capturing it. Fahrmbacher did not feel the Lorient defenses were adequate to defend against an attack until 10 Aug. By that time the Americans had decided to let Lorient sit out the war.

Once the initial 4th Armored attacks on Lorient were met with resistance, General Wood wanted to hand the city over to an infantry unit and get back to moving east. Exactly what the situation in France was at that moment was not quite clear, and both Patton and Middleton wanted Wood to hold up outside Lorient until they could figure out how things were developing. In any event, there were no spare infantry units available to relieve the 4th.

Wood would later say that he felt the decision to pull him back from his eastern direction, in pursuit of a disorganized enemy, to sit outside Lorient *"was one of the great mistakes of the war."* Middleton would

probably have agreed, if it were not for the fact that the VIIIth Corps had suddenly gone from being the most important corps in Europe, to the least. The entire Normandy front had broken open and Patton was pouring his other troops through the hole in an attempt to encircle the main German forces in France. Middleton knew that he was not about to get any more assistance or troops from the Third Army while Patton had an opportunity to destroy the bulk of the German Army elsewhere. Wood bought his complaint directly to Bradley on 4 Aug. He remarked, *"I protested long, loud and violently. But no, we were forced to adhere to the original plan - with the only armor available and ready to cut the enemy to pieces. It was one of the colossally stupid decisions of the war."* It may have been a lost opportunity, but the senior commanders in the ETO were all focused on cutting off and destroying the main German combat forces in the west which they felt was more important.

Wood was told to keep his main forces at Lorient, but he was allowed to send some reconnaissance units to the east to make contact with the American 5th Infantry Division outside Nantes. Wood sent Colonel Clarke's CCA to Nantes and in a daring move this unit, with the assistance of the local FFI, entered Nantes and captured it. On 15 Aug. Wood finally was allowed to turn responsibility for Lorient over to the 6th Armored Division and attack with his division east into France.

Middleton later remarked that Wood had probably been right to want to forget the ports and drive as far east into the heart of France as possible before the Germans had a chance to react. This was assuming the Germans had been stopped at Mortain. Had they broken through to the sea, sending the 4th Armored further east would have been a major mistake. The question remains that if Wood had been allowed to move east, could the 4th Armored have been kept supplied over such a vast distance with German troops wandering about his supply lines.

The price the Americans paid for not grabbing the necessary port facilities became apparent as the supply lines grew longer and longer. Shortages of every kind plagued the Americans until the large ports were finally opened in 1945. There were shortages of ammunition, gasoline, jerry cans, tires, and even cigarettes. In the Ardennes that winter American soldiers would freeze while their winter clothing sat on ships offshore waiting for space at the docks.

Top.
The size of the gun barrel and the shape of the mantle identifies this as the 105mm howitzer version of the Sherman tank. These replaced the lighter M8 assault guns in the medium tank battalion headquarters company. They were used to fire a heavier high explosive round than the 75mm guns found in the majority of American tanks.
(National Archives)

THERE WERE ALWAYS "AT LEAST 200 GERMANS" IN EVERY DIRECTION.

Above.
***Yank Magazine* illustrator Cpl. Jack Coggins traveled with the 4th Armored Division during its drive from Rennes to the coast. This is his impression of 4th Armored soldiers asking the local population where the Germans were.**

Chapter 3

**The main railroad line running from Brest
to Rennes ran along the north coast of Brittany. If
Brest were to prove an effective port, this rail line
was vital to move material inland. Along
the route it crossed a number of lengthy bridges,
especially at Saint-Brieuc, Guingamp
and Morlaix.**

If the Germans destroyed these bridges it would take a long time to
get the railroad back into operation. One study concluded that if the
Germans destroyed every bridge over 100 feet in length, it would take
22 1/2 engineer battalion months (the work one engineer battalion could
do in one month) to get the line working again. While the 6th Armored
Division was directed to push up the center of Brittany, a special task
force was put together to drive up the northern coastal route to Brest
in an attempt to capture the rail line and bridges intact.

Task Force A (TFA) was formed on 31 July 1944 under Brigadier
General Herbert L. Earnest, commander of the 1st Tank Destroyer
Brigade. Originally intended for this one brief mission, TFA would
remain operational for 53 days and play a number of roles in the Brittany campaign.

The headquarters for TFA would be the command elements of the
1st Tank Destroyer Brigade. The main combat units were the 15th Cavalry Group (composed of both the 15th and 17th Cavalry Squadrons)
and the 6th Tank Destroyer Group (composed of the 705th Tank
Destroyer Bn.). Engineer support was provided by the
159th Engineer Combat Battalion, and light bridges
could be constructed by the 509th Engineer Light
Pontoon Company. Originally, no infantry or
medical support was provided.

The plan called for TFA to push along the north
Brittany coastal road as fast as possible. This road

TASK FORCE A

THE ALSOS MISSION

Alsos is the Greek word for "grove," and the Alsos Mission was
named after General Leslie Groves who was in charge of the American project to build an atomic bomb. The Alsos Mission was a group
of American scientists sent to recover as much German scientific
information as possible from newly liberated territories. Their primary job was to evaluate German progress towards an atomic bomb,
but their secondary objective was to look for any information regarding the direction or progress of German scientific research. To prevent such information from being looted or destroyed by the igno-
rant they had to travel right behind the combat troops.

After a brief stint in Italy, the Alsos Mission first entered France
in an attempt to find the famous French scientist Dr. Joliot-Curie.
Curie had been reported at his summer home in the town of L'Ar-
couest on the northern Brittany coast. Although Curie was not known
to be working on an atomic bomb, the Allies felt that a scientist of
his stature may have heard valuable gossip among his peers, or might
have suggestions as to where the mission should look.

At noon on 12 Aug. a single jeep bearing Col. Boris Basch and
his driver entered the command post of Task Force A and explained
to General Earnest their objective. As Task Force A advanced through
Paimpol the Alsos jeep located a local relative of Joliot-Curie who
showed them where the summer house was located. A quick survey
of the building showed it was not only deserted, but totally empty
of any furnishings. Gone were the hopes of finding any notes or scientific journals. As Basch and his driver were examining the house
they were caught in a fire fight between the advance guard of Task
Force A and a group of Germans passing through the area, but they
escaped unharmed.

With increased personnel the Alsos Mission later entered Rennes
as soon as it was liberated. There they found important documents
at Rennes University. Such simple things as course listings from
other universities would tell the Alsos Mission what scientists were
still teaching (and not working full time in a lab) and where they
had been located. Alsos then moved onto Paris, finding Joliot-Curie
safe at home. As the war progressed the Alsos mission was to uncov-
er many important documents, as well as a load of German urani-
um which was sent back to the States and utilized in the American
bomb program.

was a few miles inland from the sea, and there was a good network of
paved smaller roads along the way which would allow for TFA to by-
pass points of enemy resistance. Although the 79th Infantry Division
was originally selected to provide follow-up infantry support for TFA,
the 79th was diverted for an attack on Fougères so any assistance from
the infantry would have to come from the (further away) 83rd Infantry
Division.

To quote General Earnest's speech to his men on 1 Aug. 1944 at
Coutances:

*"This thing, as far as we are concerned, is a race to the sea… Our
general plan is to move down the north road, secure as many railroad
bridges as possible, and aid in the capture of Brest. In going down
there, we are bypassing resistance. I am going to designate certain
phase lines along here, but don't hold up on account of phase lines
unless we are in a fight."*

The vehicles of TFA were supplied with rations for seven days and
enough gas for 250 miles. Because they would be operating behind
German lines the officers were issued with escape kits containing a
silk map, a small compass, and a small hacksaw. Hedgerow cutters
were fitted on four M5A1 light tanks in each company so, if need be,
they could cut their way across country.

On 2 Aug. 1944 the 15th Cavalry Group, along with B/159th Engineers, and C/705th TD Bn. started the advance through the Avranches bottleneck. So tightly scheduled was the road system in this area
that the task force was given only 3 hours to move their 3,500 men and
their vehicles through Pontaubault. Earnest was told his troops must
arrive there at 0200 hrs. Aug. 3, not one minute before. The Task Force
must then be clear of the town by 0500 hrs. - not a minute later.

Once past Pontaubault, the column was subjected to Luftwaffe activity which delayed them by a few hours. Earnest had been told that they
would be following in the path of the 6th Armored Division as far as
Dinan, at which point the 6th would turn off to the south. Only then
would TFA be venturing into enemy territory. Thinking that the 6th
had cleared the path ahead of them, TFA moved along at a fairly fast
pace of 35-40 miles per hour. What they did not know was that the 6th
Armored had turned off to the south sooner than expected.

Colonel John B. Reybold, commanding the 15th Cavalry Group,
had moved up to the front of the column to assist in moving through
the congestion at Avranches. Thinking he might be needed up front in

Above.
**Charlie A. Kearns started off in the
15th Cavalry as a communications
sergeant. He was later given a
battlefield commission and served
in the 15th Cavalry HQ Troop. This
photo was taken at the end of the
Brittany campaign on the Crozon
Peninsula. The 15th Cavalry patch
is visible on his M43 jacket.**
(Courtesy Bill Parker)

Left.
**The 15th Cavalry Squadron was one
of the few American units smaller
than a division that had its own
shoulder sleeve insignia. This
example was worn by Bill Parker
during the Brittany campaign. The
red and white colors are taken
from the old cavalry guidon. The
crossed blades represent the kris
and kampilan swords used by the
Moro tribesmen during the
Philippine insurrection. The unit
served in France during WW1 at
Bordeaux, and the lion comes from
the arms of that city.**

Right.
**When the 15th Cavalry Regiment
was broken up into the 15th and
17th Cavalry Squadrons in
March 1944, the 1st Squadron of
the 15th Cavalry Regiment became
the 15th Cavalry Squadron and
kept the regimental insignia. The
2nd Squadron of the 15th Cavalry
Regiment became the 17th Cavalry
Squadron and adopted this
modified version of the design for
itself. The outer yellow band is the
branch color of the cavalry.**

19

COMPOSITION
OF TFA
on 31 July 1944

HQ, 1st Tank Destroyer Brigade

● 15th Cavalry Group
● 15th Cavalry Group HQ
● 15th Cavalry Squadron
● 17th Cavalry Squadron

HQ, 6th Tank Destroyer Group

● 705th Tank Destroyer Bn.
● 159th Engineer Combat Bn.
● 509th Engineer Light Pontoon Company

Above.
The famous Mont Saint-Michel sits just off the shore on the northern coast of Brittany, near Avranches. While moving past the area the author's father asked for a few hours off to visit it, but was told by his commander *"Don't you know there's a war on?"* The Germans respected the religious background of the structure, although it would have made a wonderful fortification had they chosen to garrison it.
(National Archives)

case they ran into the tail end of the 6th Armored, he remained near the front of his men. Moving along the Pontorson-Dol road on the morning of 3 Aug., TFA ran into an ambush as the column cleared the hill to the west of Baguer-Pican. As the lead vehicle reached the turn at the bottom of the hill the Germans struck and knocked out Reybold's command jeep. Heavy machine gun and antitank fire swept the column, which was unable to get off the road due to the ditches and hedges to either side. TFA was too bunched up to be able to maneuver since they had thought they were moving down a cleared road.

The assault guns immediately fired upon the German positions with smoke and high explosive shells, while Troop A (second in line) covered the withdrawal of Troop C (which had been in the lead). Only three men from the point platoon made it back. Col. Reybold was thought to be killed (however, at the end of the war it was discovered that he and four other men had been captured and spent the war as POWs on the Isle of Jersey). Col. Logan Berry, the commander of the 6th TD Group, took over the 15th Cavalry Group. It was not a good start for the mission.

At 0900 hrs. the word arrived to bypass the roadblock to the south. The cavalry patrol probing out in front received information from the French that there were more German units in the town of Dol. A request was sent back for infantry support from the 83rd Infantry Division to help reduce this position. However, the 83rd was still far behind, having much further to travel than the original support unit, the 79th Division.

After the losses in this initial engagement TFA needed replacement vehicles, equipment, and men. On the night of 3-4 Aug. the first supply convoy was run back through the area known to have German troops wandering about in it. The point vehicle was a jeep with a .50 cal. machine gun. Following that was an M8 armored car and then the

This photograph was taken as TFA liberated their first French village in Brittany. the townspeople have come out to the street to see the Americans pass by. The Red Cross flag is flown from the front of Dr. Parker's jeep.
(Courtesy Bill Parker)

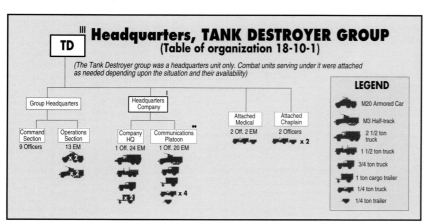

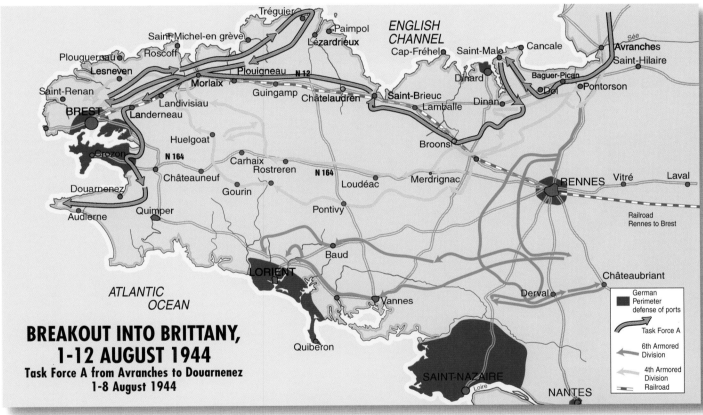

BREAKOUT INTO BRITTANY, 1-12 AUGUST 1944

Task Force A from Avranches to Douarnenez 1-8 August 1944

Map labels:
Tréguier, Saint-Michel-en-grève, Paimpol, ENGLISH CHANNEL, Lézardrieux, Cap-Fréhel, Saint-Malo, Cancale, Avranches, Plouguernau, Roscoff, Saint-Hilaire, Lesneven, Plouigneau, N 12, Dinard, Baguer-Pican, Pontorson, Saint-Renan, Morlaix, Guingamp, Châtelaudren, Saint-Brieuc, Dol, Landivisiau, Dinan, BREST, Landerneau, Lamballe, Huelgoat, Broons, Crozon, N 164, Carhaix, Rostreren, N 164, Loudéac, Merdrignac, RENNES, Vitré, Laval, Châteauneuf, Gourin, Douarnenez, Pontivy, Railroad Rennes to Brest, Audierne, Quimper, ATLANTIC OCEAN, Baud, Châteaubriant, LORIENT, Vannes, Derval, Quiberon, SAINT-NAZAIRE, NANTES, Loire

Legend:
German Perimeter defense of ports
Task Force A
6th Armored Division
4th Armored Division
Railroad

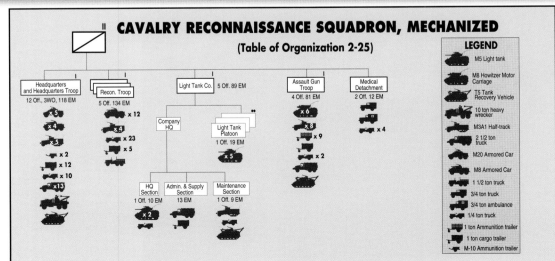

CAVALRY RECONNAISSANCE SQUADRON, MECHANIZED
(Table of Organization 2-25)

Headquarters and Headquarters Troop — 12 Off., 3WO, 118 EM
Recon. Troop — 5 Off. 134 EM
Light Tank Co. — 5 Off. 89 EM
Assault Gun Troop — 4 Off. 81 EM
Medical Detachment — 2 Off. 12 EM

Company HQ
Light Tank Platoon — 1 Off. 19 EM

HQ Section — 1 Off. 10 EM
Admin. & Supply Section — 13 EM
Maintenance Section — 1 Off. 9 EM

x12, x4, x2, x12, x10, x13, x12, x23, x5, x6, x8, x9, x2, x4, x5, x2

LEGEND
M5 Light tank
M8 Howitzer Motor Carriage
T5 Tank Recovery Vehicle
10 ton heavy wrecker
M3A1 Half-track
2 1/2 ton truck
M20 Armored Car
M8 Armored Car
1 1/2 ton truck
3/4 ton truck
3/4 ton ambulance
1/4 ton truck
1 ton Ammunition trailer
1 ton cargo trailer
M-10 Ammunition trailer

Above. A jeep from C Troop, 15th Cavalry Squadron entering Morlaix. A brightly colored aerial recognition panel has been tied to the hood of the jeep. The flowers have been tossed onto the vehicle by the liberated inhabitants. The front bumper is used to carry additional machine gun ammunition.

Opposite page, center. This top view of an M-8 armored car shows extra supplies stacked on the rear deck underneath the aerial recognition panel. The circle was added around the white star when the Americans discovered that, from a distance, the star could be mistaken for a German cross. Task Force A was out in front of the rest of the American Army and wanted to make sure the Air Force knew they were Allied troops.

Left. This 2 1/2 ton truck bears the nickname "Rough Ride." Various patriotic sayings have been chalked on the sides by the local inhabitants. Gasoline cans were always in short supply. This truck carries a few captured German cans next to the driver.

Bottom left. The bumper markings on this jeep are very clear. On the left they read: "3A/17C" standing for Third Army, 17th Cavalry Squadron, and to the right "B-38" indicating the 38th vehicle of Troop B. In the center is the invasion bar code and unit serial number "46591." When landed in France the vehicle should have had the left hand bumper makings obscured, with only the bar code and serial number visible. The bar code was similar for all equipment in the company or troop, and based on the last two digits of the unit serial number.
(All photos Pillet Collection)

supply trucks. At this time not every truck had been equipped with a .50 ring mount, so only every third truck was armed with a machine gun. In the middle of the column was a half-track with a .50 cal., and two .30 cal. machine guns. The rear was protected by a second M8.

When the supply column reached Pontaubault it had to split up to visit the different supply dumps. The ammo trucks had to go all the way back to Omaha Beach to get ammo for the tank destroyers, replacement personnel were at Granville, while gas and replacement vehicles were scattered at other locations. All vehicles rendezvoused at the task force rear headquarters and waited until daylight to move out. They decided that all supply trains would move only in the daylight hours when they could have air cover, and to help avoid being ambushed in the dark. As TFA moved further to the west it became harder and harder to keep it supplied. In tribute to the rarely heralded quartermasters, the task force may have passed out of communications at times, but never ran out of food, ammo, or gasoline. To prevent the German forces in Saint-Malo from withdrawing to Brest, TFA was given an order to contain them until the infantry of the 83rd was brought up. This delayed them in their drive for the railroad bridges. At the base of the Saint-Malo Peninsula the lead elements of TFA came under antitank fire. A brief moment of hesitation ensued among the green American troops, but a dismounted attack was quickly organized and the German position destroyed.

On the morning of 3 Aug. the Americans had secured the base of the Saint-Malo Peninsula, and TFA begin to probe north towards Châteauneuf. Allied air strikes destroyed the German gunboats in the nearby estuary and the coastal artillery guns that had earlier shelled the

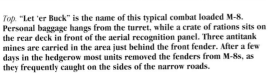

Top. "Let 'er Buck" is the name of this typical combat loaded M-8. Personal baggage hangs from the turret, while a crate of rations sits on the rear deck in front of the aerial recognition panel. Three antitank mines are carried in the area just behind the front fender. After a few days in the hedgerow most units removed the fenders from M-8s, as they frequently caught on the sides of the narrow roads.

Above right. How do you say "Where is the Cognac?" This happy jeep driver carried his M-3 "grease gun" on the hood along side the flowers tossed by the locals. The M-3 was a cheaply produced submachine gun, designed to replace the heavier and more expensive Thompson. Generally not well liked by the troops, it was useful for tank crews that had limited space.

Right. The driver (right) and assistant driver (left) of an M-8 armored car worked in very confined spaces. On the hatch in front of them is a small vision slit and a periscope. Many M-8 crews kept the 37mm gun loaded with canister ammunition. This ammunition was similar to a large shotgun shell and was devastating to personnel, and likely to scare an armored target long enough for the M-8 to get away. *(All photos Pillet Collection)*

Americans. The advance was further delayed because the Germans had flooded the lowlands. This prevented the mechanized units from moving off the roads. A roadblock at Châteauneuf stopped the advance. It was composed of angled steel bars set in concrete and flanked by concrete blocks. A ditch in front of it prevented any vehicle from bypass-

Above.
The Germans had fortified potential landing sites along the Atlantic Coast, which included beach obstacles to prevent Allied boats from getting ashore easily. This beach, near Saint-Michel en Grève, was protected by obstacles designed to rip out the bottom of Allied landing craft at high tide. These are very similar to those used at the Normandy invasion beaches.

ing it. Lt. Bob Dwan took an eight man patrol through the swamps to the east into Châteauneuf and, after fighting their way back out, was able to provide valuable information regarding the German positions.

The largest railroad bridge in France

The next day a rifle company of the 329th Infantry (sent up from the 83rd Infantry Division) was badly shot up trying to capture the roadblock. The reconnaissance company of the 15th Cavalry dismounted and took heavy casualties while allowing the engineers to place explosives on the rails of the roadblock. Tank destroyers then fired point-blank at the steel rails without causing visible damage. Finally Lt. Col. Templeton ordered up a heavy M32 tank retriever. He sent the M32 to try and crush the metal rails sticking up from the road, which he hoped had been weakened by the explosives. This tactic worked and the roadblock was removed by 1500 hrs. After this engagement it became clear that Saint-Malo was heavily defended and would not fall without a fight. TFA was relieved by the 83rd Division at 2200 hrs. on 5 Aug. Task Force A had driven the Germans up into Saint-Malo and 665 German prisoners had been taken, but the operation had delayed them, by roughly two days, in reaching the railway bridges.

Left
After the beaches at Saint-Michel-en-Grève were cleared by Task Force A, LSTs (Landing Ship, Tank) were used to bring supplies into Brittany. The LSTs beached themselves during high tide. Then, at low tide their cargo of trucks could be driven off the LSTs and onto the shore. Using small ports such as this enabled the Americans to stretch the limited tonnage able to be brought in over the invasion beaches. *(National Archives)*

Left.
Smaller vessels, such as these LCTs, were able to travel up the river to the center of Morlaix, where standard engineer cranes were used to shift supplies right onto trucks. The railway bridge in the background was one of the key objectives the Americans needed to capture intact, if they ever wanted to get the Brittany railway operating again.
(National Archives)

Dr. Bill Parker is seen here on the left with Captain Isaiah Lukens, the 15th Cav. Squadron surgeon, who wears a newly issued M43 jacket. Parker's jeep, named the "Ruptured Duck," is covered with Red Cross markings and flags to make sure the Germans knew it was a medical vehicle. Parker was on the road most of the time coordinating the medical support in Task Force A, and ran a high risk of bumping into German stragglers. To the rear of the jeep can be seen an added storage compartment covered by a tarpaulin.
(Courtesy Bill Parker)

Once troops of the 83rd Infantry Division began arriving at Saint-Malo, TFA prepared to resume its original mission. General Earnest left a platoon of tank destroyers to assist the 83rd. Local Frenchmen informed TFA of strong German positions in Dinan, so the column by-passed the city by about 11 kilometers to the south. To ensure that TFA was not held up by another roadblock, the 3/330th Infantry and C/323rd Field Artillery were attached to Earnest's task force. On 6 Aug. the column was briefly halted by a blown bridge over the Ille River, but the engineers constructed a way across and soon the troops were moving again. That night cavalry patrols entered both Lamballe and Saint-Brieuc without encountering any Germans. French Colonel Eon of the FFI was already in the town and the three railroad bridges there were taken intact. An engineer company was detailed to guard the bridges, as well as operate a POW camp for the Germans that had already surrendered.

Although the main mission of TFA was to secure the railroad bridges, French SAS troops, OSS Group Donald, and a number of Jedburgh teams had been sent into Brittany with the job of keeping the Germans from blowing the bridges before the Americans got to them. However, there are conflicting records about who actually captured which bridges and when. This is partially due to the number of different bridges, the secrecy of the covert units, and the rapid movement of TFA. Bill Kraft, the S-2 (intelligence) officer for TFA, said that when they got to Saint-Brieuc they found the bridge already in safe hands. He recalled it was very clear to them at the time that the Germans were much more interested in withdrawing to their strongholds than demolishing bridges, so the staff of TFA no longer worried about the safety of the bridges. In this joint operation, which could not have occurred without the support of the truly dedicated members of the FFI, the various allied units were able to capture every major bridge along the rail line intact.

At Saint-Brieuc the French Resistance reported that 500 -1,000 Germans and Russians were camped five miles west of the town. The French felt the Germans would surrender if approached by Americans. Lt. Col. Fuller of the 15th Cavalry and both a French and a British officer from a Jedburgh Team drove out to visit the Germans under a white flag. The Germans opened fire and wounded the three officers, then fled the area heading west. TFA was able to call for fighter-bomber air strikes upon this enemy column which devastated them.

American engineers remove mines from the small port of Roscoff on the north coast of Brittany. The small German garrison was captured by men from Operational Group Donald, which freed Task Force A so they could proceed south to Brest. Roscoff, now a major ferry terminal, was used as one of the minor ports to bring in supplies for the Americans at Brest.
(National Archives)

The next day a roadblock at Châtelaudren was overrun by the combined efforts of light tanks and engineers. German forces could be seen withdrawing westward on horse drawn wagons. Heavy resistance was expected at Guingamp because it was a German central supply base for the area. The FFI claimed 2,000 German troops were in the town, but TFA ran into only weak roadblocks and scattered mines. With the assistance of the FFI and a few air strikes Guingamp was in American hands by midnight and the city was turned over, along with 398 German POWs, to the French.

On 8 Aug. General Earnest detached the 17th Cavalry (less one troop), the tank destroyer recon platoon, an infantry company, and an engineer company and gave them the job of dashing ahead to Morlaix and capturing the railroad bridges. One was the largest railroad bridge in France. It was a stone bridge one thousand feet long and two hundred feet high. The remainder of TFA would push on along the N12 behind the advance force. Just east of Plouigneau the 17th Cavalry ran into two 40mm guns under a railroad trestle bridge. Two of the light

GERMANS CAPTURED BY TFA	
● Lesneven	550
● Guingamp	398
● Lannion- Saint-Michel	589
● Ponvanen-Tréguier-Lézardrieux	756
● Paimpol-Plounez	231
● Plougastel Peninsula	69
● Crozon Peninsula	1,679
● Douarnenez Peninsula	322
Total	**5,656**

TFA casualties
55 KIA, 201 WIA.

Top.
At Saint-Pol de Léon the word was spread that medical help was needed right away for the German prisoners. When the medics arrived they found that the Germans were not sick or wounded, just dead drunk. They had broken into the stocks of alcohol before surrendering and drunk themselves into a stupor. *(Courtesy Bill Parker)*

Above, left.
These French women were accused of collaborating with the Germans. Once the town was liberated by the Americans, the citizens shaved their heads to punish them and show everyone they were collaborators. *(Courtesy Bill Parker)*

Above.
Every American soldier will recognize this sign. It indicates a "Prophylactic Station" where treatment for possible exposure to venereal disease could be obtained. Even in the fast moving dash across Brittany the medical units of Task Force made sure the treatments were available if needed. *(Courtesy Bill Parker)*

tanks moved ahead and knocked out the guns. Without any other antitank weapons, roughly 70 Germans in the area surrendered. The column pressed on and ran into the rear of a withdrawing German convoy. The cavalrymen were told to put out marker panels and call in fighter-bombers in the area to attack the Germans. After the air strikes the advance group of TFA continued along the main road, while Troop A attempted to move to Morlaix along side roads to the south, and Troop B to the north. Neither were successful due to minefields and roadblocks.

About noon, the lead jeep was fired upon by light German guns on the outskirts of Morlaix. Moving his tanks down the main road, the squadron commander realized the Germans must know the Americans were in the city. The attached infantry company was ordered to make a run for the main railway bridge and hold it at all costs. They moved through the town and took the bridge with only minor casualties. Lt. Paul Quelen and the nine other SAS troops of the "Derry II" mission had apparently already secured the bridge with the assistance of some local Frenchmen. The German soldiers holding up in the castle at the center of Morlaix surrendered after being fired upon by the infantry. Compared to 1,460 German POWs, TFA had so far suffered only 21 KIA, 42 WIA, and 14 MIA.

The task force trains had established the SOP that each night an advance party would scout ahead for a bivouac area. As soon as the vehicles arrived at the designated area they were camouflaged and security posts were set up. The armored vehicles were used as outposts for an all-around defense. Crew members rotated guard duty, but always worked in pairs. This attention to security proved important on the morning of 9 Aug. when the supply trains of the 15th Cavalry were attacked in the vicinity of Plouigneau.

In a heavy fog a German unit of 200 men and horse drawn antitank weapons moving south discovered the American encampment. Fearing the Germans were after their gasoline, food, and ammo, the Americans tried to move their supply trucks. Unfortunately, both entrances to the bivouac field were covered by German fire and the Americans realized

they were stuck. A defensive circle was set up inside the field, in the style of a covered wagon train of the old west. A call for help went out over the radio to the rest of the task force. A cavalry troop and platoon of light tanks were sent back from Morlaix to rescue them. The column was ambushed and three tanks were lost. Eventually, with the help of fighter-bombers, the supply trains were able to disengage from the Germans and make their way to safety.

Having secured the important railway bridges, TFA was given a new mission on 9 Aug. The 6th Armored Division had passed down the center of Brittany on its way to Brest, but the German forces pushed aside were moving back onto the main supply route for the 6th (N164). TFA was ordered to clear the area north of the 6th Armored's advance.

The 17th Cav. and one TD company were left in Morlaix to guard the railroad bridges. A combat team composed of the 15th Cavalry Group HQ, HQ 15th Squadron, I/330th Infantry, C/705th TD and a battery of artillery were dispatched to capture Lesneven. While south of Lesneven, a German column was spotted moving in from the east. Again fighter-bombers were called in to strike the Germans. By chance, the small fighter-bombers arrived at the same time a group of medium bombers were attacking the city of Brest. For a moment the men of the 15th Cavalry were treated to a spectacle of Allied aircraft filling the skies and attacking the Germans to either side of them.

TFA was making good progress, but the unit still needed a supply connection with the rest of the American Army. Patrols were sent out to make contact with the 6th Armored Div. operating to the south. Convoys of TFA continued to make the dangerous run back to Avranches though territory filled with scattered German units. On 9 Aug. Major Ralph K. Johnson, the supply and personnel officer of TFA, was leading a column of five light tanks and three trucks. These were replacements for damaged vehicles and were unmanned except for a single ordnance corps driver in each. At the village of Plounevez-Moedec Johnson was told that German soldiers had blocked the road ahead. The ordnance drivers were organized into one tank crew, and with a single light tank Major Johnson ventured out to contact the enemy. Entering rough terrain Major Johnson left the tank and proceeded on foot underneath a white flag. He was able to convince the Germans that they were cut off by Americans and the entire German unit, four officers and 107 enlisted men, surrendered to him.

On 10 Aug. elements of the 15th Cavalry moved further back to the east to attack an enemy position at Plougerneau. The majority of the Germans withdrew to positions along the coast. While TFA was preparing to go after them a new order came in. TFA was to capture the coastal town of Saint-Michel-en-Grève (70 km away) and secure the beaches so LSTs could land supplies there. To prevent delay from roadblocks the cavalrymen split into smaller columns moving along three parallel secondary roads. They entered Saint-Michel finding it abandoned by the Germans, but surrounded by minefields and roadblocks. That afternoon on 11 Aug. three LSTs came ashore. The TFA engineers went to work and by the next day had removed most of the mines and obstacles on the beach, as

OPERATIONAL GROUP DONALD

One of the black painted B-24Ds used by the OSS to drop agents and supplies into occupied Europe. These special squadrons, known as the "carpetbaggers," were painted for low visibility during their nighttime missions. Even the American star is subdued to reduce visibility. *(National Archives)*

Below. **This remarkable group photo taken in Guimillau on the 6th of August 1944 shows all but one member of OSS Operation Group Donald. 1st row from L-R, T/5 Robert Reppenhagen (radio operator), Sgt. Maurice Burke, S/Sgt. P. Bolen, 1st Lt. H.R. Kern, Capt. Cadalen (French), 1st Lt. Rafael Hirtz, T/Sgt. Walter Cabe. 2nd row L-R, Pvt. Edward Chaput, S/Sgt. S. Davis, Pfc. Jack Riley. Missing from the photo is T/4 Leo Tetreault. In the center is Captain Cadalen, a former French Army captain who played a major role in the resistance.** *(Y. Creach)*

The British sent SAS teams into France to assist the resistance, but the Americans had their own special units for the task under the command of the OSS. Operational Groups (OGs) were small parties of highly trained OSS men that were sent behind enemy lines to perform specific military tasks, normally in conjunction with local resistance members.

OG "Donald" was the only such OSS unit to drop into Brittany. On the night of 5/6 Aug 1944 eleven members of OG Donald jumped just east of Landivisiau with their primary mission of protecting the bridges around Landivisiau. There they were to meet Jedburgh Team "Hilary," which was supposed to be able to provide information on the region, as well as introductions to the local Resistance forces.

OG Donald originally consisted of 25 men and 5 officers under command of Lt. Col. Serge Obolensky. One of their three aircraft had mechanical trouble and was forced to abort the mission. The second was unable to identify the drop zone and returned to England with its

passengers. The third aircraft was able to drop its load of 11 men successfully. With their original commander back in England, this small group was led by lieutenants Raf D. Hirtz and H.R. Kern.

Making contact with the local FFI, OG Donald quickly secured the bridge at Guimiliau and trained some of the local FFI to take over guarding it. Containers filled with weapons and ammunition had been dropped along with the OG and these were distributed to the Frenchmen who volunteered to help guard the bridge. Due to the confusing situation in Brittany, Jed Team Hilary, which was supposed to be the liaison between Donald and the FFI, never showed up. All of Donald's radio equipment had been packed on the two aircraft that did not drop their containers in France, so the small group was left without communications back to their headquarters.

When the men of OG Donald felt the bridge was firmly under Allied control they decided to see what else they could do in Brittany. Traveling to Lesneven they met General Earnest and Task Force A and learned about the gen-

eral situation in Brittany. After returning to check on the status of the bridge, OG Donald led a small party of men to capture 22 Germans at Guiclan, a small town five miles from Landivisiau. Then they traveled on to the coastal town of Roscoff where the Germans had a small position defending the Roscoff Harbor. 30 Germans surrendered when approached by the American led group, mostly customs officials and naval officers.

Finally on 13 Aug. a patrol from OG Donald made contact with Jedburgh Team Hilary in Morlaix. Through Hilary radio contact with England was established and a request was made to drop more arms for the FFI. While in Morlaix the men of Donald ran into General Earnest again who mentioned that he had heard of a large group of Germans in Roscoff. OG Donald was pleased to be able to report they had already taken care of the Germans and the small port was clear. On 17 Aug. an American civil affairs unit finally, arrived to take over administration in the region and OG Donald started back to England.

well as roadblocks cutting off the seashore. In the next 6 weeks 60,000 tons of supplies would be landed on those beaches.

The success at Saint-Michel-en-Grève led the Navy to consider Morlaix as a place to bring in supplies. They sent PT Boats 502 and 504 to reconnoiter on 8 Aug. At first they were met with small arms fire from the shore, until the crews were able to convince the local population they were Americans, and on 25 Aug. a convoy of two liberty ships and ten LCTs arrived at Morlaix. Further east the minor port of Roscoff was also used to bring supplies directly from England into Brittany. Word now reached TFA of a German force building up in the area to the south of Morlaix-Guingamp. Although a reconnaissance patrol made the long sweep from Morlaix, through Carhaix and Rostrenen, no Germans were found. How-

ever, scattered German outposts and separated units moving to Brest continued to pose problems for the task force. A large group of Germans was located in the coastal area north of Guingamp and TFA was sent, along with Colonel Eon and his Frenchmen, to eliminate them. The deal struck by Middleton was that the Americans would get the German POWs and the French would get the weapons and supplies captured.

The assault against these Germans started on 14 Aug. They engaged the Germans at Tréguier, but the enemy withdrew and blew the bridge over the Jaudy River to cover their escape. The Germans stubbornly resisted, but with the aid of 300 men from the FFI the area was secured by the end of the day. The next day the objective was the German garrisons in the coastal towns of Lézardrieux and Paimpol. These were important to the Germans as they represented one of their last connections to the Channel Islands. After a sur-

Above.
This shot of a destroyed M8 Howitzer Motor Carriage nicknamed "Wild Terror" was taken by Sergeant George Martin of the 603rd Engineer Camouflage Battalion - part of the 23rd Special Troops deception unit - somewhere outside Brest.
(Courtesy George Martin)

Above.
Brigadier General Earnest is seen here addressing the men of Task Force A upon the completion of their mission and the disbanding of the unit. TFA had been organized for one short operation (the capture of the railroad bridges), but was kept together as a fighting force for over 60 days.

render ultimatum was refused by the German commander of Paimpol, TFA moved in. Heavy minefields kept the vehicles from entering Lézardrieux, but dismounted troops forced their way in and, with only minor casualties, pushed the Germans out of the town. German morale was very poor and the defenses collapsed soon after.

On 16 Aug. the cavalrymen continued to eliminate small pockets of German resistance. A/15th Cavalry located a German position on the small offshore Ile à Bois. A narrow causeway led from the mainland to the heavily defended island. The situation was a stalemate, with no way to advance on the island and the American assault guns having no effect on the concrete emplacements. The troop commander, Captain Wheelock, continually changed his guns' positions to make it appear he had more tanks. While directing this action Captain Wheelock was wounded by a German sniper. The Germans finally decided that they were greatly outnumbered and sent up a white flag.

While the French and TFA were fighting at Paimpol, a battalion of the 8th Infantry Division (3/28th) was sent to the Cap Fréhel area. The Germans surrendered there on 15 Aug. With the capture of Cap Fréhel, and Paimpol on 18 Aug., all organized German resistance in the northern region of Brittany from Saint-Malo to Brest was eliminated.

On 18 Aug. TFA moved back to the west and took up patrolling between Landivisiau and Landerneau. Special precautions were taken to guard the bridges over the Elorn River near Brest, and patrolling was extended to the south across the base of the Daoulas Peninsula. The reconnaissance patrols quickly discovered the main German defensive line on the peninsula which was anchored on the left flank by the town of Daoulas.

The Daoulas Peninsula sticks out into the water just opposite the port of Brest. Possession of this land would allow the Americans direct observation and artillery fire right into the heart of the city. The Germans also understood the importance of the Daoulas Peninsula and had dug in along major terrain features. The area was too congested for the mechanized cavalry troops of TFA to take on alone, so the decision was made to form a new task force much heavier in infantry. Task Force A was not disbanded, but assigned to this new larger force called Task Force B.

Under TFB the cavalrymen of TFA would assist in capturing the Daoulas Peninsula and then move on to screen the base of the Crozon Peninsula (located further to the south). The men of TFA would continue to play a part in the siege of Brest until they captured the last positions on the Douarnenez Peninsula far to the south.

THE DENTIST OF TASK FORCE A

In the rush to organize Task Force A no one had given thought to medical support for the unit. A cavalry group was only a headquarters unit and the only medical personnel it had was a dentist. Each of the units in the task force had its own small medical staff, but they were only designed to handle the needs of a few men. A few ambulances were initially provided for evacuation of casualties, but after the first engagement these ambulances went back with the wounded and were never seen again.

As TFA moved further and further west, more and more men became wounded. With no way to care for the casualties they were left in the care of local Frenchmen. At one point the dentist for the 15th Cavalry, Captain Bill Parker, was forced to leave a wounded man bundled up by the side of the road hoping that someone able to take care of him would come along. This lack of medical support infuriated Parker and he stormed up to General Earnest and verbally exploded about the problem. The general calmly asked Parker what he thought was needed to handle the problem, and was told a collecting company assigned to the Task Force was the answer. Earnest got on the radio and the 429th Collecting Company was designated to move casualties back to the evacuation hospitals.

Parker found himself now coordinating the medical support for the entire task force. He would attend the briefing each night, then travel in turn to visit each of the doctors assigned to the combat units. After gathering their suggestions he figured out how to best handle the casualties and made sure they were taken care of. This was normally the task of the unit surgeon (the title given to the senior doctor in any unit), but the young dentist handled the job well.

Later on in September a medical doctor arrived at the TFA headquarters and reported in to General Earnest as the new task force surgeon. Earnest reportedly said, *"Where the hell were you when I needed you? I've got a young kid here doing a fine job and I don't want anyone messing it up."* He then threw out the new doctor and went back to work. What resulted was that "Doc Parker" continued to run the medical side of the unit, but each night the new doctor would sign the paperwork to keep the higher authorities happy.

Doc Parker also played another important role in the history of Task Force A. He was a dedicated amateur photographer. He shot many rolls of film throughout the war. Some he even developed huddled in the darkness of his sleeping bag. Other rolls were sent home with wounded men to escape the censors. A handful of rare color shots made their way back to the States through friends in the French embassy. His photos are some of the only visual records of task force A in Brittany and provide excellent coverage of a cavalry unit throughout WW2.

Bill "Doc" Parker, the 15th Cavalry Group dentist, stands next to his jeep "Ruptured Duck" somewhere on the Crozon Peninsula.
(Courtesy Bill Parker)

THE 6TH ARMORED DIVISION

Chapter 4

The narrow roads and hedgerows of Brittany were ideally suited for German tank-hunter teams. A single brave German soldier could hide in a foxhole dug next to the road and spring up to fire the panzerfaust as the tank drove by. No matter how powerful a tank was, when buttoned up the crew had limited visibility and needed friendly infantry close by to protect them.
(National Archives)

When the 6th Armored Division landed in Normandy on 18 July 1944, the first man ashore was the division commander, Major General Robert W. Grow. On 28 July the 6th, or "Super Sixth" as it would be called, entered combat and crossed the Ay River in Normandy. After crossing the Sienne River they were sent to clear the town of Granville and move down the coast to Avranches. They continued to advance south against sporadic enemy resistance until reaching the base of the Cotentin Peninsula at Avranches.

On the afternoon of 31 July Grow was ordered to move the 6th Armored Division to Pontaubault and hold awaiting orders to advance. Before his troops had even reached the city he was given new orders to drive through it on into Brittany. Passing through the Avranches bottleneck was not easy for the tankers, who had to share the narrow roads with the 4th Armored Division. The Luftwaffe was taking a special interest in the bridges over the Sélune River. During the two days the 6th was in the area their attached antiaircraft unit (the 777th AAA Bn.) took credit for shooting down 18 German aircraft, and was awarded the French Croix De Guerre for defending the vital bridges from Luftwaffe attacks.

Once past Pontaubault the 6th Armored was ready to spring into Brittany and capture the corps objective of Dinan. General Patton personally gave Grow a verbal order to by-pass Dinan and "take Brest." He also told Grow that he had made a five pound bet with Montgomery that the Third Army would have Brest by Saturday night. With this general directive, and confirmation from Middleton that indeed he was

Tanks of the 6th Armored Division move through Bréhal on their way south to Avranches. The jeep is covered with bedrolls and other personal items. Unlike these mechanized troops, the regular infantry could only take what they could carry on their backs.
(National Archives)

to take Brest, Grow sent General James Taylor's CCA south to cross the Couesnon River at Antrain. Colonel Hanson's CCR, followed by Col. Read's CCB, would cross the river at Pontorson.

Normally in an armored division CCR would not be used to spearhead an attack. Due to the difficulty of moving the unit through the Avranches bottleneck, CCR was in the lead when it ran into a German position at Brée. The Germans had a perfect position for an ambush. Their antitank guns were well camouflaged and commanded a long stretch of road. Allowing the American advance guard to move in close to their guns before opening fire, the first units of CCR had passed through the ambush zone before the Germans opened fire. The Germans then destroyed the lead two M7s of the main column. This blocked the road to the front. They then hit a half-track 3/4 of a mile back to block off the rear.

For many of these men this was their first time in combat, and they reacted surprisingly well. The advance party continued on to their objective and grabbed the river crossings at Pontorson. The main column immediately left the road and took up positions. Knowing that the men of A/231st Field Artillery Bn. were stuck in the ditches by the side of the road, Major Goodin ordered his other two batteries to fire within 30 yards of the side of the road. This close in support from the M7s

"Let's Do it" is an M5 tank from CCA Headquarters of the 6th Armored Division. The photo was probably taken outside Brest during the time that General Taylor's CCA was holding the perimeter waiting for more troops to arrive. During this time these men earned the nickname "The Brassiere Boys." Every available inch of storage space on the vehicles has been put to use for the drive through Brittany. They did not know when, or if, they would be resupplied, so extra cans of water and boxes of rations were taken along.
(Courtesy Sgt. Allen Walker)

was credited with breaking up the initial German attack. While the 15th Tank Bn. fired on the German positions, the troops of the 9th Armored Infantry Bn. dismounted and moved in. By chance one German bullet went right down the barrel of an M7 and penetrated the base of a fired shell casing, much to the amazement of Sgt. Gerding who was pulling it out of the breech.

Sgt. Worton, the first sergeant of Battery A, was awarded the DSC for his actions at Brée which included driving off seven Germans attacking his vehicle. He shot three with his carbine and the other four ran off. He then moved up and down the line encouraging his men and shooting at the Germans. Captain Robert Leoffer, the battalion surgeon of the 9th Armored Infantry Bn., was awarded the Silver Star for moving up the road and providing aid to the wounded while his medics evacuated the casualties, two at a time, in a jeep. Morphine was particularly welcomed by men burned in the vehicle explosions.

With the assistance of a liaison aircraft spotting for the artillery, the Germans were eliminated after a three hour fight and the 6th moved on. Once at Pontorson the 6th formed into two columns of CCA and CCB, with CCR following whichever combat command was making better headway. The reconnaissance units were to constantly probe ahead to find the path of least resistance and maintain contact between the two columns.

On the road to Pontorson the 6th ran into a group of American sailors pinned down by the side of the road. It seems that Captain Norman Ives, commander of the naval base at Cherbourg, had taken a party of 97 men down the Cotentin coast to examine the smaller ports. While in Granville they heard a false rumor that Saint-Malo had been captured and headed there at top speed. Outside Pontorson they were ambushed by Germans and suffered five killed and eight wounded. Pinned down, the sailors held out, refusing to surrender, until finally rescued by the 6th Armored.

CCA on the southern flank traveled with no serious German opposition. CCB, to the north, ran into only minor German defenses until it hit the outskirts of Dinan. With the assistance of fighter-bomber cover Read's CCB by-passed Dinan to the south and halted for the night at Bécherel. In a staff conference that night General Grow was able to tell his officers to ignore Dinan and focus on their new objective, Brest. The 6th Armored was now faced with traveling over 200 miles across enemy controlled territory without a secure line of supply.

Originally the 6th, like Task Force A, had been promised infantry support from the 79th Infantry Division, but that unit had been diverted by General Bradley to the east. In a few days the 83rd Infantry Division was expected move up to help the 6th, but for the time being the tankers were on their own. The only non-divisional support they could count on was the 174th Field Artillery Battalion (self-propelled 155mm guns) and some air cover.

Throughout the Brittany campaign fighter-bombers really proved their value. Time and again the fast moving armored columns were able to call upon air support to help them break through German resistance. This was mainly due to a technique that had been developed only recently in Normandy. Pilots were put into tanks, so they would be up at the front, and were given radios that could communicate with the aircraft overhead. This meant that there was a skilled observer on the ground where the action was who knew just how to explain to the aircraft overhead what was needed. Much is made of this technique in Air Force histories, however, many armored veterans do not ever recall hearing about such a thing during the battle.

At noon on 3 Aug. the Super Sixth moved off again and CCA quickly got into a fight at Mauron. After a few hours the Germans there were eliminated and CCA moved on. To the north CCB was moving unopposed when it was ordered to stop. General Grow had just received new orders not to bypass Saint-Malo or Dinan. The 6th had now been ordered to assist Task Force A with the reduction of Saint-Malo, to be followed by the capture of Dinan. Grow immediately sent off a messenger to Middleton requesting that his mission to Brest be reinstated and sadly turned CCA to the north towards Dinan. He kept CCB where it was, ready to proceed west in the hopes of new orders.

Also on 3 Aug. a platoon of the 603rd Tank Destroyer Bn. entered the town of Broons and was confronted by the crew of an American

6th ARMORED DIVISION "THE SUPER SIXTH"

The 6th landed in France 18 July 1944, and helped break out of Normandy. Drove to Brest then moved to Lorient. Then they turned east and reached the Saar in November and Germany in December. The 6th was heavily engaged in the Ardennes fighting, and drove the Germans back across the Our River in Jan. In Spring 1945 attacked through the Siegfried line and reached Rhine in March. After capturing Mulhausen in April and Buchenwald. They took Leipzig and stopped along the Mulde River awaiting the Russians.

6th Armored Division (Bamboo)	Division Artillery (Battle)
● CCA (Bacon)	● 128th Armored Field Artillery Battalion.
● CCB (Balloon)	● 212th Armored Field Artillery Battalion.
● CCR (Back)	● 231st Armored Field Artillery Bn.
● 15th Tank Bn.	
● 68th Tank Bn.	● 86th Cavalry Recon Squadron
● 69th Tank Bn.	● 76th Armored Medical Bn.
● 9th Armored Infantry Bn.	● 128th Armored Ordnance Bn.
● 44th Armored Infantry Bn.	● 25th Armored Engineer Bn.
● 50th Armored Infantry Bn.	● 146th Armored Signal Co.

General Grow awards the Silver Star to assistant division engineer Captain Ed Clark. Captured while searching for a water point, Clark was taken as a POW to Jersey Island. He escaped from the Germans by boat in January 1945.
(National Archives)

B-24. They had been shot down in Brittany and had been hiding from the Germans for 105 days. The same day word of the American advance reached the German command post at Pontivy and they evacuated to Lorient. Pontivy was the German communications center in Brittany. This disrupted the ability of the Brittany defenders to coordinate their actions in the region.

Around 1100 hours on 4 Aug. General Patton appeared at Grow's HQ near Merdrignac to award the Bronze Star to Grow. According to his aides Patton "whooped with joy whenever they ran off one map and had to go onto the next." Therefore, it wasn't surprising that, upon arrival at Grow's HQ Patton became very angry that the 6th had stopped. When Grow presented Patton with a written copy of the corps order to take Dinan and Saint-Malo, Patton told Grow to ignore it and proceed to Brest; he would deal with Middleton. When the two generals later met, Patton told Middleton there was probably no more than 500 Germans in Saint-Malo and not to worry about it. According to Middleton's memory, Patton told him that there probably weren't more than a thousand Germans left in Brittany and to push the 6th Armored out to Brest. On the same day the 6th Division records indicated intelligence reports that there were an estimated 60,000 Germans still in Brittany.

Middleton had previously been ordered by General Bradley to secure the flank at Avranches and then send the 79th Infantry Division to take up blocking positions at Fougères. But plans change, and the 79th was assigned to help sweep around the Germans trapped in Normandy. This left the 6th with no infantry support in case it got into trouble. Patton hoped that the 6th Armored could drive out to Brest and capture the port before the Germans were ready to defend it. It was a long shot, but the Americans had already had some good luck getting Germans to give up when confronted by American forces. Patton would soon begin to change his focus from Brittany and on to the grand encirclement taking place in Normandy.

Middleton's concern for Dinan stemmed from a misunderstanding at headquarters. Grow's report that he had by-passed Dinan was misread as he had passed through Dinan. When Task Force A ran into German forces in the Dinan area, that they assumed had been cleared by the 6th, Middleton worried his forces were becoming too separated and that the Germans were moving in behind them. From the scattered reports he had received, Middleton thought that the 6th Armored was still close to Dinan and

that it would be simple for them to come to the assistance of TFA. The 83rd Infantry Division was still too far away to get there in a reasonable amount of time. Having to turn about in preparation to attack Dinan cost the 6th a day's time in which they could have continued on to Brest.

Some historians have faulted Middleton for this, and have proposed that if the 6th had arrived at Brest one day earlier they may have been able to grab the city. Although it is possible that the 6th may have been able to arrive at Brest a day earlier, it is very doubtful that this armored unit would have been able to capture the fortified port city. They may have made some headway into its defensive ring, but would certainly have become hung up without more infantry to support them in the built up areas. Brest was encircled by 90mm and 105mm antiaircraft guns in concrete emplacements, just the thing to stop an armored attack. After the war ended the German General Fahrmbacher stated that there were enough defenders dug into Brest to keep the 6th from taking the city. He also noted that he was aware of the American advance as early as

Top. **General Spang of the German 266th Infantry Division was captured just north of Brest when he drove into the 212th Field Artillery Bn. His division had been ordered to abandon their positions in northern Brittany, and move to Brest as reinforcements. Although a handful of his men did make it to Brest, the majority of the 266th Division was destroyed or captured by the 6th Armored Division.**

Above.
In the tight confines of small roads bordered by hedges like these, the German 266th Infantry Division was destroyed by the 6th Armored Division. Key to the American attack was the ability of their tanks to cut through these hedges using steel prongs welded to the front of the tank hull. This allowed the American tanks the freedom to move off the roads and strike at will. Had the Germans reached Brest the city might have been able to hold out for a longer period of time. *(National Archives)*

COMMUNICATION PROBLEMS

Lt. Colonel Bill Given was the 6th Armored Division's Signal Officer in Brittany. In charge of all communications matters for the unit, he had a nightmare of a task to keep his unit in contact with VIIIth Corps headquarters. Using a combination of radio, telephone, and jeep messengers he was able to keep the division in touch with the rest of the American Army.
(Courtesy Bill Given)

At the start of the move into Brittany, Middleton's VIIIth Corps command post was located just north of Avranches. Eventually he was able to move it slightly further south. He had wanted to move further into Brittany, but he was not allowed to shift out of telephone range from the Third Army command post. The radios used by the American Army at the time were the best in the world, but they were not built to transmit the distances required in Brittany. By 2 Aug. Middleton had, for the most part, lost communications with his armored columns.

According to the official histories, a special directional high frequency radio Teletype team had been attached to the 6th Armored and told to aim their broadcast to a specific hill near Avranches. The receiving team set up their antenna at Bréhal instead and was not able to get the signal. Surprisingly, the 6th Armored Division signal officer, Bill Given, denies any knowledge of such a team attached to his division in Brittany. He definitely stated that no radio Teletype unit accompanied the 6th Armored into Brittany, or joined it at Brest.

Why this story was added to the record remains a mystery. According to Given the 6th was rarely in direct communication during the drive to Brest. It was not until the French telephone lines at Pontivy were used to connect the division with corps HQ that communications were reliable. Until then communications were an intermittent system of messengers and brief radio connections.

Communications in the VIIIth Corps mainly depended upon messengers in jeeps. Getting a message from division to corps could take most of a day, if it got there at all. Brittany was considered "Indian Country" with scattered German troops wandering the countryside. These stragglers might avoid a large combat unit, but a lone truck or jeep was an easy target. Some of the light liaison aircraft assigned to the artillery units were also used as messengers, but many of these aircraft had been damaged in the fighting, and the units were moving too fast to allow the aircrews time to develop decent landing fields.

General Patton had set up his own communication system independent of the standard channels. He had taken the 6th Cavalry Group, under Col. Edward "Joe" Fickett, and turned it into what was officially called the Third Army Information Service (A.I.S.). The former reconnaissance squadrons were tasked with monitoring the battalions and regiments on the front lines and reporting directly back to Third Army HQ. This by-passed the division and corps HQ and speeded up the information flow to Patton. The 6th Cavalry Group was also known as "Patton's Eyes and Ears," as well as "Patton's Household Cavalry."

By having a separate flow of information heading right to his HQ, Patton was often better informed of the situation on the front lines than his divisional commanders. However, this could also create problems when Patton issued orders based on information his subordinates did not yet have. Normally, it took eight hours for reports to get from an infantry battalion up to Army headquarters, but with the A.I.S. the reports arrived in two and a half hours.

At Brest the A.I.S. unit was the 1st Platoon of Troop A, 28th Cavalry Recon Squadron under command of 1st Lt. James A. Dunlop. The system was not always infallible, as on 6 Aug. they radioed to the Third Army that *"Brest is ours."* A while later they had to send the correct *"Brest is not ours. Probably not fall until tomorrow."* There is no record of what was sent when they had to correct the second message.

THE BRASSIERE BOYS

When Grow moved his division to Lorient on 12 Aug. he left behind a small contingent to contain the Germans at Brest. Because of their mission it was only a matter of time before someone gave them the nickname "the Brassiere Boys." The original Brassiere Boys were General Taylor's CCA; the 50th Armored Infantry Bn.; 2 companies of the 68th Tank Bn.; the 603rd TD Bn.; troops A&E/86th Recon Squadron; A/ 777th AAA Bn. and the 1/28th Infantry.

These men had a rough job. They needed to convince the Germans in Brest that there was still a large force outside the city. Between 13 and 18 Aug. the Germans conducted a number of raids out of the city. The most celebrated was that of paratrooper Lt. Lepkowski. 130 German paratroops from the 7th FJ Regiment, captured at Huelgoat, were being held prisoner by the FFI in a school at Brasparts 50 kilometers from Brest. A few escaped and brought word back to Brest of their location, and that they had been robbed and mistreated by their French guards. German records claim the men were actually sent by the French to tell the Germans in Brest if they did not surrender the prisoners at Brasparts would be executed. On 16 Aug. Lepkowski led his men on a rescue attempt. Traveling in a convoy of 18 vehicles and three tanks (many of them captured American vehicles), Lepkowski freed the prisoners and, with only three of his men lightly wounded, brought them safely back to Brest. For this act of bravery Lepkowski was promoted to Oberleutnant and awarded the Knight's Cross.

The FFI report on the raid is slightly different. It claims that the convoy consisted of two tanks, 12 trucks, and 50 men. They said that white stars were painted on, and French and American flags were flown from, the vehicles to fool the FFI guards along the way. The FFI states that the Germans lost 50 men in the raid, and that 26 of their own troops as well as 15 French civilians were taken prisoner. The captured Frenchmen were not executed as might be thought, but taken to the POW camp near Le Fret.

The 1/28th Infantry arrived outside Brest on 11 Aug. after a 24 hour drive from Rennes. The infantrymen were given an initial assignment of capturing the airfield to the north of the city, which was surrounded by a large number of concrete emplacements. At first the 1/28th advanced over 2,400 yards to push the Germans off the airfield. Greatly outnumbered by the defenders, and without support or reserves, the Americans pushed back a force larger than their single battalion to take most of the airfield. The next morning the Germans brought up reinforcements and counterattacked to retake the area. After defending against German attacks for the rest of the day, the 1/28th attacked again on the afternoon of 12

This photo of Eric Lepkowski was reportedly taken at Brest and shipped to Germany on one of the last U-boats to leave the port. His famous rescue of over a hundred captured Germans from the French Resistance made him a well known figure. After the war he would return to duty in the newly formed Bundeswehr and continued to serve as a paratroop officer.
(Courtesy Ramcke family)

Aug. Progress was slowed by heavy German artillery fire, and ammunition had to be brought up to the front line in tanks. At last General Taylor, commander of CCA, realized the infantry was in danger of being encircled. He ordered a withdrawal and at 0330 hrs. the 1/28th pulled back under cover of darkness. They continued to defend against German probes until the remainder of the 8th Division began to arrive on 18 Aug.

Once the 8th Infantry Division was in position outside Brest, General Taylor moved CCA to Lorient on 21 Aug. Left behind were the 50th Armored Infantry Bn., A/603rd TD Bn., A/777th Bn., and A&E/86th Recon Squadron. These units were under command of Lt. Col. Arnold R. Wall. They would later become the basis for General Van Fleet's Task Force B which operated on the Daoulas Peninsula.

A light M-5 tank from CCA of the 6th Armored division moves through Rostrenen. These tanks were armed only with a 37mm gun - hardly enough to scratch the paint of most German tanks. They were fast though and the 37mm, along with their two machine guns, were effective against German infantry and gun positions.
(National Archives)

5 Aug., when the 6th arrived at Huelgoat, and at that time any chance of surprising the Brest garrison was lost.

Intermittent communications difficulties kept Middleton from staying in touch with the 6th Armored. All of the light aircraft used by the division's artillery units had been either shot down or damaged in landing. On 3 Aug. a light observation aircraft from VIIIth Corps finally located the 6th Armored's actual position. When Middleton found how far away from Dinan the 6th really was he revised his orders and told Grow that Saint-Malo and Dinan would be dealt with by TFA and the 83rd. He initially asked Grow to spare one combat command for the operation, but then sent a message stating: *"I had wanted you to assist in the capture of Saint-Malo, however, it is apparent that your advance precludes this. Proceed with your original mission to take Brest."*

The diversion to Dinan of the 6th Armored was extremely frustrating as communications problems delayed orders and reports (upon which the orders were based) for hours at a time. Most of 4 Aug. was spent by Grow trying to sort out exactly what his orders were, and by VIIIth Corps and the Third Army trying to figure out where Grow was and what he was doing. The further Grow moved into Brittany the worse the communications problems became. It was not until the night of 4 Aug. that Middleton finally sure that Grow was again moving on Brest. At times reports could take up to 36 hours to get from the 6th Division to VIIIth Corps.

One of the complicating factors in this campaign was that Grow had served as General Patton's operations officer in the 2nd Armored Division. He and Patton knew each other well and, although Patton

This M-18 tank destroyer named "Bataan" has been identified as belonging to Company B of the 603rd TD Bn. On 28 Aug. Bataan was at the village of Concarneau, and came under fire from a flak ship roughly 5,000 yards offshore. With only six rounds Bataan hit the small ship. The local German garrison surrendered saying, *"any weapon that can sink a boat three miles offshore is too much for us."*
(National Archives)

should have sent orders to Grow through the corps headquarters, he frequently by-passed the chain of command and went right to the division itself. Until Patton received command of other corps in his army, it sometimes seemed he had forgotten he even had a commander of VIIIth Corps and had taken on that role himself. Complicating the issue more was that Patton's "Household Cavalry" had a detachment with the 6th Armored, and with their own radio circuits were often able to get information from the 6th Division to the Third Army HQ long before Middleton at corps headquarters found out what was going on.

Moving west the 6th Armored had been delayed by destroyed bridges at Loudéac and Pontivy, so Grow pushed his men on a nighttime march under the full moon of 4 Aug. Passing through Pontivy CCA captured the main German communications center for the area. The FFI reported to Grow that 2,000 German paratroopers were defending Carhaix, so on 5 Aug. the 6th by-passed the town to both sides. Once they were cut off the Germans evacuated Carhaix, blew some bridges there, and withdrew to Huelgoat.

The tankers were making very good progress and it seemed they would be at Brest in time to win Patton's bet. Then CCA ran into the German paratroopers at Huelgoat. This was Colonel Erich Pietzonka's 7th FJ regiment. General Ramcke wanted the unit to withdraw, but the region was under command of General Rauch of the 343rd Infantry Division. Rauch ordered Pietzonka to stay at Huelgoat and delay the Americans so work could proceed on the Brest defenses.

The wooded areas nearby gave the Germans excellent defensive positions and only after very hard fighting did CCA break through. In this combat Oberfeldwebel Adolf Reininghaus, a platoon leader in the 14th Company, 7th FJ Regiment, won the Knight's Cross for bravery under fire. The 7th FJ Regiment found itself nearly surrounded by the Americans and was ordered to fight its way out and proceed to Brest.

CCB drove north to the outskirts of Morlaix where, finding German resistance, they swung west to Lesneven. On the same day (6 Aug.) CCA moved slowly west over small country roads and by nightfall it was just west of Morlaix. The sight of American tanks in Lesneven triggered the order for German coastal defense forces to withdraw to their designated fortresses. Units defending the coast against amphibious landings abandoned their positions, destroyed what they could not take with them, and headed for Brest. When the 7th Army received the report of Americans in Lesneven they could not believe

Above.
S/Sgt. Horace Lennon of A/25th Armored Engineer Bn., was awarded a Bronze Star in Brittany when he spotted a German convoy in the distance, then directed accurate artillery fire upon it. Later he was awarded a Silver Star for his outstanding leadership in CCB during the Brittany campaign. Often overlooked, the engineers in an armored division kept the tanks moving by clearing mines and building bridges. *(Courtesy H. Lennon)*

The hood of a reconnaissance jeep in Brittany is covered with a camouflage net, and festooned with grenades and spare magazines for the M-3 grease gun. The M-3 submachine gun was a replacement for the heavier and more expensive Thompson. Troops in Brittany never knew when they might run into a cut off German unit heading for their own lines.
(National Archives)

it. They thought their men were seeing ghosts, and were furious that the 343rd Infantry Division had destroyed the 280mm guns at Paimpol. The 266th Infantry Division was ordered to return to their positions north of Morlaix. Had they been allowed to continue on to Brest the 266th would have been able to add a great deal to the city defenses.

On the morning of 6 Aug. VIIIth Corps HQ received the message that Middleton had been afraid of. Grow reported that the Germans in Brittany were hampering his supply operations. He said, *"if additional troops are not furnished to keep supply routes open, the division must live off the country, which cannot furnish gasoline or ammunition. Air support essential, but ground security is equally essential at once."* Now Middleton had to worry that the dash to Brest would fall apart and his armored columns would be cut off and destroyed by Germans sweeping in behind them.

One of the problems wandering German soldiers created for the 6th Armored is illustrated by the fate of the assistant division engineer, Captain Ed Clark. He had set out in a jeep to look for a water point for the unit and had been captured near Saint-Dominieuc by a group of Germans passing through the area. He was sent as a POW to Jersey, but to his unit it appeared he disappeared without a trace. Later on, in January 1945, he made a perilous escape from the Channel Islands in a small boat along with an observation plane pilot (George Haas) who had crashed and also been captured in Brittany.

By now Grow was no more than 15 miles from Brest. The radio links to Middleton were not working, so he made radio contact with a fighter-bomber overhead and asked it to relay a message back to corps HQ stating that he thought Brest was well-defended and that he would need an infantry division to attack it. Hearing this Middleton got a message back to Grow to stay at Brest and develop the situation there. Middleton wanted the circumstances clearer before he sent more troops to the distant port.

Many of the Germans that General Grow had run into were poorly trained and demoralized. They were rear echelon soldiers who had never expected to find themselves on the front lines and had given up when confronted by American tanks. With the situation as fluid as it was, and some Germans readily surrendering, Grow hoped that with luck he might have a chance at capturing Brest. In order to show as much force as possible he deployed his troops into three different

T/Sgt. Wilmer Jones from the 9th Armored Infantry Bn. discusses a patrol route in Brittany using the back of his jeep as a table. Note the SCR-300 radio sitting in the driver's seat. *(National Archives)*

columns and on the morning of 7 Aug. sent them to test the city's defenses.

On the right, CCB passed through minor opposition - destroying a large antiaircraft warning system - until it was about 7 miles from Brest (near Millizac). There it came under intense artillery fire and was stopped. In the center, CCR reached Gouesnou roughly four miles from the city, and on the left, CCA made it to Guipavas. It was obvious that the Germans were not only ready, but willing to defend the port. In order to give himself time to reorganize for an all-out assault Grow sent German speaking Master Sergeant Alex Castle and the 6th Armored Division intelligence officer Major Ernest Mitchell in a jeep, draped with white sheets and flying a white flag, into Brest on 8 Aug. to try and bluff the German commander into surrendering.

The Germans blindfolded the Americans and brought them to an underground bunker. There Sgt. Castle translated the surrender ultimatum into German.

*"Headquarters 6th Armored Division,
Office of the Commanding General
APO 256, U.S. Army*

*8 August 1944
Memorandum to: Officer Commanding German Forces in Brest
1. The United States Army, Naval and Air Force troops are in a position to destroy the garrison of Brest
2. This memorandum constitutes an opportunity for you to surrender in the face of these overwhelming forces to representatives of the United States Government and avoid the unnecessary sacrifice of your lives.
3. I shall be very glad to receive your formal surrender and make the detailed arrangements any time prior to 1500 this date. The officer who brings this memorandum will be glad to guide you and necessary members of your staff, not exceeding six, to my headquarters.
R.W. Grow, Major General USA, Commanding"*

The German fortress commander, Col. Hans von der Mosel, was not taken in by the ruse and told them he would not surrender. Mitchell took back the ultimatum and the two Americans were blindfolded and returned to their lines. At this point General Ramcke and the 2nd FJ Division had not yet arrived at Brest. It was not until 9 Aug. that the 2nd FJ slipped into Brest by way of Daoulas. Three days later, on 12 Aug., Ramcke assumed com-

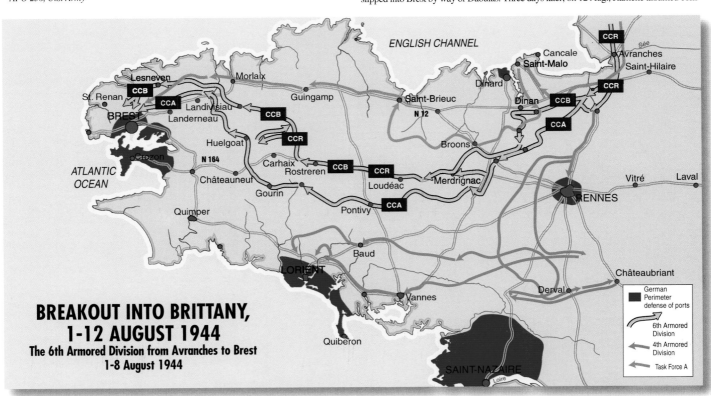

BREAKOUT INTO BRITTANY, 1-12 AUGUST 1944
The 6th Armored Division from Avranches to Brest
1-8 August 1944

German Perimeter defense of ports
6th Armored Division
4th Armored Division
Task Force A

mand of Brest, with von der Mosel becoming his chief of staff.

Grow prepared to make a thrust into the city of Brest to again test the defensive perimeter. He realigned his forces to the north of the city into two columns and requested heavy air bombardment for the next day. He asked for no less than 3 hours of constant air attack on German positions. Everything was set for a major attack on 9 Aug. to show the Germans what they would be facing.

At this point Middleton's VIIIth Corps was composed of five main combat units: the 4th and 6th Armored Divisions, located at Brest and Lorient; Task Force A in northern Brittany; the 8th Infantry Division in Rennes; and the 83rd still moving up from Normandy. Middleton

Above.

A half-track ambulance from the 76th Medical Battalion moves up to the front to pick up casualties. Men wounded during the drive to Brest faced many uncomfortable hours of riding in a ambulance or truck before they got to the nearest hospital. Fortunately, the Germans respected the red cross markings and did not attempt to interfere with men being evacuated.

(National Archives)

was greatly overextended and it was only due to the lack of German organization that his troops were not cut off. Now that the breakthrough in Normandy was developing into a major operation Middleton knew that any spare troops the Americans had would be sent there, not to bail him out of a mess in Brittany.

From all the intelligence that had been gathered it appeared that it would take an assault force of one armored and two infantry divisions plus heavy artillery to capture Brest. Those were troops he did not have. Middleton decided the best course of action was to start reducing the Brittany ports one by one, as originally planned, starting with Saint-Malo. It posed a serious threat on his right flank. Troops stationed there could easily venture forth and cut the Avranches bottleneck, upon which all of his forces depended for a supply route. There was also the possibility that the German 319th Infantry Division garrisoning the Channel Islands would be evacuated to Saint-Malo in order to build up for a counterattack. However, the 6th Armored really did need some additional manpower so one infantry battalion from the 8th Division at Rennes (1/28th Infantry) was put onto trucks and sent to assist Grow outside Brest.

Communications had grown so difficult by this point that again a liaison aircraft was sent out to locate the 6th Div. HQ. Unable to find a field large enough to land in, the aircraft dropped a message to Grow and was able to pick up a reply that was hung suspended between two poles. Attempts to carve a landing strip out of the hedgerows failed because the selected area was too short for the aircraft. As the plane started back to the Allied lines the pilot radioed to the 6th, "*See you tomorrow. Get a longer field.*"

The end of the German 266th Division

While Grow was preparing his attack on Brest reports started coming into his HQ of curious activities to his rear (the north). German troops and vehicles drove into his rear outposts. Men behind the lines were coming under scattered gunfire. Finally the 6th Division trains approaching from the east reported that they were unable to proceed further as they were running into German forces. Late in the day the 212th Armored Field Artillery Bn. captured a German general and his staff. Generalleutnant Karl Spang, commander of the 266th Infantry Division, had previously sent some of his troops to bolster the defenses of Dinan and Saint-Malo. Now he was bringing the remainder of his division to assist in the defense of Brest. Without any idea that Americans were so far out into Brittany, Spang was traveling in advance of his unit to arrange for the proper reception facilities for his men and had driven right into the American position.

Faced with the 266th Infantry Division coming in behind him, Grow was able to contact Middleton and said, "*I'm in front of Brest. I've got a German division in front of me and one in the rear of me. What shall I do?*" Middleton replied, "*Well Bob, you've always wanted to use your own judgment; now's your chance to use it.*" This was not a flippant reply, but confirmation that Middleton knew that Grow was in a better position to decide a course of action and was deferring to his judgment.

Grow was in quite a predicament that evening with an enemy unit advancing on his rear and strong fortifications to his front. He canceled the attack order on Brest. He directed that the reconnaissance troops were to leave a screen in front of Brest to prevent any German attack from that direction, while his combat commands were ordered to reverse direction (at night) and prepare for an attack to the north. In case he was overrun preparations were taken to prevent the Germans from capturing his code machines. Soldiers were stationed at all vital equipment with thermite grenades so they could destroy the equipment at the first sign of trouble.

The telephone lines in the 6th AD position were cut by Germans moving through the area. Grow did not want to risk breaking radio silence so he sent written orders to his units. Acknowledgments came back from CCB and CCR, but the message sent to CCA was delayed. As part of Grow's continuing good luck the German 266th ran into the CCB and CCR positions, but not CCA which was still oriented to the south.

According to veterans from the 6th Armored Division a supply of alcohol had been captured by the men of CCA and on the night the attack order came in the message center sergeant had had a little too much to drink. He fell asleep before seeing that the order was passed on and the next day CCA again started to attack to the south, not knowing they were headed in the wrong direction.

What is generally not known about the attack of the 266th Division is that General Ramcke was aware of the trouble his reinforcements were having and personally led an attack to try and clear a path for them. As soon as he arrived in Brest he scraped together two companies of his paratroops and two platoons armed with panzerfausts. They were supported by some army artillery and two naval flak batteries. The combat group attacked north into Gouesnou, but ran into trouble with the naval flak units. They had never been trained for ground combat and fired into their own forces. The Germans got into Gouesnou, but were unable to open a route into Brest for the 266th. This is a testament to the ability of Lt. Col. Albert E. Harris and his 86th Recon-

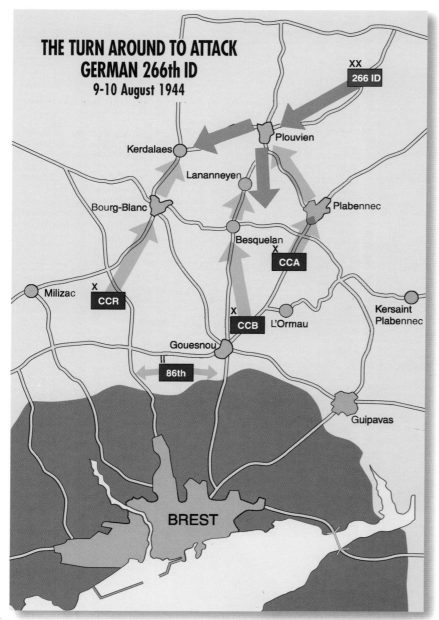

THE TURN AROUND TO ATTACK GERMAN 266th ID
9-10 August 1944

XX
266 ID

Plouvien
Kerdalaes
Lananneyen
Bourg-Blanc
Plabennec
Besquelan
X
CCA
Milizac
X
CCR
X
CCB
L'Ormau
Kersaint Plabennec
Gouesnou
II
86th
Guipavas
BREST

naissance Squadron whose thin screen kept the Germans at bay.

Light skirmishes early on 9 Aug. developed into a full scale battle as the German 266th moved south. CCB and CCR attacked headlong into the German forces. Fighter-bombers requested for the aborted assault on Brest arrived and were redirected to strike the 266th Division supply column convoys to the north. At Lananneyen a large group of Germans surrendered after they had monitored American transmissions on a captured radio and discovered that American tanks had by-passed their position and were moving in behind them.

At Bourg Blanc the heavy weapons company of the German 851st Regiment ran headfirst into the security element of CCR. With only one 57mm antitank gun and two heavy machine guns the CCR detachment wiped out the German company. After the orders finally reached CCA, Taylor quickly turned his men about and attacked the Germans at Plouvien. At one point the Germans were only two fields away from the 6th Division headquarters. With machine gun fire passing overhead, and bullets hitting water and gas cans stacked next to the radio trucks, the Division Signal Officer, Lt. Col. Bill Given, ordered the message, "*Under attack, codes in danger may destroy*" sent in the clear (uncoded) to VIII Corps. He knew that the radio operators at corps HQ would recognize the distinctive "fist" or signature of his radio operator and if they were overrun there would be no question that he had kept the codes from German hands. Needless to say, this was a disturbing message to receive 200 miles away at Middleton's headquarters. The reason Given was so concerned about the code equipment was apparently he had been given a SIGABA machine for the operation. The SIGABA, also known as the ECM Mark II in the Navy, was a high level cypher machine normally not used so close to the front lines. Like the German ENIGMA machine it used a series of rotors to encrypt messages, but the ENIGMA used three rotors, and the SIGABA used 15. Supposedly the SIGABA was the only cypher machine

Above.
Pvt. W. Outlaw of 6th Armored Division MP platoon chats with a POW at Plouay in late August. He has acquired one of the new M-1943 field jackets, which were just beginning to arrive at the front lines. Curiously he wears his helmet chin strap behind the steel pot, but the thin leather liner strap under his chin.
(National Archives)

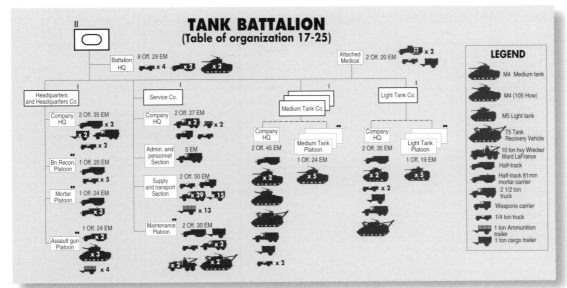

TANK BATTALION
(Table of organization 17-25)

Battalion HQ — 8 Off. 29 EM
Attached Medical — 2 Off. 20 EM

LEGEND
- M4 Medium tank
- M4 (105 How)
- M5 Light tank
- T5 Tank Recovery Vehicle
- 10 ton hvy Wrecker Ward LaFrance
- Half-track
- Half-track 81mm mortar carrier
- 2 1/2 ton truck
- Weapons carrier
- 1/4 ton truck
- 1 ton Ammunition trailer
- 1 ton cargo trailer

Headquarters and Headquarters Co.
Service Co.
Medium Tank Co.
Light Tank Co.

Company HQ — 2 Off. 35 EM
Company HQ — 2 Off. 27 EM
Medium Tank Co.
Company HQ — 2 Off. 45 EM
Medium Tank Platoon — 1 Off. 24 EM
Company HQ — 2 Off. 35 EM
Light Tank Platoon — 1 Off. 19 EM

Bn Recon. Platoon — 1 Off. 20 EM
Admin. and personnel Section — 5 EM
Mortar Platoon — 1 Off. 24 EM
Supply and transport Section — 2 Off. 50 EM
Maintenance Platoon — 2 Off. 30 EM
Assault gun Platoon — 1 Off. 24 EM

Below.
This German Luftwaffe signalman (note the sleeve insignia) was captured at Pont Croix, and is being processed by a 6th Armored Division sergeant at Plouay. This must be far from combat because the sergeant is only wearing his helmet liner, not the steel pot. The German soldier's soldbuch (pay book) often contained lots of useful intelligence information about where and when he had served and in what units.
(National Archives)

used in WW2, by any country, that was never broken. It was retired in 1956, and although information about was declassified in 1996, the veterans questioned about its use in Brittany refused to discuss it.

Part of the problem was that the captured German general had been brought to the 6th division HQ. Men from the Division signals section were assigned to guard him, but he had been able to walk about in the open. One of his men must have spotted the general and directed an attack to free him. Thus the German attack was unknowingly directed right at the division HQ and caused a great many problems for the 6th Armored. American veterans recall that General Spang was very angry at having been captured. This may have been aggravated by someone stealing his leather coat (years later a 6th Division man would claim responsibility for souveniring the garment). Another GI stole Spang's watch, but General Grow ordered it returned. The next morning Grow ate breakfast with Spang before evacuating him from the area inside a tank so he would not be spotted. By the end of the day Grow's men had captured over 1,000 prisoners and wiped out the remaining German units. 200 vehicles and 20 antitank guns had been captured or destroyed. The 266th was actually a "static division," with less firepower and transportation than a standard infantry division. After contributing men to the Dinan and Saint-Malo garrison it was estimated to be roughly equal to a full strength regiment. Even at this the ability to turn a division 180 degrees during the night, with no radio or phone communication, 200 miles from friendly lines, and destroy an enemy so thoroughly is a great tribute the skill of the 6th Armored division. On the night of 9 Aug. a near catastrophe was averted by none other than the members of the 6th Armored Division band. The 80 sup-

Col. George W. Read commanded CCB of the 6th Armored division in Brittany. He was considered one of the best officers in the Division, and was promoted to brigadier general soon afterwards.
(National Archives)

6th AD OUTSIDE BREST, 8 August 1944

CCA
- 68th Tank Bn.
- 44th Armored Infantry Bn.
- Co. A and Recon Co. 603rd Tank Destroyer Bn.
- A/777th AAA Bn.
- B/25th Armored Engineer Bn.

CCB
- 15th Tank Bn.
- 9th Armored Infantry Bn.
- A/50th Armored Infantry Bn.
- D/69th Tank Bn.
- C/25th Armored Engineer Bn.
- B/777th AAA Bn.

CCR
- 50th Armored Infantry Bn. (-)
- 69th Tank Bn. (-)
- 25th Armored Infantry Bn. (-)
- 603rd Tank Destroyer Bn. (-)
- 1/28th Infantry Regiment (8th Inf. Div.)

Division Artillery Command
- 128th Field Artillery Bn.
- 212th Arm. Field Artillery Bn.
- 231st Armored Field Artillery Bn.
- 83rd Armored Field Artillery Bn.
- 174th Arm. Field Artillery Bn.

Division Trains
- D/15th Tank Bn.
- C/9th Armored Infantry Bn. one platoon
- C/603rd Tank Destroyer Bn.
- C&D/777th AAA Bn.

ion from the 8th Division had arrived. A crew from the 6th Division was able to restore telephone service from the former German communications center at Pontivy. The telephone exchange had been destroyed, but many of the phone lines were still in place. This provided telephone connections for the Americans throughout most of Brittany.

Still hoping that Brest was undermanned, Grow directed CCA and the 1/28th Infantry to take the high ground near the Guipavas Airport on 12 Aug. When these attacks failed Grow called for heavy artillery support from VIIIth Corps. The corps artillery was then in use at Saint-Malo and Middleton would not move it up before he captured that city. Middleton told Grow, "*I feel it unwise to become too involved in a fight at Brest unless you feel reasonably sure of success. I prefer you watch the situation and wait until an infantry division arrives. Heavy artillery will arrive with the infantry division.*" Middleton's VIIIth Corps intelligence felt the German garrison at Brest was roughly 8,000 men. By 12 Aug., according to German records, the garrison actually numbered about 35,000 men.

On the evening of 12 Aug. Grow was ordered to leave one combat command at Brest and relieve the 4th Armored Division at Lorient and Vannes. Leaving CCA and the 1/28th Infantry behind to keep an eye on Brest, the remainder of the 6th moved south to let Wood's 4th Armored head deeper into France. On 15 Aug. Grow relieved the 4th AD in what he later recalled was the shortest relief in history; Wood called out from his departing vehicle to Grow, "*We're off, it's all yours.*"

The actions of the 6th Armored in Brittany were amazing by any standard. The 200 mile drive to Brest was the most extended operation by a single division in the ETO. They had taken over 4,000 prisoners and lost only 130 KIA, 400 WIA, and 70 MIA. This was in addition to maintaining a supply route 200 miles back to Avranches and functioning with only limited communications with higher headquarters. The 3916th QM Gas Company, and 3398th and 3803rd QM Truck Companies had been attached to the 6th to provide for the long haul from the supply point at Pontorson and performed splendidly.

Gasoline is vital to an armored division. At one point in the campaign the 6th Armored Division learned that an LST had landed at Morlaix with 200,000 gallons of gas on board. It was to be issued to the VIIIth Corps, and since the 6th Armored was a VIIIth Corps unit they quietly took the gas and thanked the ship's captain. It was not until long after the gas had been used that the VIIIth Corps discovered what had happened to it.

The quartermasters of the 6th were able to keep up with almost every need the division had, with one major exception. Maps of Brittany were in very short supply. At times some of the 6th Armored really did run off the end of their maps. This shortage was partially rectified by confiscating civilian Michelin maps from gas stations or the local population.

To carry wounded men back to the American field hospitals the medics of the 6th had to keep their casualties consolidated in the combat area until enough had been collected to warrant a trip by ambulance back through Brittany.

Unless their wounds prohibited it, each casualty was administered a high dose of 6 grains of sodium pentothal to get them through the rough trip. The 76th Armored Medical Battalion was assisted in this by a platoon from the 53rd Field Hospital and the 595th Ambulance Company. Many of the 39 ambulances available to the division spent 18 to 20 hours on the road trying to get wounded men back to where they could be properly cared for.

ply trucks carrying gasoline for the 6th were ordered by the Third Army quartermaster to head back after 130 miles. Supposedly this was by direct order of General Patton who wanted the trucks back to supply his columns to the east. The gas cans were taken off the trucks and dispersed over a few fields near Lesquern. This supply dump was guarded by four light tanks and 20 men from the division band. According to local legend a French traitor alerted the Germans to the location of the American gasoline and approximately 120 German paratroops set out to destroy the supply dump. When the Germans attacked they destroyed one of the tanks and a truck, then set fire to 5-7,000 gallons of gasoline in one of the fields. The handful of bandsmen, under command of Warrant Officer Thompson (the band leader), quickly rallied and drove off the attackers, saving the majority of the gasoline supply. The next day the Frenchman was brought out by the FFI and was shot while trying to escape.

For the next two days the 6th Armored would continue rounding up the stragglers of the destroyed German division. The area was combed for the scattered Germans, because every man that was kept out of Brest would be one less to man the defenses of the city. Things had finally started to shape up for the VIIIth Corps. A new higher radio antenna restored regular radio communications between corps HQ and the Brest area, an airstrip was built to allow liaison planes to land, contact was made with Task Force A in the north, and the infantry battal-

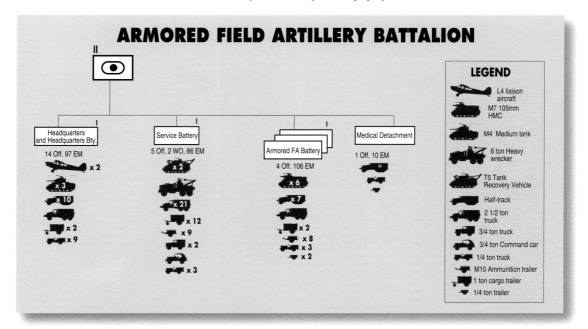

Reports indicate that both German soldiers and the Luftwaffe generally respected the red cross markings on the ambulances. German wounded were sent to a facility in Morlaix where they were treated by four captured German medical detachments.

At Plouvien Captain Albert Rothman, the battalion surgeon of the 25th Armored Engineers, was captured. Four hours later he was released due to the insistence of German casualties that he had given them the same treatment as his own men.

Throughout the Brittany campaign both sides attempted to play by the rules of war when dealing with medical facilities, and as word spread this may have helped many Germans decide to surrender.

The 6th Armored at Lorient

Grow was mad about his new assignment. He was ordered to sit still and contain the German garrisons in Lorient and Saint-Nazaire. He attempted to convince Middleton that the local FFI units could handle the job, but remained stuck in a static position better suited for an infantry unit. Not releasing the 6th Armored Division for the glamorous task of pursuing the Germans into Germany may have been hard on the commander, but for the men of the division it was a chance to get some rest. They had been in action or moving since 18 July.

The 6th took part in limited patrolling actions and harassing the German positions with light artillery fire. The 9th Armored Infantry Bn. found an old car and modified it to run on railroad tracks. They filled it with 750 pounds of explosives and fit a detonator to the front bumper. One night they let it drive down the tracks under its own power, hoping to intercept the daily German supply train that ran from Lorient to

Quimperlé. At 2300 hours a massive explosion was heard roughly 3 miles behind the lines at Geste, but no one ever found out exactly what they had destroyed.

On 25 Aug. 1944 General Grow held a division formation at Plouay to pay tribute to the men who had lost their lives in the ten day, 250 mile drive to Brest. The division chaplain suggested a battery of tank destroyers fire a salute, directed so the shells would fall into Lorient. When Patton heard of this he remarked, *"That's great work, why can't we promote that chaplain?"*

The next day Grow drove 300 miles to visit Patton and plead for a new assignment. Grow, like Wood, wanted his tanks pushing the Germans to the east, not sitting still around a port. He felt that the FFI were fully able to keep the Germans bottled up in the ports. Patton agreed with him, but gasoline was then in very short supply. The majority of the Allied supplies were being sent to Montgomery's army in the north. Grow told Patton he already had enough gas to get him to the front lines, but he was unable to change Patton's mind. Patton promised he would see

GENERAL ROBERT W. GROW

The commander of the 6th Armored Division began his military career as a private in the Minnesota National Guard in 1914. He attended the University of Minnesota and graduated in 1916 with a degree in Civil Engineering, as well as a commission as a cavalry lieutenant. The lack of cavalry positions in WW1 led Grow to attend artillery school. After the war he served a brief stint in Germany with the Army of Occupation. In 1929 he attended Command and General Staff school. In 1940 he served as operations officer to General Patton in the 2nd Armored Division. Moving through various armored commands, in May 1943 he assumed command of the 6th Armored Division which he commanded until July 1945.

Grow was a cavalryman like Patton and strongly believed that men needed to be led, not ordered from the rear. He was always out in front. On 5 Aug. 1944 he needed to move from CCB south to the CCA column. Normally he traveled with one jeep and one half-track. This trip meant 15 miles of German infested countryside. He borrowed 2 tanks and made the trip anyway. Arriving at CCA he felt the unit was moving too slowly, and led the advance with his own four vehicles into Huelgoat. As he entered the town the Germans were withdrawing out of it. His aide later recalled that Grow felt the Germans were more interested in retreating safely than getting into a fight.

At Bastogne Grow had a run-in with General MacAuliffe of the 101st Airborne. This incident returned to haunt him after the war in 1952 when Grow was the military attaché in Moscow. Communist agents stole Grow's personal diary and this breach of security, which might normally be overlooked, was used as an excuse to retire him. Sources familiar with the situation maintain that it was General MacAuliffe, then one of the top generals in the Army, getting his final revenge.

Left.
On 25 August 1944 at Plouay, General Grow addresses the 6th Armored Division in a tribute to the men killed in Brittany. This event was held within reach of the German guns at Lorient. A salute to the casualties was fired from tank destroyers, using live ammo, and aimed into Lorient itself. *(National Archives)*

ply situation. Lee, with a massive problem keeping the troops already at the front supplied, told Bradley it would add more strain to his already overstretched supply lines. Bradley kept the 6th at Lorient and Saint-Nazaire, but did allow them to relieve the 35th Infantry Division east of Orleans.

Grow ordered his men to develop their combat skills by engaging in patrolling actions, mining the perimeter, and "mouse-trapping" enemy patrols. This was accomplished by establishing 12 artillery observation posts along the division front. Enemy patrols were allowed to advance unmolested until they reached an open area, then a massive artillery barrage was called down on them. At times German patrols were allowed to penetrate American lines, then were cut off and destroyed. Eventually these actions brought German patrol activity down to a minimum.

On 3 Sept., with the fight at Brest still raging, the Ninth Army took over in Brittany. Grow drove to Brest to confer with the new Army commander, Lt. General William H. Simpson. Simpson agreed that the 6th Armored should be allowed to move east, but that it had to wait until the 94th Infantry Division moved up to take its place at the Brittany ports. While Grow was waiting at Lorient his CCB was extended over 400 miles from 6th Armored HQ. On 11 Sept. it contacted French units under General Patch, making the first link up between the Third and Seventh Army in France. Finally, on 16 Sept. the 94th Infantry Division took up positions at Saint-Nazaire and Lorient and the 6th moved off

The advance across Brittany by the 6th Armored was one of the finest (and unrecognized) examples of armored troops in a breakout that was seen during WW2. General Grow attempted to get the Distinguished Unit Citation for his division. Grow argued that for 8 days in August the 6th Armored functioned superbly while out of contact with corps headquarters and against a numerically superior enemy force. He claimed that "the extent and speed of the operation and the results obtained are believed to be without parallel for a single division, operating alone, in the entire European campaign."

777th AAA AUTOMATIC WEAPONS BN. (SELF-PROPELLED)

Award of the French Croix De Guerre with Silver Gilt Star.
"This unit was engaged in the battle of the Channel and particularly distinguished itself in the region around Avranches, from 1 to 3 August 1944. By valor and accuracy of fire it brought down a great number of enemy planes, which eased the task of the 6th Armored Division engaged in the attack."

Above.
Lt. Col. Joseph Henry Twyman Jr., commander of the 777th AAA Bn. This unit was awarded a French Croix De Guerre for protecting the bridges vital to the breakout into Brittany. The 777th was attached to the 6th Armored Division for the Brittany campaign. Once the German Luftwaffe disappeared from the skies, the antiaircraft weapons were used to protect headquarters and supply dumps against ground attacks.
(National Archives)

what he could do and allowed Grow to move a combat command down to Orleans.

Conferring with Patton about the 6th Armored, General Bradley went to the Quartermaster General in the ETO, General John C.H. Lee, and asked how moving the 6th Armored Division up to the front would affect the sup-

German infantryman, 266th Division
This German soldier is one of the few survivors of the 266th Division's destruction around Plouvien that made their way into Brest. He is armed with the standard Mauser 98K rifle and an egg-shaped grenade, hanging from his belt. The shovel in his belt could be used in hand-to-hand fighting, but was more practical for digging holes to hide from the American fighter-bombers. He wears the reed green herringbone twill jacket and trousers, over a gray collared knit shirt. The white piping on his shoulder boards identifies him as an infantryman. Instead of jackboots he has the short marching boots and canvas gaiters. He has discarded his gas mask and its metal carrier, but will later regret this when the mask would protect him from the smoke and dust that blanketed Brest during the street fighting.
(Reconstruction by Militaria Magazine)

The request was sent to General Middleton who disapproved it. It was then forwarded to General Patton who also turned it down, probably as he did not want to overrule a subordinate. After pushing the citation request up the chain of command Grow was told that the War Department had decided that no more full divisions could be given this award, only elements of a division.

With the unspoken threat that forcing the issue could jeopardize his military career, Grow finally backed down. He always felt that the confusion over the drive on Dinan resulted in Patton losing confidence in Middleton, and that Middleton ended up taking it out on the 6th Armored by turning down this award.

THE 23rd SPECIAL TROOPS IN BRITTANY

Due to their top secret nature, the 23rd never wore an insignia of their own. At the end of the war their official report of wartime actions bore this proposed design of a ghost patch. The unit was disbanded before the troops could consider having it made, and not one such patch was ever produced.
(National Archives)

The 23rd Special Troops is one of the last great secrets of WW2. It was the tactical deception unit for the Americans in the ETO. The operations of the 23rd still remain shrouded in mystery, as the members of the unit were sworn to secrecy for a period of no less than 50 years.

The 23rd, commanded by Col. Harry L. Reeder, was composed of four main units: the 603rd Camouflage Battalion, Special (composed mainly of artists); the 244th Signal Operations Company, Special (for sending deceptive radio messages); the 406th Engineer Camouflage Company, Special (to set up and maintain rubber dummy guns and vehicles); and the 3132nd Signal Service Company, Special (used for sonic deceptions).

The 3132nd was often referred to as a Sonic Deception Company. Its job was to play recordings of various sounds over loudspeakers carried on the unit's half-tracks. A complete library of recordings, ranging from tanks moving forward to bridges being built, had been recorded onto large phonograph records. These could be combined and mixed together as needed onto wire recorders for use in the field. Special charts had been developed that used such factors as temperature, wind speed and humidity to determine how loud the recordings were to be played to achieve the desired effect at specific distances.

The 23rd landed in France in late June. Their first operation, code named "Elephant," took place at the start of July in the forest of Cerisy. The mission was to conceal the movement of the 2nd Armored Division as it moved from a reserve position to the front. The mission was not well planned at higher headquarters and the 23rd found itself attempting to fool the Germans while the real 2nd Armored had only moved a few miles away into combat.

The first major operation of the 23rd started on 9 Aug. with a deception on the Brittany Peninsula. The 23rd was broken down into four groups, each to simulate the movement of a task force from four different divisions away from the actual fighting in France and into Brittany.

The hope was to fool the Germans into thinking that part of, if not the entire, 35th, 80th and 90th Infantry Divisions and the 2nd Armored Division had changed direction and were headed west to

Brittany instead of east to surround the Seventh German Army in France.

This operation was mainly composed of what the 23rd called "special effects." The men and vehicles used the insignia of the unit they portrayed. Men dressed as MPs posted divisional signs. At night rubber dummies were set up to allow inquisitive eyes to see a larger force at rest. The men were all too eager to talk to the locals about "their division" and where they were going. The effect was designed to fool any German collaborators or agents left behind when the Germans retreated. The final product was so good that even stragglers from those units were fooled and had to be quietly redirected back to their real units.

The radio operators of the 23rd were all trained in simulating different types of units. They knew what kinds of messages to send and how often. Only a handful of radio transmissions were needed to grab the attention of the German radio interception service. These transmissions were actual messages properly encoded so that if, for some reason, the Germans were able to read the ciphers they would continue to be fooled. The radio operators of the 23rd sent such innocent messages as reports on waterpoints or daily reports when moving into bivouac.

Force "Mike" simulated the 35th Infantry Division's 134th Infantry Regiment, plus an attached 105 and 155mm artillery battalion. It followed on the heels of the 23rd's Lt. Col. Day driving out to Brest as a phony advance party. "Mike" was supposed to be enroute to Brest to assist the 6th Armored Division. The column stopped at Dinan because they had few weapons and the area in front of them still had German units wandering about. They were supposed to link up with a supply column heading to the 6th Armored, but were unable to locate it and felt it best to stay where they were rather than risk capture.

Force "Nan" portrayed a column from the 80th Infantry Division composed of the 518th Infantry Regiment, the 314th Field Artillery Battalion, and the 80th Signal Company. It too was headed to Brest to support the 6th Armored. "Nan" stopped just west of Rennes when it also realized it was headed into German territory without an armed escort. The local Frenchmen seemed to be totally fooled as to their identity, and the Germans had jammed their radio transmissions, indi-

DECEPTION IN BRITTANY
23rd SPECIAL TROOPS
9-20 Aug. 1944

Force	Represents	Headed to	Stops at
MIKE	35th ID	Brest	Dinan
PETER	2nd AD	Saint-Nazaire	Châteaubriand
NAN	80th ID	Brest	"East of Rennes"
OBOE	90th ID	Lorient	Baud

German Strongholds
Actual unit
Capt. Cowardin advance liaison
Staging Area
Lt-Col. Day advance liaison

cating that the column had been detected and was under scrutiny by the Germans. Force "Oboe" simulated a group of units from the 90th Infantry Division, and was sent to Lorient to link up with its advance party run by Captain Cowardin. "Oboe" traveled over 600 miles and found itself under scattered sniper fire at times. At Baud, near Lorient, "Oboe" linked up with the 4th Armored Division and came to a halt. Along the way the Germans had at first jammed their radio transmissions, then stopped, obviously listening in trying to figure out who the unit was.

Force "Peter" simulated an armored column from the 2nd Armored Division headed to Châteaubriant. They simulated an armored infantry battalion, an armored field artillery battalion, and a tank battalion. When "Peter" got to Martigné the men were told to roam the streets and tell anyone that cared that they were from the 2nd Armored Division. Some were dressed as MPs from the 2nd Armored and placed at key positions in Châteaubriant. A few German planes were seen to circle the dummy encampments indicating they had been spotted. The locals warned the Americans not to talk to two specific Frenchmen who had been very friendly with the Germans. When these two men approached the American troops, the Americans were all too happy to let them know they were the 2nd Armored Division on their way to Lorient. "Peter" was quite sure they had been spotted by groups of Germans hiding in the woods, and when they left they told the locals that any vehicles heading north were just going back for supplies.

While this operation was going on the bulk of the American Army was attempting to encircle the German Army. The Germans obviously paid attention to the ploy, as about the same time the German high command reported that elements of the XVth Corps had stopped moving east and were now moving west. The reports of radio jamming make it clear the Germans knew that units were on the move. The German radio interception service was extremely good and would certainly track the sources of transmission. An evaluation of the jamming indicated it was centered on the frequencies used by the 23rd, and that no other Allied units in the area were using those frequencies.

No direct evidence has surfaced to indicate that the 23rd convinced the Germans that the American Army was spreading out to Brittany and not focused on encircling the Germans. However, it remains a possibility that this previously unknown deception operation may have contributed to the ultimate defeat of the German 7th Army in the Falaise pocket. It would make sense that if the Germans thought the Americans were pulling troops from their flank to move west into Brittany, that they need not be in such a hurry to withdraw from France. It was the failure of the Germans to withdraw from the trap sooner that caused the destruction of the main German forces in France.

After "Operation Brittany" the 23rd sent another Task Force to Brest to try and fool the Germans into thinking the 6th Armored Division tanks were still outside the city, when in fact they had moved away to the south. They also experimented with misdirecting German counter-battery fire through the use of dummy artillery positions and simulated muzzle flashes.

One platoon of the 3132nd Sonic Deception Company was sent to Saint-Malo in an effort to use their high-powered speakers to convince the Germans on offshore islands to surrender. These speakers could be heard up to 15 miles over water, but this attempt to use the unit for propaganda broadcasts was not successful.

Right.
The inflatable decoys proved to be tricky to work with. During the day the sun would expand the air inside, stretching them to their breaking point. At night the cooler air would cause the dummies to slowly collapse unless kept topped off. Nothing could spoil the effect better than an artillery barrel dropping to the ground.
(National Archives)

Below.
By themselves, the rubber decoys were not very realistic when viewed up close. However, when seen from a distance, and with the appropriate cover and emplacement, they could fool even the most experienced eye. This is a dummy artillery position created by the 23rd later on near the German border.
(National Archives)

Bottom right.
The inflatable rubber dummies were the mainstay of visually fooling German spies that there was an American armored unit in the area. The decoys would be set up under appropriate camouflage netting, and in areas where they could only be observed from a distance. Proper unit markings were also painted on each decoy.
(National Archives)

Below.
Perhaps the most important lesson the 23rd learned at Brest was to be sure and coordinate closely with the local combat troops. In the 2nd Division sector the sound of tanks moving into the area caused the Germans to bring in more antitank weapons. The following tank attack by D/709th Tank Battalion was stopped with many casualties, probably due to the increase in German defenses.
(National Archives)

DECEPTION IN BRITTANY OPERATION BREST
23rd SPECIAL TROOPS 20-27 Aug. 1944

23rd BASE

Key
- Real units
- 23rd Units
- Real attack
- Simulated threats

Lesneven → Morlaix

XXX
VIII

XX 29
XX 8
Plabennec

II 69 Tk Bn
Milizac

XX 2

II 15Tk Bn
Rennes →

II 37 FA Bn
Landerneau

Saint-Renan

Gouesnou
Guipavas

Saint-Mathieu
BREST

XX TFB

Brest Roadstead

Daoulas

1

1

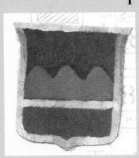

2

3

This is one of the hand painted 6th Armored division patches used during the Brest Operation. It was the last time the 23rd would have to rely on painted shoulder insignia. Complaints to 12th Army Group paved the way for the deception troops to have access to the correct embroidered insignia for the rest of the war.
(National Archives)

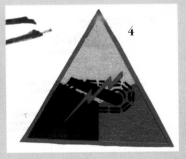

4

During most operations the 23rd used some of their men to portray MPs. Here a man from the 1st Platoon of the 406th Engineer Combat Company, during a later operation in Luxembourg, plays the role of a 95th Division MP. Great care was taken to make sure the MP helmet markings matched those used by the original unit.

The 3132nd Signal Service Company was designed to play audio recordings of military activities (tanks moving up or bridges being built) to fool enemy listening posts. Large banks of speakers were mounted in M-3 half-tracks to broadcast the recordings in the field. Each of the company's three sonic platoons was composed of a command half-track and five half-tracks with mounted loudspeakers.

Above.
The 23rd found itself with a difficult problem during the Brittany operation. They had to simulate troops from four different divisions, but were unable to obtain the correct patches from the quartermasters. The 23rd was a secret organization and could not tell the quartermasters why they needed to requisition insignia from units they were not assigned to. The artists in the 23rd solved the problem by hand painting a number of divisional patches on shelter-half material. These field expedient insignia were worn by the men of the 23rd. These are actual samples of the painted insignia used in Brittany kept as a reference by the 23rd.
1. 90th Infantry Division
2. 80th Infantry Division
3. 35th Infantry Division
4. Independent Tank Battalion

THE 83RD INFANTRY DIVISION AT SAINT-MALO

Chapter 5

The 79th Infantry Division had originally been expected to follow the 6th Armored Division out to Brest. However, the fear of a German counterattack cutting off the Americans in Brittany led General Bradley to order the 79th to take up a blocking position at Fougères. This put the 83rd Division next in line to be moved into Brittany, and the first priority for the 83rd was the capture of Saint-Malo.

Saint-Malo was considered a key position in Brittany. It was a small port on the northern coast and the main source of supply for the German bases on the Channel Islands. The city was perfectly situated to allow German forces based there to cut off American supply routes into Brittany. General Middleton felt he had to eliminate the threat from Saint-Malo before he could safely move the bulk of the VIIIth Corps into Brittany.

Saint-Malo had been named by Hitler as one of the "German Fortresses." The fortress commander here was Colonel Andreas von Aulock, who vowed to turn Saint-Malo into another Stalingrad. He is quoted as saying, *"I was placed in command of the fortress. I did not request it. I will execute the orders I have received and, doing my duty as a soldier, I will fight to the last stone. I will defend Saint-Malo to the last man, even if the last man is myself."*

To prepare the city for combat von Aulock tried to get the French population to leave. They, in turn, asked him to vacate the city and spare the historic architecture. Aulock relayed the request up through the chain of command to Hitler, who supposedly replied, *"In warfare there is no such thing as an historic city."*

Saint-Malo is an ancient walled town that contains the 15th century chateau of Anne of Brittany. It sits on the eastern shore of the Rance Estuary. Outside the city wall was the modern suburb of Paramé and to the south was the harbor area of Saint-Servan. On the waterfront between Saint-Malo and Saint-Servan was a fortress known as the Citadel, which would be the main German command post. Across the Rance a mile to the west was the smaller city of Dinard. Both Dinard and Saint-Malo had been fortified over the years of occupation and the defenses included coastal artillery in fortifications built on the offshore islands. The approaches to both cities had been heavily mined and the German troops were dug in. Low lying areas had been flooded as an obstacle to the Americans.

The Channel Islands of Jersey, Guernsey, and Alderney could furnish supplies and receive casualties (as well as POWs) so the Ger-

mans at Saint-Malo never felt they were actually trapped. As judged by the German high command, the Saint-Malo defenses were the most advanced of any fortress in France. The emplacements were connected by underground telephone wires, supplies were plentiful, and strongpoints ringed the approaches. The French claimed that at least 10,000 Germans were in the city, but the Americans felt it could be no more than 3-6,000. In reality, German troops throughout Brittany had fled the rapid advance of the 6th Armored Division and Task Force A and joined the Saint-Malo garrison. There were roughly 8,000 German troops in Saint-Malo and another 4,000 in Dinard.

General Patton originally wanted only one regiment of the 83rd Infantry Division to attack Saint-Malo. He did not think it would be hard to capture, but the initial attacks on the outskirts by TFA told a different story. Middleton realized that the Germans were well dug in and ordered the entire 83rd Division to attack the city. He did not want to leave such a strong German position, which could be reinforced from the Channel Islands, behind him when he moved further into Brittany.

At first General Bradley was also ready to by-pass Saint-Malo, but upon seeing how scattered the VIIIth Corps was throughout Brittany he too became worried about leaving it alone. As an added bonus, the capture of Saint-Malo would allow a small amount of supplies to be landed in the area to help supply the troops in Brittany. Once the 83rd started to arrive at Saint-Malo General Earnest and his Task

Force A pulled out to continue their advance. Earnest left a platoon of his tank destroyers to assist the 83rd, but was given a battalion of motorized infantry and a battery of 105mm howitzers in their place.

On 5 Aug. the 83rd Division sent a battalion of infantry across the Rance River in assault boats to cut the Dinan - Dinard road. These men ran into heavy German resistance and were recalled. The same day the Germans abandoned their positions to the east in Cancale. The 331st Infantry moved in to check the area and immediately plans were made to land supplies there. The next day the Germans withdrew from Dinan and pulled back to the north, tightening their lines. They left a few hundred men in Dinan who let it be known they were more than willing to surrender to American troops, but not to the FFI. They were afraid of what the French might do to them.

While an American unit was sent to accept the surrender in Dinan, the 83rd was preparing for the assault on Saint-Malo. The three regiments of the 83rd were put into the line in a semicircle with the 329th on the left, the 330th in the center, and the 331st to the right. Seeing that the Americans were ready to attack, the Germans evacuated the French civilians under cover of a white flag on 5 Aug. Once they had left, the German artillery on the Ile de Cézembre opened up. One of the first shells fired struck the spire of the Saint-Malo Cathedral - this was considered a bad omen by the French. Soon after fires started throughout the city.

It was never known if these were accidental or started on purpose,

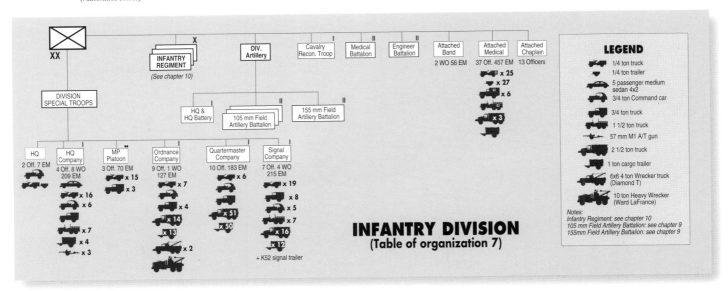

INFANTRY DIVISION
(Table of organization 7)

REDUCTION OF SAINT-MALO

Cézembre · Paramé

SAINT-MALO

Dinard

Cancale

Saint-Servan

6 August

Saint-Benoît
des-Ondes

Baie du Mont
Saint-Michel

330
6 August

12 August

8/12 Aug. · Pleurtuit

9 August

331
5 August

7 August

Dol
de Bretagne

4 August

329

Map Key

→ Axis of advance

〜 German
Defense Line

▬ German
Strongholds

◯ 3/121st Infantry
(8th Division)
surrounded

121

Rance River

331
9 August

Dinan

The commander of the 83rd Infantry
Division, Major General Robert
Macon (Left), and his assistant
division commander, Brigadier
General Claude Ferenbaugh, observe
artillery fire directed at the Ile de
Cézembre. When Macon took charge
of the assault on Dinard he left
Ferenbaugh in command of the main
attack on Saint-Malo.
(National Archives)

but rumors claim they were started by the Germans burning their secret documents. The fires were a major problem because the Americans had cut off water supplies to the city and there was no way to fight them. On 7 Aug. the German demolitions in the dockyards were set off. The Germans did a very thorough job and the facilities were completely destroyed.

The advance to Saint-Malo looked like it would be tougher than expected so General Macon was given the 121st Infantry Regiment (from the 8th Division) and a company of tanks to assist him. Most of the VIIIth Corps artillery was moved to the area and an increase in air support was requested. The 121st was sent around the Rance River to work its way up to Dinard, while the 83rd would focus on Saint-Malo.

The 83rd, however, was having a very hard time moving forward. The Germans were well dug in and resisted stubbornly. After two days of artillery and tank destroyer fire 400 Germans on the key point of Saint-Joseph's Hill finally surrendered on 9 Aug. This broke the German defensive line and the 83rd started moving forward to the city. The 331st under Colonel York drove through the defenses to capture Paramé on the coast.

This cut off the German positions on the eastern edge of the defensive perimeter. On the left flank the 329th, under Col. Crabhill, moved

through Saint-Servan right up to the Citadel. It took five days of heavy fighting, but the 83rd was at the edge of the city.

Dinard and the Lost Battalion

Col. John R. Jeter's 121st Infantry (Georgia National Guard) of the 8th Infantry Division was attached to the 83rd for the Saint-Malo operation. On 7 Aug. he sent a detachment to take the surrender of the Germans in Dinan while his main force crossed the Rance River and moved north to attack Dinard. There they ran into very strong

This heavy machine gun keeps a
careful watch on Fort National in
the Saint-Malo Harbor. When the
Americans finally assaulted this
fort it was found to be unoccupied.
The beach defense obstacles used
to keep the Allies from landing at
Saint-Malo are seen here during
low tide.
(National Archives)

German emplacements and the advance slowed. The Germans were well-positioned and camouflaged. What appeared to be typical farm-houses suddenly burst into life with enemy fire and turned out to be concrete strongpoints.

On the afternoon of 8 Aug. the 3/121st under Lt. Col. Gordon Eyler moved up to the town of Pleurtuit four miles south of Dinard. I/121st had opened a gap in a line of German antitank obstacles and the entire battalion moved through. 2/121st was unable to advance in its sector and remained behind. That night the Germans circled around 3/121st, replaced the roadblock in the antitank line, and cut the battalion off.

Not until the next morning did the Americans realize they had been surrounded, when they started to take fire from their rear. Eyler tried to break back through the German line, but was stopped by strong artillery and mortar fire. When Col. Jeter learned what had happened he ordered Eyler to hold his position until the rest of the regiment could come to their aid.

The 121st tried but was unable to get through to the 3rd Battalion. German artillery and tanks attacked the cut off unit mercilessly. Artillery fire poured down on the area and the battalion command post was shelled, killing the S-3 and other key personnel. As casualties mounted the supply of blood plasma ran short. On the afternoon of 8 Aug. two liaison planes from the 56th Field Artillery attempted to drop vitally needed medical supplies to the battalion. The plasma was dropped, but the two aircraft collided in midair and their crews were killed. Soon afterwards a third liaison plane on a similar mission was shot down by German fire. Before the battle was over two more aircraft would also collide and crash attempting to drop blood plasma.

On the night of 8 Aug. the Germans attempted to penetrate into the 3/121st position by driving up in a captured American vehicle (reportedly an armored car). The trick was discovered, the vehicle destroyed, and ten Germans taken prisoner. The 3rd Battalion would become known as the "Lost Battalion of Dinard" even though it was never really lost, just cut off from their own lines.

One GI from the unit later recalled: "*I was hit on the first day when the shell wacked the CP. They carried me to a little farmhouse where the medicos had set up. It was called the Purple Heart Hotel. There were no medical officers in that place, just a bunch of GIs. They worked like the devil to keep us going.*

They tore up shirts, underwear, and any clothing the French house-keeper could find to wrap up our wounds. We ate green apples, sugar beets, and raw potatoes. There must have been about 50 of us there. You just didn't groan because you knew the fellow next to you

was hurting more. God how those medics worked. There were Jerries there too. And the medics treated them just like another dough. I recall a Jerry officer who was all shot up. He seemed to be about 17 years old. The medics gave him the next to the last shot of morphine. They worked and worked on him for days but he finally passed away.

I particularly recall the day a Jerry shell hit that place. It was miraculous how any of us are left to tell the tale. That shell tore off a couple of rooms. There was plaster, bricks and blood about me- I had to pinch myself to make sure I was alive!"

Captain Lew Atkinson was a forward observer for the 56th Field Artillery Bn. attached to the 121st. Throughout the fight he left his radio operator at the 121st CP. This radio was the only communications the battalion had back to American lines. Whenever the Germans attacked Atkinson moved to the action, bringing a field telephone with him. He would call for artillery and his radio operator,

Above. **American GIs examine the underground living quarters of the German garrison at Saint-Malo. This shelter was probably in the Citadel. The living quarters were well-equipped and provided good protection from the air and artillery attacks.** *(National Archives)*

Below.
At Saint-Malo a captured German medic is treating one of his countrymen under the watchful eye of a few GIs. Many German medical units were kept intact when captured to operate medical facilities for their own troops. This freed American medics to work on Allied troops.
(National Archives)

Cpl. Onofrio Patti, would relay it over the radio. With the help of well-directed artillery the battalion was able to hold its position for three days.

Once the key point of Saint-Joseph's Hill, south of Saint-Malo, was captured General Macon turned his attention to Dinard. He wanted to eliminate it as a possible retreat avenue for the Germans, stop the artillery fire from the Dinard positions, and of course rescue the lost battalion. He reorganized his troops on the Saint-Malo side of the Rance, moved the 331st across to support the 121st, and took personal command of the Dinard operation.

1&2/121st were fighting hard to break though to their comrades, but were unable to make any headway. A battalion from the 331st Infantry was sent to assist them, along with a company of tanks and a company of tank destroyers. After combat patrols on 12 Aug. were still unable to contact the lost battalion the rest of the regiment went into the attack with the newly arrived support.

It took two regiments (121st and 331st) plus massive corps artillery support to finally break the German defenses. On the afternoon of 12 Aug. contact was finally restored with the 3rd Battalion. During this period the battalion suffered 31 killed, 106 wounded and 16 missing. Two men from the 121st were awarded the DSC for their actions while surrounded.

On 14 Aug. the attack north to Dinard was again under way. At one point G/121st was held up by a small fortification heavily garrisoned by the Germans. Sgt. William Vaughan discovered a small tunnel that seemed to lead to the German position. He led three other men into the tunnel which ran under the German defenses. Suddenly appearing inside the fortification allowed the four GIs to capture the strongpoint and take 200 Germans prisoner.

"And for every stone we must fight "

The Germans in Dinard were commanded by Colonel Bacherer. His forces were primarily composed of combat veterans from the 77th Infantry Division. To a surrender ultimatum he replied, "*Every house must become a fortress, every stone a hiding place, and for every stone we must fight.*" However, late in the afternoon after a spectacular air strike with jellied gasoline, the Americans finally captured the city. Over 1,300 prisoners were taken in the advance to Dinard and half of those on the last day alone. When Bacherer's command post was captured it was found to be very well-supplied and equipped, even including air conditioning. He had obviously not fought to the last round.

Originally, General Macon of the 83rd had felt that Col. Jeter and the 121st had not performed very well. When he learned that one of their battalions had been surrounded he thought it must have been from poor leadership. However, after commanding the 121st in the final drive to Dinard he changed his mind. On the evening of 11 Aug. General Macon radioed to Corps HQ, "*I want Monarch Six (General Middleton) to know that the resistance we are meeting south of Dinard is more determined than I anticipated.*" Later on he would say in defense of the 121st, "*It is hard to tell what they have been up against. Sometimes these things go very slow for a while, then all of a sudden they break...*" It was his way of telling Middleton that it was a rough fight and the 121st was not to be blamed. With Dinard finally in American hands the 121st Infantry was sent to rejoin the 8th Infantry Division at Brest.

The 3rd Battalion of the 121st Infantry was later awarded a unit citation of the French Croix de Guerre with Silver-Gilt Star. The citation reads,

"*A brilliant unit which especially distinguished itself in the Brittany Campaign on 8 August 1944. Installed in front and inside enemy defense installations, cut off from its communications, sustained without yielding six enemy counterattacks preceded by heavy artillery and mortar fire. This unit succeeded in reestablishing contact and inflicted serious losses on the enemy, forcing it to abandon its attacks, destroying one tank and taking 60 prisoners.*"

Siege of Saint-Malo

While General Macon had been dealing with Dinard he had left his assistant division commander, General Ferenbaugh, in charge of the Saint-Malo operation. On 9 Aug. Ferenbaugh concentrated on the smaller German positions at Saint-Ideuc and La Varde with attacks by the 330th Infantry. After three days of artillery barrages the Germans at Saint-Ideuc gave up, and La Varde was taken the following day.

The fighting in the city of Saint-Malo was a taste of what the VIIIth Corps would find later on at Brest. Progress was measured street by street, and the troops learned to blow holes in the walls of the buildings to move forward under cover. On 11 Aug. the casino at the end of the Paramé-Saint-Malo causeway was captured. This gave the Americans access to the old city area where the chateau was. The thick walls of the chateau were finally targeted by the American guns, but neither tank destroyers, 8" guns, nor Air Force bombers had any effect on them.

Fires still burned in the city. On 13 Aug. a truce was held to allow any remaining French civilians to evacuate the area. The Germans in the chateau were insulated from the fires by the thick stone walls, and the burned-out buildings posed a difficult obstacle for the advancing Americans. Finally, on 14 Aug. they reached the chateau, but machine guns kept the American engineers from placing demolition charges on the thick walls. The Germans inside, however, had finally had enough and 150 POWs were taken.

Once the old chateau was captured all of the organized resistance on the north shore of Saint-Malo stopped. The job was not yet finished as all artillery fire from the Saint-Malo area had to be stopped if supplies were to be landed at Granville and Cancale. There were German positions on two small offshore islands that still had to be dealt with. There had been no activity from them, but the Americans did not want to be taken by surprise. At low tide on 16 Aug. a company from the 329th Infantry waded out to Fort National and found it unoccupied. Then, under cover of a smoke screen they moved to

THE 83rd
"THE THU...

After only two months in England, the 83rd arrived in France on 18 June 1944. The division immediately entered the hedgerow fighting south of Carentan. Assisting in Operation Cobra, the 83rd broke the German lines in Normandy, then turned west to capture Saint-Malo and patrol central Brittany. It moved to Luxembourg in September, where it advanced to the Siegfried line, fought in the Hurtgen Forest and took part in the Ardennes battle at Rochefort. In March the 83rd took part in Operation Grenade and crossed the Rhine. Moving through Germany the 83rd captured Halle and passed through the Harz Mountains to the Elbe where it met the Russians. The division insignia contains the letters "OHIO" from the state in which it was organized during WW1.

DIVISION,
DIVISION"

83rd Inf. division (*Blackstone*)
● 329th Infantry Regt. (*Blackjack*)
● 330th Infantry Regt. (*Blackfish*)
● 331st Infantry Regt. (*Blackboy*)

Division Artillery (*Blackbird*)
● 322nd Field Artillery Bn. (*Blackberry*)
● 323rd Field Artillery Bn. (*Blood*)
● 324th Field Artillery Bn. (*Blank*)
● 908th Field Artillery Bn. (*Blackdog*)

● 83rd Division Special Troops
● 308th Engineer Combat Bn. (*Blimp*)
● 83rd Recon Squadron (*Bluecoat*)
● 308th Medical Bn. (*Blueberry*)
● 783rd Ordnance Co. (*Blacksmith*)
● 83rd Quartermaster Bn. (*Bluebeard*)
● 83rd Signal Co. (*Bluejay*)

Attached units
● 802nd Tank Destroyer Bn. (*Blackjoe*)
453rd AAA Bn. (*Mayfair 453*)

Grand Bey and, taking the garrison there by surprise, captured 150 Germans.

The Citadel

The command post and last defenses at Saint-Malo were located in a fort known as the Citadel. The basis for the Citadel was an 18th century fortress. It housed six artillery pieces and a number of mortars. Supplies had been stockpiled and the garrison could hold out for quite a while. The defenses to the landward side were very strong, and entire buildings had been knocked down by the Germans to clear good fields of fire. The seaward side was supported by artillery fire from the Ile de Cézembre three miles offshore. Any attempt to storm the Citadel could be stopped by artillery barrages from Cézembre.

Middleton considered leaving the Citadel alone, but thought that allowing it to remain would boost the morale of other German defenders in Brittany. Once it was eliminated he would be able to use the full 83rd at another location. The VIIIth Corps artillery battalions, consisting of 8" guns and 240mm howitzers, pounded the fortress, but made little impact on the thick stone walls. At this point American supplies of artillery ammunition were starting to run low and some guns were reduced to only 5 rounds per day. Thousand pound bombs dropped by the AF had little effect, so other ways to take the Citadel were tried.

The sewer system was explored to see if there were any passages that went close enough to the fort to allow explosives to be used. A captured German chaplain was sent into the fort to convince Aulock to surrender, but he refused. A French female friend of the colonel was convinced to call him on a telephone line and ask him to give up, but he refused to speak with her. A psychological warfare unit broadcast requests for the German surrender, and other programming to lower German morale, over loudspeakers.

After the battle the defenders claimed the only reason they did not give up sooner was that Col. Aulock forbid it. What they did not

know was that Aulock had been told of the forthcoming Mortain offensive. He thought that all he had to do was hold out a little longer and German forces would soon link up with them. At last he announced the news of the offensive to his men and stated that "*anyone deserting or surrendering is a common dog.*"

On 11 Aug. a group of medium bombers again blasted the Citadel. Afterwards a rifle company from the 329th Infantry moved in supported by combat engineers. They used a flamethrower to keep nearby positions from interfering as they blew gaps in the barbed wire with Bangalore torpedoes. A group of roughly 30 men assisted by three French volunteers climbed up the wall and got inside. They dropped explosive charges down air vents, but after seeing no visible damage they were driven off by machine guns and artillery fire from Cézembre.

Col. Crabhill's 329th Infantry then formed two special assault teams to breach the walls. Each was composed of 96 infantrymen along with demolition and security teams and a special heavy demolition group. While preparing for the final assault tank destroyers fired at weak places in the walls. On 13 Aug. another flight of bombers hit the city and a white flag appeared. To the dismay of the riflemen it was only to arrange the truce allowing more French civilians to leave the town.

On 15 Aug. the assault teams went in after another air strike. They were driven back by machine gun fire. 8" guns were set up only 1,500 yards from the wall and directed to fire at openings and ventilators. Two companies of 4.2" mortars shelled the fort with white phosphorous rounds and there were more air strikes with (the then experimental) jellied gasoline. Just before another ground assault was to jump off another white flag appeared. Aircraft already in route were diverted to drop their load on the Ile de Cézembre.

Aulock had finally decided to surrender because the 8" guns had penetrated the firing apertures and destroyed some of his guns. This broke up his interlocking fields of fire and meant that it was only a matter of time before a ground attack would succeed. The psycho-

logical warfare unit had driven the men's morale down, and with the failure of the Mortain offensive it seemed pointless to continue. For his defense of Saint-Malo Aulock was awarded the Oakleaves to his Knight's Cross. Aulock had destroyed a port that was important to the Allies, and held up a full division with corps support for more than two weeks when they were desperately needed elsewhere. With Saint-Malo in American hands the 83rd Division then took over responsibility for the Rennes-Brest area as far south as the Loire River. Two battalions of the 330th Infantry were assigned to patrol the coastline for German infiltration from the Ile de Cézembre.

Ile de Cézembre

Attention now turned to the fortified island 4,000 yards off the coast. These guns had to be captured before the local beaches and small harbors could be used to bring in supplies. They controlled the sea approaches to not only Saint-Malo, but also Granville and Cancale. The commander of Cézembre was Oberleutnant Richard Seuss, who had been awarded the Oakleaves to his Knight's Cross for holding out at Saint-Malo. There were six ex-French 194mm guns on the island along with a 150mm gun, an Italian manned 75mm battery, and a light flak battery. The guns were positioned to fire either out to sea or be turned around to fire inland.

When Saint-Malo had fallen the Channel Isles received a message from Cézembre saying they were low on food, water, and ammo, and that their radio was in poor shape and they needed a replacement.

The island garrison had run out of 194mm shells, but the 150mm gun happened to be an old naval gun that could be supplied from Jersey. German ships from the Channel Isles visited Cézembre almost every night bringing supplies and taking off casualties. These visits showed the garrison they had not been forgotten, and the Germans were ready to keep fighting. The problem was that a large part of the garrison was composed of Russians and Italians who wanted to give up. Three Italians actually stole a small boat and sailed to Saint-Malo where they surrendered. Allied bombers regularly attacked Cézembre from 9 Aug. on. Finally General Macon sent Major Joseph M. Alexander, two enlisted men, and a motion picture cameraman to demand the German surrender. Seuss refused, saying his last order had been to continue to hold out, and he still had plenty of ammo. However, the island defenses were in poor shape from the bombardment and the jellied gasoline had severely damaged the garrison morale.

The 330th Infantry was given instruction in amphibious techniques for a planned assault on the island. The Navy trucked 15 LCVPs overland on trailers from Omaha Beach. This movement proved that landing craft could be transported by truck and the concept was later used

UNIT CITATION 2nd BATTALION, 330th IR

"The 2nd Battalion, 330th Infantry is cited for outstanding performance of duty in armed conflict with the enemy. At 0830 on 7 August 1944, the 2nd Battalion, 330th Infantry launched an attack toward Saint-Joseph, France. By 0930 the leading company began receiving intense artillery, machine gun, and small arms fire. All through the rest of the day heavy fighting went on, and the two leading companies were able to advance another three hundred yards before darkness came and the defensive positions were prepared for the night. Before dawn on the 8th, the German artillery began a concentration which blanketed the entire battalion area and lasted for forty-five minutes, and its intensity delayed the jump-off time of the battalion's attack. The battalion sector was some 1,800 yards in width and ran through woods of varying density and over bald open hills that were under direct enemy observation and subject to all their fire power.

At about 0800, the battalion resumed its attack. Here the battalion bore the brunt of the attack, being almost in the center of the division sector. It encountered the strongest of enemy installations, including permanent gun emplacements hewn out of the granite rocks of a quarry and an extensive series of foxholes and trenches reinforced by stone walls and barbed wire entanglements. Several times hand-to-hand combat was needed to reduce

these positions. Even though outnumbered, it continued the attacks against fanatical opposition in the face of intense artillery concentrations, including multiple barreled rocket projectors, antitank guns, 88mm guns, mortar and machine gun fire.

Through aggressiveness, determination and sheer courage, by 1030 it had gained 600 yards of bitterly contested ground. Then the enemy counterattacked. The numerically superior enemy closed in upon the battalion and a furious hand-to-hand battle raged. Radio operators, runners, and liaison personnel all joined in the battle to muster every available weapon to force the enemy back. Finally the fighting skill and spirit of the 2nd Battalion showed its effect. Those enemy who were not killed, wounded, or captured were put to rout and their morale broken.

Without respite the battalion's attack continued. When one company was suffering heavy casualties and became disorganized by fire from a self-propelled gun, the last remaining officer in the company, at great risk to his life, knocked it out with a bazooka. Such leadership and disregard to personal safety characterized the actions of all members of the battalion.

By nightfall it had advanced to within 500 yards of the Saint-Joseph fortress, and by constantly pouring fire from small arms, mortars and artillery into the fortress,

they prevented the enemy from manning their gun positions atop the fortress, thus being able to clean up the outposts of the enemy that surrounded the fortress. The heavy shelling shook the fortress continuously throughout the night. The next morning, the German commander of the fortress, his troops decisively defeated and thoroughly demoralized, and seeing the hopelessness of his situation, surrendered the fortress.

Battalion losses during the three day action were 154 killed, wounded, or missing. An estimated 261 Germans were killed, 428 taken prisoner, and 178 wounded. Five enemy assault guns, three self-propelled guns, five antitank guns, seven antiaircraft guns, one tank, and seven mortars were destroyed. An undetermined but large amount of enemy small arms ammunition and food stores was captured or destroyed. Thus during the three day period from 7 August to 9 August 1944, the 2nd Battalion, 330th Infantry with a notable display of courage, combat skill, and determination, broke stubborn enemy resistance at Saint-Joseph and the approaches to Saint-Malo, decisively defeated the enemy, and prevented them from denying our entry into the Saint-Malo-Dinard area.

The undaunted courage and unswerving devotion to duty shown by each man of the battalion reflects the highest traditions of the armed forces."

MAJOR GENERAL ROBERT C. MACON

The commander of the 83rd Infantry Division graduated from the Virginia Polytechnic institute with a degree in mechanical engineering in 1912. He entered the Infantry and served in WW1 as a captain. In 1942 he commanded the 7th Infantry Regiment (3rd ID) during the North African campaign with such success he was sent back to the States as the assistant division Commander to the newly formed 83rd Infantry Division. He assumed command of the unit in January 1944, and led the division through Europe. He continued to command the unit during occupation duties until January of 1946.

Major General Robert Macon - commander of the 83rd Infantry Division
(National Archives)

in the Rhine River crossing.

On 31 Aug. a major air strike was made against the island with the primary target being the water tanks. This came from a comment the German commander had made - that he would fight to the last drop of water. On 1 Sept. there were more air strikes along with shelling from the 15" guns on the HMS Warspite. Again Seuss was asked to surrender and he replied he had no permission to do so.

Seuss radioed the Channel Islands telling them he now had 277 wounded men on the island and he needed them evacuated. In desperation the Germans sent the hospital ship Bordeaux to help him, knowing it would probably be captured. The ship was spotted in the daylight and taken over by the Allies. With this Seuss was finally ready to give up. He radioed that "*the men would rather fight with bare fists than sit in the ruined bunkers and bleed to death.*"

The Jersey garrison told Seuss to hold on and they would evacuate them off the island, but their rescue mission was prevented by bad weather. Finally Seuss was given permission to surrender and he had the code books burned. On 2 Sept., with the 330th ready to assault, a white flag was raised over the island. The landing craft were sent out and Seuss, 320 men, 12 female Red Cross workers, and 2 Italian officers were taken prisoner. The final blow for Cézembre was that the water distillation plant had been destroyed in the bombing and the garrison had run out of water. With Cézembre captured the eastern section of Brittany was fully in Allied hands.

Chapter 6

Above and page 54.
A motion picture cameraman filmed this group of GIs from Task Force B moving up on the Daoulas Peninsula. As the men pass before the camera they provide good examples of what the soldiers wore and carried. This BAR man carries his weapon by hooking the front straps of M-1936 suspenders under the magazine. Careful examination reveals he also wears an M-1928 pack. Like many soldiers he has removed the bipod of the weapon to make it lighter.
(National Archives)

Below and opposite page, bottom
Senior officers from Task Force B examine a map outside their headquarters building. Clearly the men were more concerned about fighting the Germans than making sure they had fancy signs for their command post.
(National Archives)

TASK FORCE B ON THE DAOULAS PENINSULA

On 21 June 1944 Task Force B, under the command of General James A. Van Fleet, became operational. Van Fleet, the assistant division commander of the 2nd Infantry Division, was given the job of clearing the Plougastel-Daoulas Peninsula. This peninsula, just to the southeast of Brest, was known to the Germans as the Armorique Peninsula and to the Americans as the Daoulas Peninsula.

Van Fleet divided his troops into two main groups. In the south he had the bulk of Task Force A, now reinforced with the 50th Armored Inf. Bn. and the 83rd Armored FA Bn. The northern end of the peninsula was assigned to a force built around the 38th Infantry Regiment. They were supported by the 3/330th Infantry, B&C/705th TD Bn., A/68th Tank Bn., and A/603rd TD Bn. Artillery support came from the 174th Artillery Group, composed of the 2nd Field Artillery Bn., 561st Field Artillery Bn., and C/323rd Artillery Bn.

Task Force B was responsible for not only capturing the Plougastel Peninsula, but also for screening the left flank of the Americans at Brest. Mobile patrols were constantly run down the coast as far south as Châteaulin and Douarnenez to make sure no Germans were moving up from the south.

The Germans knew that the Daoulas Peninsula was key to defending Brest. It was a perfect location to place artillery to shell the approaches to Brest. If captured by the Americans it would allow them to shell Brest from both the north and south. The German defensive line along the base of the peninsula ran from a strongpoint on Hill 154 down to the town of Daoulas. Most of the naval and antiaircraft guns in the area were mounted for a 360 degree traverse so they could engage ground targets.

The terrain was generally open with good fields of fire over the loose rocky ground. The main defensive position was on Hill 154 with a double system of trenches protected by belts of barbed wire. Eight

concrete pillboxes protected against artillery fire and the entire area was ringed with mines and trip wires. Although the American records indicate these pillboxes were made of concrete, examination of the area today reveals they were only wooden structures covered with earth. At least 25 machine guns were dug into the hill along with a few high velocity guns and some mortars. The defenders were infantry from the German 266th Division, stiffened by a backbone of paratroops from the 2nd FJ Division.

On the afternoon of 22 August the 3/38th Infantry under command of Lt. Col. Olinto M. Barsanti attacked the hill. L/38th was on the left and I/38th took the right flank. Each company had been reinforced with a section of heavy machine guns from M/38th. K/38th was in battalion reserve.

L/38th, under Captain Robert L. Utley, moved by slowly creeping up the hill. They clung low to any cover and the Germans had a hard time spotting them. While the Germans were concentrating on L/38 to their front, I/38 under Captain George Van Hoorebeke was moving up on the right. They were able to by-pass Hill 154 to the north and move around the German flank. I/38th occupied the high ground to their front without much trouble, but this movement had opened a gap between the two forward companies that the Germans would later take advantage of.

When the 3rd platoon of L/38th first came under fire from a machine gun position on Hill 154, the lead scout turned to his partner and said, *"This is my baby, I'll take care of it."* He worked forward under cover until he was in a position to fire on the machine gun crew. He shot the gunner then the assistant as he tried to take cover. The German ammo bearer ran off, and the scout motioned to his squad to move up.

L/38th found itself held up at the base of the hill by a 75mm self-propelled gun. A runner, Pvt. Clifford Nolan, and an ammo bearer, Pvt. Leo Bose, crawled out in front of the American lines with a bazooka. Nolan later said, *"We fired and ran like hell, but nothing happened so we returned and fired once more. Kabloom, the 75 just wasn't."* T/Sgt. Hubert D. Deatherage found a German bazooka abandoned in front of the hill and strapped it to a tree. He fired the captured ammo back at the German pillboxes.

Hill 154 was one of only a few times the 2nd Division used flamethrowers at Brest. Three M1A1 flamethrower teams, each consisting of the flamethrower operator, an assistant operator, and two BAR men, were sent forward to try and knock out the pillboxes on the hill. The operator in the first team was killed by machine gun fire, which also damaged the flamethrower tanks so the assistant could not take over. The second team was able to move up to the hill, but the hydrogen line had been torn loose in crawling up the hill so the flamethrower would not function. The third team made it to their objective and succeeded in shooting flame at a pillbox aperture. Supporting troops were then able to move up and eliminate the German position.

When night fell the Germans began to infiltrate the gap between companies I and L. This was not discovered until dawn on the next day when the Germans were spotted by a supply detail returning to the battalion command post. Two German platoons had come close to cutting off both rifle companies. The battalion command group, about 40 men, grabbed their weapons and counterattacked the Germans. This fire fight got the attention of I/38th and their mortars assisted in driving the Germans back with heavy losses. K/38th moved up to fill the gap between the two forward companies, letting L/38th swing to the left and flank the hill. Then the Americans went back to slowly inching forward. It was not unusual for a man to be pinned down in the same spot for hours before being able to advance.

Both I&L/38th had moved well into the German lines, but were pinned down. TDs from the 705th TD Bn. were called up to fire at the German pillboxes. This forced the Germans to stay under cover so the Americans could move on up the hill. The enemy tried to reinforce the hill defenses, but was unable to bring up more men. The fight dissolved into the slow digging out of well-fortified Germans. Offers to surren-

On the Daoulas Peninsula the headquarters staff of Task Force B is hard at work. This photo was taken on 25 Aug. 1944 and shows some of the men behind the scenes (L-R Sgt. Leo Rein, Capt. George Fisk, Maj. Daniel Webster, 1st Lt. George Fitsbugh, M/Sgt. Howard Mitchell). Notice how the field telephones have been suspended underneath the wooden folding tables, providing more working space on top.
(National Archives)

Major General James Van Fleet was the assistant division commander of the 2nd Infantry Division. He was given command of Task Force B and ordered to clear the Daoulas-Plougastel Peninsula of German resistance.
(National Archives)

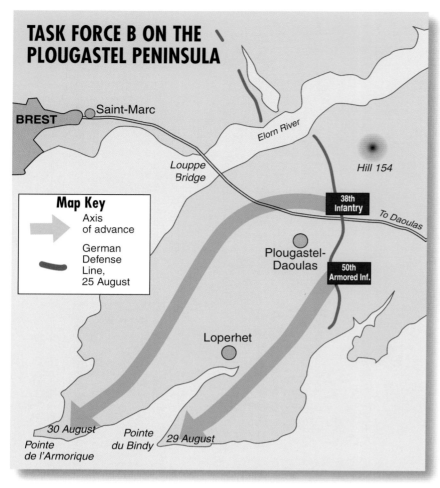

TASK FORCE B ON THE PLOUGASTEL PENINSULA

BREST
Saint-Marc
Elorn River
Louppe Bridge
Hill 154
38th Infantry
To Daoulas
Plougastel-Daoulas
50th Armored Inf.
Loperhet
30 August
Pointe du Bindy
29 August
Pointe de l'Armorique

Map Key
Axis of advance
German Defense Line, 25 August

Americans were light considering the strong German positions. Only seven were killed and 28 wounded, as opposed to 100 Germans killed and 143 taken prisoner.

One German Stabsfeldwebel of the 5th Battery, 811th Naval AA Bn., later said, *"I was sent out as an observer on Hill 154. I could see the village of Kerudu, parts of the main road south of the hill leading from Plougastel to Landerneau, and could also see as far back as Loperhet. My phone was dead. Even if I had connections with my battery I could not have been able to phone back any targets as I could see no vehicles, troops or movement of any kind. I knew that the enemy was coming up the hill because I heard shooting, but I looked and could not see any enemy troops. I saw the first American troops when they were real close and approaching our dugout from the flanks. The Americans used cover and concealment to the fullest advantage when they attacked Hill 154."*

Once Hill 154 was captured it became clear to the Germans that they could not hold the peninsula. They blew the Albert Louppe Bridge (Pont Albert Louppe) that connected the peninsula to Brest and withdrew to a second line of defenses at Plougastel. Upon examination, Hill 154 was shown to be one of the most heavily defended areas on the peninsula and was a marvelous observation point for the area. 3/38th brought up their 57mm antitank guns to Hill 154 and were able to fire over the heads of their men right into the German lines at Plougastel. The 3/38th would earn a Unit Citation for their actions at Hill 154 and Staff Sergeant Alvin P. Carey would be posthumously awarded the Medal of Honor for his heroism during this fight.

To the South

On the southern flank TFA had exchanged the 3/330th (83rd Div.) for the 50th Armored Infantry Bn. The 159th Engineer Bn. had been replaced by the 35th Engineer Bn. Artillery support was to be provided by the 83rd Armored Field Artillery Bn. The initial attack of TFA on 22 Aug. captured the town of Loperhet and they continued to advance against light resistance. The cavalry units in the task force continued to patrol the mainland to the south, and were told by the FFI that 10,000 Germans were dug in on the Crozon Peninsula.

Continued advances were made until the morning of 27 Aug. when the Germans finally turned the Americans back at Hill 63. 18 French Hotchkiss machine guns were dug into the hill and it required heavy artillery barrages to knock them out. These guns had been captured in 1940 and then issued to the rear area German troops. As the peninsula narrowed, the units from Task Force A were pulled out and sent further south to watch for a possible build-up on the Crozon. The remainder of Task Force B kept pressure on the Germans and finally broke through the last German defensive line. All that remained was to mop up scattered resistance. The peninsula was finally considered clear on 30 Aug. Task Force B had taken 3,000 POWs and captured 50 large antiaircraft and naval guns ranging in size up to 120mm. Most of these guns would have been able to provide vital defensive fire for Brest positions had they not been captured.

The 50th Armored Infantry Bn. was awarded the French Croix De

A 60mm mortar team is seen with one man carrying the complete mortar. Although it could be broken down into three parts, the 60mm mortar was normally carried fully assembled by one man, leaving the rest of the crew fraee to haul more ammunition. His assistant follows behind lugging two bags of ammunition.
(National Archives)

der were refused and resistance was very stubborn until the hill was finally overrun. At 1500 hrs. on 23 Aug. Hill 154 was fully in American hands.

A German unit of roughly 125 men had been dug in on the reverse slope of Hill 154. Once they realized they had been flanked they attempted to pull back to the next defensive line at Plougastel. The American forward observers with the infantry were perfectly situated to call in artillery fire, and the Germans were subjected to 11 full volleys of battalion fire. Those surviving the bombardment were finished off as the American infantry moved forward off the hill. Casualties among the

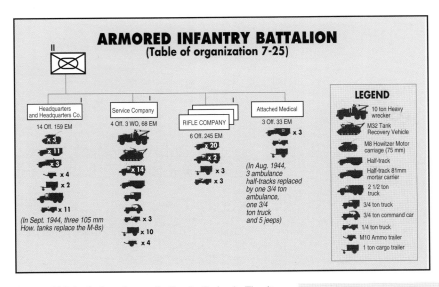

ARMORED INFANTRY BATTALION
(Table of organization 7-25)

Headquarters and Headquarters Co.
14 Off. 159 EM

Service Company
4 Off. 3 WO, 68 EM

RIFLE COMPANY
6 Off. 245 EM

Attached Medical
3 Off. 33 EM
× 3

x 20
x 2
x 3
x 3

(In Aug. 1944, 3 ambulance half-tracks replaced by one 3/4 ton ambulance, one 3/4 ton truck and 5 jeeps)

× 3
× 11
× 3
× 4
× 2
× 11

(In Sept. 1944, three 105 mm How. tanks replace the M-8s)

× 14
× 3
× 10
× 4

LEGEND
- 10 ton Heavy wrecker
- M32 Tank Recovery Vehicle
- M8 Howitzer Motor carriage (75 mm)
- Half-track
- Half-track 81mm mortar carrier
- 2 1/2 ton truck
- 3/4 ton truck
- 3/4 ton command car
- 1/4 ton truck
- M10 Ammo trailer
- 1 ton cargo trailer

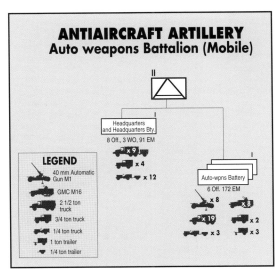

ANTIAIRCRAFT ARTILLERY
Auto weapons Battalion (Mobile)

Headquarters and Headquarters Bty.
8 Off., 3 WO, 91 EM
× 9
× 4
× 12

Auto-wpns Battery
6 Off. 172 EM
× 8
× 8
× 19
× 2
× 3
× 3

LEGEND
- 40 mm Automatic Gun M1
- GMC M16
- 2 1/2 ton truck
- 3/4 ton truck
- 1/4 ton truck
- 1 ton trailer
- 1/4 ton trailer

Guerre with Palm for its actions on the Daoulas Peninsula. The citation reads, "*A unit which distinguished itself by its courage in battle in the region of Brest. On 26 and 29 August 1944, it was tasked with taking a position which was firmly held, from which the enemy dominated the rest of the front. Rushing courageously to the attack, in spite of the intense fire, it drove the enemy away after a hard battle. The sacrifice made by this unit gave the artillery an excellent observation point from which it reduced enemy positions and permitted the victorious advance of the Allied forces.*"

General Ramcke was not pleased with the defense of the Daoulas Peninsula. In his memoirs he recalled that one of the regimental commanders of the 343rd Division caused him great difficulty. He thought this officer had been spoiled from garrison life in France with its good food and wine and was not suited for a combat command. This officer did not evacuate the civilians from his sector and neglected to occupy important defensive positions on the peninsula. It is not surprising that afterwards most of Ramcke's key officers at Brest were chosen from his own Fallschimjäger-Division.

Once the Daoulas Peninsula had been cleared of Germans the 38th Infantry was sent back to the 2nd Division to take part in the main attack on Brest. The 50th Armored Infantry Bn. and 3/330th Infantry were assigned to garrison the area to prevent the Germans from reoccupying it. It cannot be overstated that the Daoulas Peninsula was a key location for the defense, or attack, of Brest. The peninsula was perfectly sited to allow artillery and heavy machine guns to fire into Brest from the south. Once the Peninsula was in American hands the Germans soon learned to stay out of sight, as any movement on the mainland was quickly shelled by tank destroyers and observed artillery fire.

S/SGT. ALVIN P. CAREY, MEDAL OF HONOR

38th Infantry Regiment, 2nd Infantry Division

"For conspicuous gallantry and intrepidity at the risk of his life, above and beyond the call of duty, on 23 August 1944. S/Sgt. Carey, leader of a machine gun section, was advancing with his company in the attack on the strongly held enemy Hill 154, near Plougastel, Brittany, France. The advance was held up when the attacking units were pinned down by intense enemy machine gun fire from a pillbox 200 yards up the hill.

From his position covering the right flank, S/Sgt. Carey displaced his guns to an advanced position and then, upon his own initiative, armed himself with as many hand grenades as he could carry and without regard for his personal safety started alone up the hill toward the pillbox.

Crawling forward under its withering fire, he proceeded 150 yards when he met a German rifleman whom he killed with his carbine. Continuing his steady forward movement until he reached grenade-throwing distance, he hurled his grenades at the pillbox opening in the face of intense enemy fire which wounded him mortally. Undaunted, he gathered his strength and continued his grenade attack until one entered and exploded within the pillbox, killing the occupants and putting their guns out of action.

Inspired by S/Sgt. Carey's heroic act, the riflemen quickly occupied the position and overpowered the remaining enemy resistance in the vicinity."

A heavy machine gunner carries the M1917A1 water-cooled machine gun on his shoulder. This weapon was too heavy to carry on its tripod so the load was always split between two men. The next soldier in line can be seen with a can of .30 caliber ammunition in each hand.
(National Archives)

To take advantage of this position the 2nd Division Artillery organized a provisional battalion for what they called "Operation Ivory X."

Ivory X was named after the 2nd Infantry Division Artillery headquarter's code name "Ivory." Initially, it was referred to as Task Force X, but quickly became known as Ivory X. It used 57 .50 caliber machine guns, normally the antiaircraft defenses for the field artillery battalions, as well as twelve tank destroyers and eight 40mm antiaircraft guns. Each gun was tied into a telephone line so that fires could be massed on specific targets rapidly. Any motorcycles, vehicles, flak positions or apparent German defenses in Brest were fired upon by the Ivory X guns. To prepare for the final assault on the Brest city wall Ivory X fired more than 72,000 rounds of .50 caliber ammo in one afternoon. A total of half a million rounds of .50 caliber ammo was fired at Brest by Ivory X, making life in the city very difficult for the Germans. The Ivory X guns were also used to fire on the southern slopes of hills in the 2nd Division sector to their north.

3rd BN. - 38th INFANTRY
UNIT CITATION FOR HILL 154

General Order Number 15, 1945

"The 3rd Battalion, 38th Infantry Regiment is cited for outstanding performance of duty in action. On 22 August 1944, while engaged in operation against the enemy in the vicinity of Brest, France, the 3rd Battalion, 38th Infantry Regiment was assigned the arduous mission of assaulting and reducing the heavily fortified enemy strong point Hill 154. This formidable enemy position was a dominant terrain feature, commanding excellent observation, the seizure of which would deny the enemy his last high observation point from which he could accurately direct fire on our units attacking the Daoulas Peninsula and the city of Brest. Hill 154 was elaborately defended by light steel and concrete reinforced pillboxes well concealed and dug in, a complete network of circular trenches and intercommunication trenches crowned the hill, and an outer defensive ring of single apron barbed wire protected the base. Excellent fields of fire were afforded the enemy 40mm and 88mm flat trajectory weapons, machine guns, mortars and small arms, and approximately two reinforced companies of the enemy manned this seemingly impregnable bastion. Fully cognizant of the immensity of their task, the 3rd Battalion moved out at midday on 22 August 1944. The assault companies pushed forward under a withering fire poured down on them from the entrenchments and pillboxes on the heights. By an outstanding display of the tactical employment of infantry with aggressive and skillful maneuvering and cunning use of cover, our casualties were held to a bare minimum and the advantage gained was maintained in the face of bitter fighting. The following morning a vicious counterattack was beaten off with the death or capture of the entire attacking force and the 3rd Battalion audaciously resumed the assault with unsurpassed gallantry and indomitable fortitude. At 1600 hours, 23 August 1944, Hill 154 was taken, the entire defending force having been killed, wounded, or captured. Upon consolidating their hilltop position, elements of the battalion exploited their advantage and drove an estimated 300 enemy troops from entrenchments on the reverse slopes of the hill, annihilating with machine gun and artillery fire all who attempted to escape. The conspicuous gallantry, valorous devotion to duty, and the superb tactical skill displayed by all personal of the 3rd Battalion, 38th Infantry Regiment exemplify and glorify the noblest qualities and finest traditions of the service."

Above.
This German position was near Kerizou on the tip of the Daoulas Peninsula. The 105mm dual-purpose guns situated here were from the 1st Battery, 81th Naval Artillery Bn. They could fire into the Bay of Brest, over to the Crozon Peninsula, or inland to protect themselves against ground attack.
(National Archives)

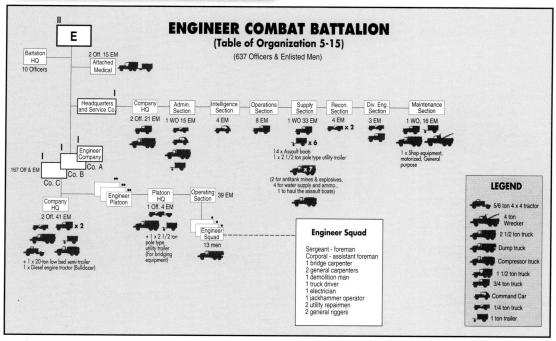

ENGINEER COMBAT BATTALION
(Table of Organization 5-15)
(637 Officers & Enlisted Men)

Engineer Squad
13 men

Sergeant - foreman
Corporal - assistant foreman
1 bridge carpenter
2 general carpenters
1 demolition man
1 truck driver
1 electrician
1 jackhammer operator
2 utility repairmen
2 general riggers

LEGEND

- 5/6 ton 4 x 4 tractor
- 4 ton Wrecker
- 2 1/2 ton truck
- Dump truck
- Compressor truck
- 1 1/2 ton truck
- 3/4 ton truck
- Command Car
- 1/4 ton truck
- 1 ton trailer

TFB CASUALTIES

21-30 August 1944

	Officers	Enlisted Men
KIA	5	78
WIA	14	417
MIA	-	8
	522 total	

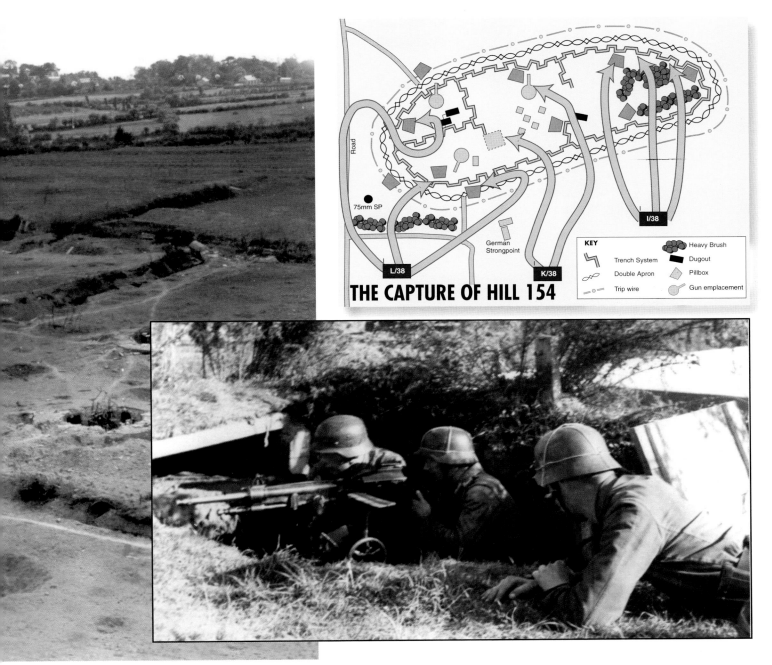

THE CAPTURE OF HILL 154

KEY

Trench System		Heavy Brush	
Double Apron		Dugout	
Trip wire		Pillbox	
		Gun emplacement	

Road

75mm SP

German Strongpoint

L/38

K/38

I/38

GERMAN UNITS ON THE DAOULAS PENINSULA

Due to the scattered nature of the German forces at Brest, it is hard to determine exactly which units took part in which sectors.

The following list is of units from which POWs were captured by TFB.

- 1/851st Infantry Regt.
- 11/852nd Infantry Regt.
- 811th AA Bn.
- 898th Infantry Regt.
- 13th Co, 7th FJ Regt.
- 2nd FJ Antitank Bn.
- 46th Minesweeper platoon
- 633rd Ost Bn.
- 56th Security Regt.

A few Brest customs guards, and 33 Italians

Above right.
This photograph was found in the German defenses north of Brest by Don Van Roosen. It shows a German crew using a captured French Saint-Etienne machine gun. These weapons were heavily used in the defenses on the Plougastel Peninsula. Such foreign, but effective, weapons were extensively used by the German Army in defensive positions.
(Courtesy Don Van Roosen)

Right. A group of German paratroopers is brought back to a POW collecting point. Behind them is a jeep from the 166th Photo Signal Company, the unit assigned to photograph the campaign. The metal strut welded to the front of the jeep is designed to cut any wires that might be stretched across the road. Before the Americans started adding this to their jeeps a few drivers were decapitated by such wires.
(National Archives)

Top left.
A German paratrooper captured on the Daoulas Peninsula explains to an American MP how his gravity knife works. The knife was designed to allow a paratrooper whose chute was caught in a tree to cut himself down one-handed. Pushing the switch allowed the blade to slide out of the handle.
(National Archives)

Left. These artillery observers on the Daoulas Peninsula are using a captured German bunker for their observation post. Judging from the pile of Lucky Strike cigarette packs in the embrasure, they are prepared to stay in this position for a while. These men will keep a close watch on the mainland and will call for artillery at the first sign of any movement behind the German lines.
(National Archives)

Bottom left.
It takes two men to carry the over 200 pound shell fired by an 8" gun. They haul it to the gun on a special carrying stand and hold it in place while two others push it into the breech. Then all four finally seat it in the gun with a mighty heave on the loading rod. These heavy guns had a slower rate of fire than the lighter 105mm howitzers, but the larger shells packed a tremendous punch.
(National Archives)

Below and opposite page.
Once it became clear that the Daoulas Peninsula could not be held the Germans blew a span on the Albert Louppe Bridge. This bridge connected the peninsula to the mainland just to the east of Brest.
(National Archives)

Above.
The Daoulas Peninsula was perfectly situated to fire upon the rear of the German defenses at Brest. Large rock formations such as these provided perfect locations for observation posts. Five jeeps are visible, hidden from the Germans behind the rocks. The artillery observers have climbed to the top of the rock to watch for German targets.
(National Archives)

Top right.
These artillerymen of operation "Ivory X" are tied into a network of field telephones. When an observer spots movement on the mainland he can rapidly call upon a large amount of firepower to target the area. This denied the Germans freedom of movement in their rear areas and forced them to remain in shelters underground.
(National Archives)

Right.
The gunner of a 105mm howitzer pulls a spent case from the gun. Smoke can be seen rising from the hot shell. This crewman wears a pouch for carbine ammunition. Even though the artillery was well behind the lines, the gun crews needed to be ready at all times in case a German patrol suddenly attacked.
(National Archives)

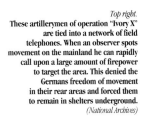

TASK FORCE SUGAR

Chapter 7

The two Ranger units assigned to northern Europe were the 2nd and 5th Ranger Battalions. Best known for their D-day exploits, the 2nd Ranger Bn. was commanded by Lt. Col. James E. Rudder and the 5th Ranger Bn. by Major Richard P. Sullivan. Although they were given a few specific assignments worthy of such special units, for the most part they were utilized as little more than infantrymen sent into the line when additional manpower was required.

The history of the Rangers in Brittany is somewhat confusing, as they were frequently split into different groups, individual companies, or groups of companies, and used as independent units in corps reserve. The actions of the Rangers as part of Task Force Sugar is found later in this chapter. The relatively small size of the Ranger companies (68 men as opposed to 193 men in a rifle company) was compensated for by sometimes assigning FFI units for additional manpower. Although some local Frenchmen performed outstanding service with the Rangers, for the most part the use of the local FFI units was a failure. However, this use of the Rangers to lead indigenous units is curiously similar to the original mandate of the later American Special Forces.

One specific incident illustrates the frustration the Rangers had with most of the FFI. While the Rangers were attacking the town of Le Conquet the FFI was nowhere to be seen. After the town had fallen the FFI suddenly appeared in the streets boasting of their ability and claiming credit for liberating the town. Similar incidents throughout the region did nothing to help the image of the FFI and most Rangers preferred to operate without them. Particularly irritating to the Rangers, and all American troops, was the tendency of the FFI to appear after the fighting had

Wearing ammunition belts across his chest in typical Russian fashion, this former Russian volunteer is now fighting alongside the French. The GI at left has the orange painted diamond insignia of the Ranger battalions, with the number "2" indicating he is from the 2nd Ranger Battalion.
(National Archives)

stopped and extract revenge upon suspected collaborators and captured Germans.

Since their landing on D-day, both Ranger battalions had spent some time in combat followed by a period of patrolling, guarding POWs, and building up their strength. During the breakout they were sent south to help guard the American right flank near Mortain. On 19 Aug. the 2nd Rangers were trucked out to Brest as part of the VIIIth Corps reserve. The Rangers were used for a variety of tasks including guarding the corps HQ against German attack. One Ranger detachment was given the task of setting up a location behind enemy lines where local Frenchmen could bring intelligence about German positions. D/2nd Rangers worked with the 86th Recon Squadron in mobile patrols of the Saint-Renan area, and companies E&F/2nd Ranger set up outposts around Saint-Renan to defend against a possible German attack from the north.

On 23 Aug. the 2nd Rangers were officially attached to the 29th Infantry Division. They were given the job of keeping an eye on the American right flank. Captain Harold "Duke" Slater (the 2nd Ranger executive officer) was put in charge of a task force of Companies B, D, E&F/2nd; one platoon from the 86th Recon; and seven light tanks from the 741st Tank Bn. On 25 Aug. "Task Force Slater" begin by moving south from Saint-Renan and cutting the Brest - Le Conquet Road. For a while these men operated in enemy territory, ambushing supply trucks heading west from Brest, and the Rangers enjoyed captured German rations as a change of diet. On 27 Aug. Task Force Slater was expanded to form the larger Task Force Sugar.

Task Force Arnold

With the danger of a German attack from the north diminishing, Companies A&C/2nd Rangers were released from guard duty and formed into "Task Force Arnold" (named after Ranger Captain Edgar L. Arnold). Task Force Arnold, assisted by some tank destroyers from the 644th TD Bn., was to move west to the ocean and clear the German

An aerial view of the Battery Graf Spee. Two of the guns are visible, directed inland, in the front and back right. The large bunker on the left protects one of the guns that is pointed out to sea. The command bunker, captured by the Rangers, is located one kilometer to the southwest near the old Saint-Mathieu Abbey.

This was the only gun of the Graf Spee Battery that could not traverse inland. It could only fire out to sea. The Germans had planned to upgrade all the guns for a 360 degree traverse, but the Americans invaded Brittany before the work could be completed. *(National Archives)*

Three of the Graf Spee guns were installed in concrete firing pits and given a 360 degree traverse. By the time the battery was captured all three of these guns had been put out of action by American artillery bombardments, but only after they had caused many casualties in the units attacking Brest. *(National Archives)*

The armor-piercing and high explosive shells used by the 280mm guns of the Battery Graf Spee are shown here in comparison to an average GI. They were the largest artillery shells fired in Brittany and had a range of 30 kilometers. *(National Archives)*

An orange diamond was painted on the rear of every 2nd and 5th Ranger Battalion helmet. The Rangers were originally trained to be night fighting specialists, and this marking was developed to help them follow one another in the dark.

held pockets south of Trezien. The first strongpoint was attacked in the fog on the morning of 28 Aug. and was captured without American casualties. At one point in the fighting a Ranger forgot to pull the safety pin as he fired a rifle grenade, yet the sight of the unexploded grenade bouncing around inside a building was enough to convince the Germans inside to surrender.

Task Force Arnold then moved onto the Pointe de Corsen three miles north of the American lines, where they found a unit of FFI and a group of 162 Russians already surrounding the German position. The Russians had been used by the Germans as laborers. When the chance came they revolted and formed their own anti-German unit under the command of their own officers. The group was supposedly led by a fellow calling himself Joseph 351 who claimed to be a White Russian. However, there is some evidence that the whole affair had been arranged by one of the Jedburgh team officers, Major John.W. Summers of Jed Team Horace. Although Summers is not mentioned in the Ranger report, the description of his activities in Brittany, coupled with the fact that this was in his assigned region, makes it a good probability. No matter who was responsible for the turned Russian unit, it formed a barrier to the south of the German position while the Rangers pressed in from the west with covering fire from the tank destroyers.

Strong German artillery fire drove back the open topped TDs and the attack bogged down. About midnight the Germans were prepared to surrender, but a sudden artillery barrage from their own artillery to the south at La Maison Blanche drove everyone under cover. That night an enemy patrol attempting to escape to the south was ambushed by the Russians and all eight Germans in it were killed. The Russians apologized to the Rangers for not leaving anyone alive to interrogate. The next morning, after more fire from the TDs, a German POW was allowed to talk his comrades into surrendering without the need for another assault.

On 31 Aug. Task Force Arnold attacked the fort just North of Kervillou, estimated to contain only 50 German troops. The guns of the TDs were unable to penetrate the fortress walls and German artillery fire

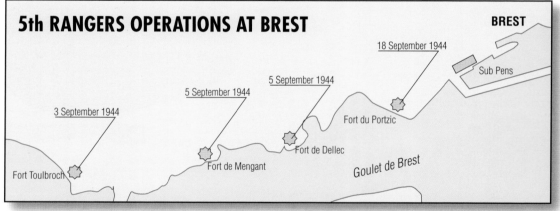

5th RANGERS OPERATIONS AT BREST

BREST

18 September 1944

5 September 1944

5 September 1944

3 September 1944

Sub Pens

Fort du Portzic

Fort de Dellec

Fort de Mengant

Goulet de Brest

Fort Toulbroch

from the Le Conquet area forced the TDs to withdraw. On 1 Sept. heavy artillery fire was directed against the fort from the VIIIth Corps artillery units. By then the Rangers had moved up very close to the fort, but it was finally decided to leave a small holding force there and move the rest of Task Force Arnold south to assist with clearing the Le Conquet area.

The Rangers left 20 Americans at Kervillou to keep the Germans bottled up, assisted by 60 of the Russians. On 4 Sept. two Germans were captured trying to slip away. They stated there were only 30 Germans in the fort, so the Americans decided they could leave a smaller contingent to watch them. Only five Americans were left, but they put 15 Russians in American uniforms to fool the Germans. For the next 10 days this small group kept the Germans bottled up inside. Later on, when two companies of Rangers arrived and were observed moving in for an attack, the German garrison decided to surrender.

After clearing their assigned area the Rangers in Task Force Arnold were drawn back into the 2nd Battalion and added to the strength of Task Force Sugar to clear the Le Conquet region.

5th Rangers

On 29 Aug. the 5th Ranger Battalion under Major Sullivan moved up to Brest, only to be broken up into three groups. Companies A&C/5th Rangers were attached to the 2nd Infantry Division. They took up positions along the Guipavas-Brest road. These Rangers ran combat patrols in the area and were under near constant machine gun fire. In conjunction with the 38th Infantry they reconnoitered the German defenses on Hills 90 and 105. E/5th Rangers was sent to Gousneau, north of Brest, to act as the connecting link between the 2nd and 8th Infantry Divisions. The Germans noticed the new unit move up and immediately attacked it to try and determine its identity. The Rangers drove off the German assault, but suffered heavy artillery bombardment in return.

The rest of the battalion operated with the 29th Infantry Division. On 1 Sept. Companies A, C, & E rejoined the rest of the 5th Battalion, which had been given the assignment of tying the American left flank into the coastline along the Channel of Brest. This area was heavily defended by a number of fortresses which had been constructed along the water route into the bay.

On 2 Sept. the 5th Rangers attacked Fort Toulbroc'h. The 1st Platoon, B/5th (commanded by Lt. Askin) was directed to attack south to the crossroads. To the west the 2nd Platoon

B/5th (commanded by Lt. Gombosi) was to hold their position and provide covering fire, but Gombosi noticed that the area to their front was not defended. With permission to advance, his platoon was able to move forward a half mile until they suddenly ran into a German counterattack. Gombosi's platoon was outnumbered by 10 to 1 so they fell back. Fearful of being cut off, so did Lt. Askin's platoon.

This prompted a general German counterattack in that area that put heavy pressure on the Rangers. Major Sullivan called for every man from 5th Ranger Headquarters to man the front lines in defense. With the help of their clerks and cooks the Rangers were able to hold their position and the next day another attack was made on Fort Toulbroc'h. F/5th covered the flank to the east and D/5th was ready to follow up behind the main assault being made by B/5th. The attack started with an air strike against the fort. Lt. Gombosi and his men followed so closely behind the strafing aircraft they were able to storm the fort before the Germans had come out of their shelters to man their positions. The 60 Rangers captured the fort this time in six minutes, taking five officers and 237 enlisted men prisoner.

The 5th Rangers then moved on to Fort Mengant just to the east. A platoon of tank destroyers from A/644th TD Bn. was attached to them. As the Americans were finding out, tank destroyers were very useful weapons in attacking German fortifications. Their high-powered guns were used against specific weak points on the emplacement such as observation or ventilation ports, gun emplacements, and doorways.

The attack began with F/5th providing supporting fire from the west while B/5th pushed down from the north. They ran into a German counterattack and without hesitation F/5th charged the German flank with bayonets. This assault so unnerved the Germans that the fort soon fell. Unfortunately, American planes then accidentally bombed F/5th thinking the area was still held by Germans. A&E/5th moved in to clean up the Germans lurking in the surrounding area and to hold against another German counterattack. By the end of the day the Rangers had taken 72 prisoners and suffered only 18 casualties. The nearby smaller Fort du Dellec was later captured after a two hour assault. B&F/5th were left to guard the forts against German reoccupation and the remainder of the battalion moved west to join Task Force Sugar. They were trucked out to Le Conquet on 6 Sept. and moved up to the German lines at night. As part of Task Force Sugar both Ranger battalions played a major role in reducing the German coastal positions near Le Conquet.

MAP KEY

✈	Light Gun
⚲	Light AA Gun
◿	Casemate
╱	German defenses
▱	Shelter
∧∧∧	Trench
Ⓢ	Supply Dump

HQ 5 Rangers Reserve — Kervahe

FORT TOULBROCH 2 sept. 1944

D/5 Rangers 1st Platoon

B/5 Rangers 2nd Platoon

B/5 Rangers 1st Platoon

TOULBROCH

Barracks

Goulet de Brest

Flak coastal artillery NCO, Batterie Graf Spee
This artillery observer wears the insignia of the coastal Artillery on his field gray wool naval uniform. The insignia, including the eagle on his sidecap, all has a distinctive yellow color. He has been awarded the black Wound Badge and the Coastal Artillery War Badge. This was awarded to coastal artillerymen who either took part in a number of engagements or showed outstanding ability. The headphones and microphone are linked to the fire direction center, but if that wire is cut by enemy action he can call for fire by using the flare pistol in the black holster hanging from his belt.
(Reconstruction by Militaria Magazine)

Task Force Sugar

At the very tip of Brittany is the Le Conquet Peninsula. It lies roughly 20 kilometers west of Brest. It is the furthest point of the French mainland to extend into the Atlantic Ocean. The Conquet, together with the Crozon Peninsula to the south, forms the natural harbor that made Brest such an important naval facility. Due to its position commanding the approaches to Brest, as well as the sea lanes off the coast of Brittany, Le Conquet had long been heavily fortified as part of the area defenses.

A chain of forts extended from the tip of Le Conquet eastward to Brest. They varied in size and quality, but the most important of these fortifications was the main coastal artillery emplacement just east of the village of

The muzzle of one of the 280mm guns of the Battery Graf Spee was damaged by American artillery fire. The Germans attempted to put the gun back into action by sawing off the damaged section, but the work was not completed by the time the battery surrendered.
(National Archives)

Lochrist. Named the Battery Graf Spee by the Germans, this emplacement housed four 280mm guns that commanded the area for miles around. Any ships passing by the coast, such as those that were expected to tow the components of the Quiberon Bay harbor, would come under the deadly fire of these guns. Three of the guns could also traverse inland to the east to assist in the defense of Brest. The forth gun position was not yet completed in 1944 and could only fire out to the sea.

Defending the main battery was an intricate defensive network of barbed wire, underground tunnels, storerooms, blockhouses, and trenches. The area was defended by a number of machine guns and both light and heavy antiaircraft guns. These guns were used to not only defend against air attack, but could also be turned on ground targets. In fact much of the Conquet area contained radar stations, antiaircraft emplacements, and artillery sites. Due to the high density of antiaircraft guns in the area it was impossible to use aircraft to spot for artillery fire.

The 29th was assigned the far right flank of Brest from the Penfeld River to the West. The main body of the 29th Division settled into the

outskirts of the city on 25 Aug., and General Charles Gerhardt formed Task Force Sheppe (named for its commander Lt. Col Arthur Sheppe, the executive officer of the 175th Inf. Regt.). Task Force Sheppe was also referred to as Task Force S, and in the phonetic alphabet of the time eventually became known as Task Force Sugar (TFS). TFS initially consisted of Companies D, E&F of the 2nd Ranger Bn., Troops A&E/86th Recon, one platoon from 3/175th Infantry, and the cannon company of the 175th Inf. (short barreled 105mm howitzers). Their mission was to clear the Conquet Peninsula of Germans and knock out the Graf Spee Battery.

TFS assembled two miles northwest of Saint-Renan, then pushed west until hitting the German defensive line on a series of hills just to the north of the Route Nationale 789. The plan was to head to the coast and seal off the Germans from the north, then move south into the Le Conquest positions. The main prize was always the Graf Spee Battery, but each strongpoint would pose its own set of difficulties. On the night of 27 Aug. TFS had cut off the area from Brest. It seemed that the Germans were slow to realize this and for days afterwards the Americans intercepted trucks heading out of Brest with cheese, sardines and other canned food (much to the delight of the GIs).

The smaller Task Force Arnold was a few miles to the north dealing with the isolated German positions at Pointe de Corsen and Kervillou. The job assigned to TFS began to take on greater importance when the men of the 29th Division were subjected to shelling from the Graf Spee Batteries. These heavy shells not only did a lot of damage when they hit, but the fact that the Germans could continue to fire such large guns at the Americans lowered the morale of the GIs. They wondered why didn't their Air Force knock those guns

The Rangers carried as little equipment as possible so they could travel quickly and without noise. This man carries only his weapon (an M-1 Garand), bayonet, ammo belt (with canteen and first aid pouch on back), and bandoleer of extra ammunition. He wears the standard wool shirt, herringbone twill fatigue pants, and the winter combat jacket. Instead of boots and leggings he wears the parachutist's jump boots commonly seen on Rangers. Initially, soldiers needing glasses could not get into the Rangers. Thus this man is probably one of the replacements brought into the unit in France to make up for invasion casualties.
(Reconstruction by Militaria Magazine)

TASK FORCE SUGAR IN LE CONQUET PENINSULA 26 AUGUST - 10 SEPTEMBER 1944

Pointe de Corsen — Task Force Arnold — 28 Aug.

Atlantic Ocean

Kermenoc

To Saint-Renan

31 Aug.

Kervillou

2 Rangers

La Maison Blanche — 10 Sept.

2 Sept. — 5 Rangers — Tremeal — 30 Aug.

Task Force Slater — 25 Aug.

Trebabu

Ty Baul

Hill 54 — 7 Sept. — Hill 63

Le Conquet — 9 Sept.

3/116

To Brest

Hill 53 — 7 Sept.

Le Cosquer

Lochrist

Graf Spee Battery — 9 Sept.

10 Sept.

Le Trez-Hir

Tremeur — 9 Sept.

Plougonvelin

Saint-Mathieu

Saint-Martin — 9 Sept.

out? On 28 Aug. TFS was shifted from 175th Infantry to 29th Division control. The 29th Division chief of staff Colonel Edward H. McDaniel took command, with Lt. Colonel Sheppe remaining as his as his executive officer. Gerhardt assigned additional troops to the task force to speed up the capture of the Graf Spee Battery.

On 30 Aug. D&E/2nd Rangers attacked the heavily defended towns of Tremeal and Ty-Baol as well as Hill 63. This hill, located just to the southwest of Ty-Baol, was an important piece of high ground. The Germans subjected the Americans who took it to continual artillery fire and probing attacks. This area was held by TFS until 2 Sept. when they moved west to the neck of the Le Conquet Peninsula. Task Force Arnold moved south and took up blocking positions to the north at Trebabu, where they were reinforced by four Sherman tanks from the 709th Tank Bn. and a few members of the FFI. Although the ground captured over the next few days was small, there was constant patrolling and probing of enemy lines. On 4 Sept. the Americans had worked their way up the German main line of resistance running across the neck of the Le Conquet. In many places the FFI was used to fill in the gaps between units and to guard the rear of the American positions. The need to capture the Graf Spee guns continued to grow, as the heavy artillery shells continued to be fired at American positions. The shells made a terrific noise, like a freight train, which unnerved the troops as they passed over the American lines.

On 6 Sept. TFS jumped off on the final assault to capture the Graf Spee Battery at Lochrist with only mild preparatory fire from the tank destroyers. The Rangers were to the north of Route 789 and 3/116th to the south. The first objectives were Hill 54 for the Rangers and Hill 53 for the 116th. The area was covered with hedgerows and the Germans had plenty of time to dig in. The advance was slowed by heavy artillery fire from the Graf Spee as well as other medium artillery units in the area. By mid day TFS was only 500 yards further from where they started.

The 3/116th had been stopped by a strongpoint manned by 100 Germans and called for tank support. The tanks, coupled with a flanking maneuver by the infantry, caused the Germans to surrender at 1430 hrs. It was later found that the defenders had no antitank weapons, so when confronted with the American tanks they felt they had no option but to give up. This allowed the 3/116th to move up to their next objective: Hill 53. The Rangers to the north were under heavy artillery fire, but had not run into any German strongpoints so by nightfall they had reached the slopes of Hill 54.

On 7 Sept. L/116th was left to take Hill 53 alone while the remainder of 3/116th moved to Plougonvelin. They met heavy machine gun fire from the nearby woods and the advance was slowed down. FFI patrols were sent to contain any Germans in the nearby Le Trez-hir beach area. When the Rangers plowed through the defenses on Hill 54 the Germans evacuated Hill 53. On the same day the assistant division commander of the 29th, Colonel Leroy H. Watson, was given command of TFS. McDaniel returned to his normal duties as Gerhardt's chief of staff. Lt. Colonel Lawrence C. Meeks became the executive officer of TFS.

TFS was reinforced by the 5th Ranger Bn. (less companies B & F) which took up the right flank. They were to attack over Hill 41 to Hill 43. They had been trucked up after capturing some coastal forts outside Brest. B&F/5th Rangers had been left behind to make sure that the Germans did not reoccupy those forts. A/86th Recon was relieved from TFS and sent back to its parent squadron.

On 8 Sept. Le Trez-hir was attacked by a platoon from K/116th, under command of Lt. Ben Snipas. They were assisted by a group of 40 members of the local FFI. A reconnaissance of the town found one high velocity gun, possibly an 88 (to Americans all German guns were

Right and Below.
This is the main command bunker and observation post for the Graf Spee Battery and all German artillery on Le Conquet. Three of the floors of this structure are above ground. This was the bunker that Rangers Bob Edlin and Bill Courtney ventured into to secure the surrender of the German garrison.
(National Archives)

88's), and at least two well emplaced machine guns. Eight foot high concrete walls in the town prohibited an easy advance. When the machine guns opened up the French troops disappeared, leaving the lone platoon to capture the town by itself. The mayor proved to be very helpful by informing Snipas that there were 60 Germans in the town. Tanks and engineer support were requested from TFS headquarters and they arrived on the morning of 10 Sept. Three tanks headed down the main road, but the second one was knocked out by the German gun. This blocked the road and kept the third tank out of action.

With Lt. Snipas on the rear of the first tank directing its action the German machine gun emplacements were kept under suppressive fire, allowing the infantry to move up. High explosive rounds from the Sherman put both machine guns out of operation. After a tank round was sent through the German headquarters in the local hotel 57 prisoners marched out to surrender.

The Air Force, meanwhile, had done its part in trying to knock out the large guns of the Graf Spee Battery. Two of the three guns able to fire east towards Brest had been knocked out of action by air strikes, most probably from the smaller P-47 fighter-bombers. On 8 Sept. the last gun able to fire inland was silenced, but the Americans had no way of knowing if, or when, any of the 280mm guns could be repaired.

With the defensive line at the base of the Conquet Peninsula broken, the Germans blew the bridge that led north over the Conquet inlet. The 5th Rangers advanced in this area finding it heavily mined. About noon on 9 Sept. the 2nd Rangers were approaching the area of the Graf Spee

This is the main observation bunker for Fort Portzic, just to the west of the city of Brest. The rubble is the result of massive artillery and aerial bombardment of the fortress. Plans were underway for the 5th Rangers to attack the fort in conjunction with the British flamethrowing crocodile tanks, but the Germans surrendered before the attack was made.
(National Archives)

COMPOSITION OF TASK FORCE SUGAR

on 6 Sept. 1944

2nd Ranger Bn.
● Troops A&E/86th Recon Squadron
● One platoon from A/121st Engineer Bn.
● 709th Tank Bn. (less one platoon)
● A/86th Chemical Mortar Bn.
● 3/116th Infantry Regt.

Artillery support from:
● A/644th Tank Destroyer Bn.
● C/ 227th Field Artillery Bn.
● 224th Field Artillery Bn.

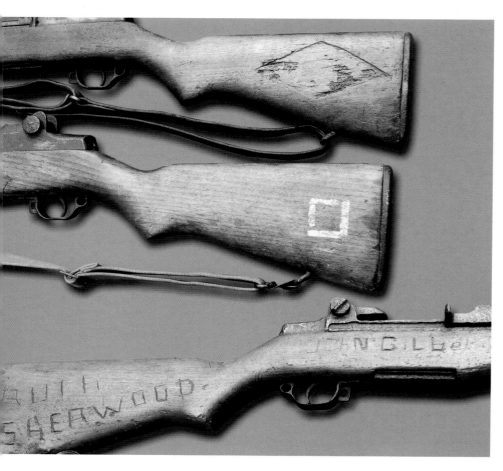

These remarkable rifles were recovered from the Fort Portzic area, just after the fighting, by a local farmer. One bears a carved diamond in which a Ranger patch fits perfectly. The other, with a painted white square on one side, bears the carved names "Ruth Sherwood" and "John Gilbert." Pfc. John Gilbert was a member of the 5th Ranger Bn. and fought at Fort Portzic. He was later killed in Luxembourg on 24 Feb. 1945. He is buried in the American cemetery in Tunisia, next to his brother who was killed in the North African campaign. Was Ruth Sherwood his girlfriend waiting for him at home? *(Courtesy Yannick Creac'h)*

Below.

Col. James Earl Rudder is a legend among U.S. Rangers. Only 34 years old, he led the 2nd Rangers on their D-day mission at Pt. Du Hoc. He finally left the Rangers in December 1944 to command the 109th Infantry Regiment eight days before the Battle of the Bulge began. After the war he went on to become president of Texas A&M University.

Battery. D, E&F/2nd Rangers took positions in a draw just to the northeast of the gun positions while A, B&C/ 2nd Rangers tried to slip around the flank.

Lt. Robert Edlin, known for his famous photo of being the first man to board the boats for the invasion of Normandy, led a four man patrol from A/2nd Rangers to investigate the local defenses. Lt. Edlin, Sgt. Bill Courtney, Sgt. Bill Dreher and Pvt. Warren Burnmaster moved carefully up to the German defenses. On the way they ran into a patrol led by Lt. Ace Parker of the 5th Rangers who had also been sent to probe the German defenses. Comparing notes the two Rangers jokingly bragged to each other that they were just going to take over the whole fort. What they were referring to was not really a fort, but a massive concrete bunker containing the command and control facilities for the battery area. Seven of the bunker's nine floors were underground, and it is still in use today by the French Navy.

Edlin's patrol moved closer to an outlying German pillbox, but was stopped by a minefield. Sgt. Courtney noticed a path worn through the mines and the four men moved forward right up to the German position. They took the pillbox by total surprise, capturing 35-40 Germans. The Germans had no idea there were any Americans in the area and had not posted a lookout.

Edlin sent back word to Col. Rudder that he had captured the position, but decided against asking for permission to try and get into the main fortification itself. One of the captured German lieutenants was fluent in English and told the Rangers he could take them into the fort and right to his commander. Leaving Dreher and Burmaster to guard the prisoners, Edlin and Courtney followed the German lieutenant through another minefield and into the main bunker.

They walked into the bunker, down a tunnel and into a hospital room. Sgt. Courtney yelled *"Hände hoch!"* (hands up!) and the doctors, nurses and patients in the room were quick to react. The German lieutenant told them all in German to stay calm and not cause any problems. He then led Edlin and Courtney past a number of guards to the commander's office. As they passed each guard the lieutenant told them to put down their weapon and let them pass.

Edlin and Courtney burst into the commander's office brandishing their Thompson submachine guns. Edlin called out *"Hände Hoch."* The commander, Colonel Fürst, spoke English as well and was quite surprised by the presence of the two Rangers. Edlin told him that the Americans had stopped the air and artillery attacks to give him a chance to surrender. He instructed the German commander to use his public-address system to order his men to surrender.

Col. Fürst wanted to use his telephone to check on how many Americans were really at his position, and this put Edlin in a tough spot. If he refused to allow the call he would have to shoot the colonel. That would leave him and Courtney stuck alone inside a German bunker with no

bargaining power. Fürst put in the call to his men then hung up awaiting an answer. In a few moments the phone rang with the information there were only the four Americans present. Fürst put down the phone and calmly told Edlin, *"You are now our prisoners. There are only four Americans, two at the pillbox and you two."*

For a moment there was silence, then Edlin asked Courtney for a grenade. Why Edlin wanted a grenade, rather than use a knife or his gun, he wasn't sure. He later said that a grenade was the first thing that came to his mind. He took the grenade, pulled the pin and held it up against the German officer telling him to *"Surrender or die."*

Fürst told him he was bluffing. The grenade would kill all three of them. Edlin threatened again to release the lever (which would trigger the grenade fuse) on the count of three. When he got to *"two"* Col. Fürst gave in and agreed to surrender his command, but in typical German style he wanted to tell his men he had surrendered to an officer higher than a lieutenant. Fürst got on the public-address system and told his men to put down their weapons and prepare to surrender to the Americans.

Looking out a vision port Edlin could see a large number of soldiers coming out to give up. It was estimated that the POW count for the total area, not just the main bunker, reached 800. While awaiting the arrival of Col. Rudder, Edlin had Fürst call General Ramcke on the phone to

A group of 5th Rangers from Company E pose with a captured German flag after the capture of Fort du Portzic.
Standing, L to R: Hubert Baker, Simon Loesch, "Beck" Beccue, Curly Lockwood, Philip Roy.
Behind the flag, L to R: Sgt Joe Pollier, Herb Moughton.
Seated: John Kiernan, Joe "Spic" Carpos.
Pollier, Carpos and Moughton will be killed later in the war, all the rest except Beccue and Baker will be seriously wounded. All of the men have pistols and belts as war trophies. These were openly displayed for the camera as the fighting had ended, but were rarely carried in the front lines during combat. *(Courtesy Nicolas Guiffant)*

see if he too wanted to surrender. Somehow he got through to Ramcke, who told Fürst that it really did not matter if the Graf Spee position surrendered or not. Edlin briefly talked to Ramcke, who spoke English well, and was told that he was in no way ready to give up.

By the time the Americans moved up to formally accept the surrender of the Graf Spee Battery someone realized that Lt. Edlin had taken Col. Fürst's pistol. Edlin was quickly found and made to give back the pistol so it could formally be presented to Col. Rudder. After the ceremony Rudder offered the pistol back to Edlin, who decided he didn't really need it as his men had taken a lot of pistols off the rest of the Germans. Many years later, when Rudder was nearing death, he made sure the pistol would be sent back to Lt. Edlin, as he felt his former lieutenant really deserved it. The surrender pistol would later be donated to the museum at Grandcamp, France, where it rests today. The final prisoner total for the whole Graf Spee defensive area was close to 1,400 men. All taken without a shot being fired.

After the official event of the day had ended Col. Rudder called Edlin aside and chewed him out for taking such a risk. Although Edlin recalls his former commander was more upset than angry at the possible risk, it must have been a relief for Rudder to be able to capture such a major fortified position without losing a man. For his actions Lt. Bob Edlin was awarded a well-deserved Distinguished Service Cross and the three men with him were awarded Silver Stars.

There was one more aspect of the German surrender that rarely gets mentioned outside Ranger circles. The Germans had a large quantity of alcohol stored in the bunker. That morning the Rangers had expected to spend the rest of the day in a fierce battle for the position, instead Company A spent it drinking their loot. Soon Company B arrived and joined in. Before long Rudder realized his entire unit might soon be drunk and had the alcohol confiscated and sent up to corps. However, as any good soldier would have done, the Rangers had kept some hidden from sight. Those that did not drink took up watch while their comrades were able to enjoy the fruits of their victory. With the surrender of the main German complex on the Conquest the remainder of the defenses soon crumbled. The 116th Infantry moved southwest against only mild resistance to clear the remaining Germans from the Pointe de Saint-Mathieu by 1700 hrs.

JED TEAM HORACE

Major John.W. Summers, code named "Wyoming" jumped into Brittany on the night of 17 July. As the leader of Jed Team "Horace" he was assisted by 1st Sgt. Zielske ("Dime") and French lieutenant Leclercq ("Levalois") in preparing the region north of Brest for an uprising against the Germans. "Horace" gathered intelligence information from the locals about the defenses of Brest, and when the 6th Armored Division arrived in the area handed over a full suitcase of documents detailing German emplacements. Summers then helped coordinate the FFI in guarding the flanks of the 6th Armored while it operated at Brest. Along with a French speaking officer of the 6th, Major Summers was able to talk the German garrison at Saint-Pabu into surrendering, and assisted the Americans with cutting off the water supply for the city of Brest on 19 Aug.

With the arrival of the American ground forces Summers was free to head back to England, but he stayed in Brittany and continued to play a major role in the fighting. While helping the 6th Armored process prisoners he discovered a Russian captain who claimed that his entire company of Russians was ready to fight for the Allies. Major Summers followed up on his story and found it to be true. He directed the Russians to change their German uniforms for civilian clothing, and

helped them work with the Rangers and Task Force Sugar. Summers also acted as the liaison between Rangers operating in the Le Conquet area and the local FFI led by Commandant Louis Faucher.

Left.
Unlike the members of most Jed teams, that wore the M43 uniform, Major John W. Summers of Jedburgh team "Horace" wears the standard M-42 paratrooper uniform. *(National Archives)*

Right.
Major General Charles Gerhardt, commander of the 29th Infantry Division, is shown here with local FFI leader Baptiste "Louis" Faucher. Faucher was a commander of the FFI in the Brest area, and is shown being awarded a Bronze Star for his assistance to the Americans on the Le Conquet Peninsula. Faucher is wearing British battle dress, dropped to the FFI before the Americans reached Brittany. *(National Archives)*

The 5th Rangers were still receiving some fire from a German position at La Maison Blanche, across the inlet from Le Conquet. A plan was made for an assault across the inlet on rubber boats which was scheduled for 10 Sept. Fortunately, the Germans had lost their will to resist after the capture of Graf Spee and the position surrendered before the risky assault was tried. Captain Arnold returned north to Kergollo with A&C/2nd Rangers to finally reduce the position there. An M12 self-propelled gun had been firing its 155mm gun at the fortification, and when it became clear to the garrison that the final assault was about to start the Germans surrendered. With the elimination of the German positions on Le Conquet, Task Force Sugar was dissolved and the different units sent back to their parent organizations. The 2nd Rangers moved on to the Crozon Peninsula and the 5th Rangers went back to continue the assault on the fortifications just west of Brest. The men from the 29th went back to their division to take part in the final assault on the city of Brest.

After Task Force Sugar

After Task Force Sugar was dissolved on 11 Sept. the 5th Ranger Battalion went back to its previous position on the Bay of Brest. The Rangers were a good choice for this flank position, as the German fortifications were extremely thick along the shore. The final fortification outside Brest was the Fort du Portzic, which was directly opposite the tip of the Crozon Peninsula. Just to the north of the fort was a battery of twin 105mm AA guns that could also be used against ground targets. Another battery of 75mm and 105mm guns was located nearby protected in concrete emplacements.

The fort had been subjected to daily harassing fire by American artillery. Some damage had been done, but the Portzic garrison continued to hold out. This fort was a particularly important position as it overlooked the Brest harbor and commanded the naval facilities, including the sub pens, on the Recouvrance side of the harbor.

The first step towards the fort was taking the town of Le Cosquer which was just to the north. D/5th Rangers was the main assault company and was forced to advance across an area which provided the Germans an excellent field of fire. Eventually 215 German prisoners were taken at Le Cosquer, compared to only 15 Ranger casualties. Unfortunately, due to poor communications American artillery shelled the town after the Rangers had captured it.

The Americans were now in the final defensive line outside Brest. The area was covered

by mutually supporting German pillboxes. A handful of the pillboxes were captured with great difficulty. In one attempt a platoon from E/5th placed a 40 pound charge in a pillbox firing port. It was detonated, but there was no visible effect. A few of the Ranger officers carefully studied the pillbox construction and came up with a new idea. They were able to recognize the air intakes on the pillboxes, so they planned to pour a can of gasoline down the intake, then detonate a shaped beehive charge on top of it. They decided to thicken the gasoline to make it stick better by adding some motor oil to it.

During the night of 17 Sept. a small patrol, led by Lt. James Green of E/5th Rangers, silently moved up to the pillbox under cover of artillery and TD fire. They poured 20 gallons of thickened gasoline into the vent, then placed two 40 pound charges of C-2 and a shaped beehive charge on the opening. Setting the fuse the patrol withdrew and at 2210 hrs. the men were treated to an enormous explosion. The pillbox continued to burn for 40 minutes while every man on the patrol returned safely. A few hours later another Ranger patrol from A/5th set off to try the same tactic on a different pillbox. However, the Germans were on full alert and had positioned machine guns to cover the outside of their emplacements. This second patrol returned without being able to get near their target and planned for another attempt the next night. That morning the word was passed that the Brest garrison was going to surrender, so the attempt was called off. When later questioned, German prisoners taken in the area admitted to being terrified by the blast and were convinced the Americans had brought up some new type of flamethrower or oil bomb.

The 2nd Rangers had been relieved from the 29th Division on 11 Sept. and returned to corps reserve. There the men were faced with a tough decision. Many had vowed not to shave until Brest had fallen, and now that they were out of the front lines they came under pressure to get rid of their beards. A compromise was reached, and a number of Rangers fought their last battle in Brittany with newly grown moustaches. On 17 Sept. the 2nd Rangers were sent back into combat to help the 8th Infantry Division clear the Crozon Peninsula. There they would help capture German fortifications along the coast right up until the very end of the fighting. During the Brittany campaign General Middleton observed Colonel Rudder with great interest and made a note of his outstanding leadership ability. Later in the war Middleton would promote Rudder to the command of the 109th Infantry Regiment (28th Infantry Division).

Chapter 8

THE OPPOSING SIDES

The two men most responsible
for the fighting at Brest were Major General
Troy Middleton (commander of the VIIIth Corps)
and General Bernhard Ramcke (commander
of Fortress Brest). Both of these men were good
officers, about the same age, and with plenty
of experience. Both had enlisted as privates and risen
through the ranks on their own ability.

Middleton was a solid corps commander who is often criticized (mostly unjustly) for not allowing his armored commanders to make bold movements. As a senior commander he was not well known to his troops. Ramcke was a paratrooper commander whose memoirs had been best sellers in wartime Germany. He was a legend to his men who had enormous respect for him.

Major General Troy Middleton

Troy Middleton had actually been in Brest twice before: once in 1918 heading to France, and again in 1919 on his way home. He was born on 12 Oct. 1889. His military career really began in 1904 when, not yet even 15 years old, he was enrolled as a cadet at Mississippi A&M College. At first he was not happy with the military styled life at the school, but he eventually rose to high ranks in the cadet battalion. After graduating in 1909 he was unable to get an appointment at

Above. **Middleton finally met Ramcke face to face after the Germans surrendered on the Crozon. The two are seen here posing for the photographers, along with Ramcke's Chief of Staff Oberst Moeller, and Ramcke's Irish Setter. Ramcke was promoted to *General der Fallschirmtruppe* during the siege of Brest.**

Left. **Troy H. Middleton, one of the youngest regimental commanders of the war, is seen here during the 1919 occupation of Germany as commander of the 47th Infantry Regiment. One of the areas they guarded was at Remagen where, in WW2, the famous bridge across the Rhine would be captured.**

West Point so he enlisted as a private in the 29th Infantry Regiment. It was during this enlistment that the Army first authorized the use of typewriters for official reports. Knowing how to type, Middleton was made a company clerk. In 1912 he took an open examination for an Army commission and passed, being made a lieutenant in the 7th Infantry Regiment.

With the 7th he landed at Vera Cruz, Mexico in 1914. He spent seven months in occupation duty there during the internal problems in Mexico. Returning to Texas, the 7th went to the Mexican border in 1916 to keep Pancho Villa from raiding into American territory. There he saw his first combat against the lightly armed Mexican rebels, but in April 1917 the 7th was sent east to prepare for action in war torn Europe.

Promotion to captain soon followed, and Middleton was put to work helping train the thousands of new officers the U.S. Army needed. Finally getting command of a company in the 47th Infantry Regt., 4th Infantry Div., he was almost left behind to train more recruits. Some-

On 19-20 August 1944 a series of messages were sent between Ramcke and Middleton, in which the German declined the offer to surrender. The Germans slowly drove up to the American lines north of Brest in this commandeered French Rosengart 1939 Supertraction, draped in white. When they entered the American lines they were blindfolded so they could not report on the American defenses when they returned to Brest. This was the standard technique when enemy troops were allowed into your lines.

1, 2. The German driver was moved to the following jeep, and an American took over driving the German vehicle. Here they are seen arriving at the 8th Division Command Post.

3, 4. General Donald Stroh, commander of the 8th Infantry Division is seen conversing with this paratroop officer. Note the German is still blindfolded. If he was allowed to see the command post he might recognize the area and be able to direct artillery fire upon it later.
(National Archives)

5. After the negotiations had ended, the German vehicle is driven back through a French town to the German lines. The jeep following the German car not only carries the German diver, but also provides protection from the local French population.
(National Archives

how Middleton made sure he sailed with the 47th for France. Landing in Brest, Middleton soon found his unit attached to the 167th Infantry Regiment of the 42nd Division. In July Middleton was promoted to major and given command of his battalion. Fighting near Sergy with the 42nd his unit took 25% casualties in their first action, but took and held their objectives.

Middleton's battalion rejoined the 4th Division and took part in the Saint-Mihiel offensive. Promoted to lt. colonel and given a staff position, Middleton asked to stay with his men for the initial attack in the Meuse-Argonne. He stayed long enough to watch his former battalion break the German lines, then left to become the executive officer of the 47th Infantry Regt. One night the entire regimental staff of the 39th Infantry was gassed and put out of action. Middleton, one day short of his 29th birthday, was given command of this regiment. It was supposed to attack the German lines that morning.

At 0100 hrs. Middleton was informed he was now in charge of a regiment he had never seen, that had no senior officers, and was scheduled for a major attack in six hours. Moving forward with his new command, the 39th Infantry was successful in their assault. Three days later Middleton was promoted to full colonel; the youngest in the American Army. When the 39th Infantry was able to get new officers Middleton was returned to the 47th Infantry and given command of his former regiment.

Colonel Middleton and his regiment remained in Germany on occupation duty until July 1919. When the 47th returned to the States Middleton was sent to help set up the Infantry School at Ft. Benning. Like most officers he reverted to his permanent Army rank (major), and was sent to Command and General Staff school at Ft. Leavenworth in 1923. Here he met and became good friends with classmate George Patton. Staying on at Leavenworth as an instruc-

tor for four years, he attended the Army War College then returned to command troops in the 29th Infantry Regiment. In 1930 he was put in charge of the ROTC program at Louisiana State University. In 1936 he was sent to Manila to help oversee the Philippine Army. A year later he retired from the Army to become Dean of Administration at LSU.

With the new war raging in Europe, in 1940 Middleton offered his services to the Army. The Chief of Staff, George C. Marshall noted on the top of the letter, "*This man was the outstanding infantry regimental commander on the battlefield in France.*" In January 1942 he was recalled to service as a lt. colonel. Middleton moved quickly up in rank through a series of units in training until he was promoted to brigadier general and made assistant division commander of the 45th Infantry Division. Eventually he would get his second star and command the 45th in the landings at Sicily and Salerno. In Italy an old football

One of the important aspects of the 19 August negotiations was an agreement that the Americans would not shell medical facilities marked with a red cross. Either Ramcke, or some of Ramcke's men, had attempted to protect German supplies by positioning them close to these protected buildings. Middleton agreed to respect the red cross markings, but if the Germans put a legitimate military target, such as an ammo dump, next to a hospital the Americans would not hesitate to destroy it.
(National Archives)

Brest is Lost!

It is only a question of time until Brest falls before the power of Allied material superiority. Neither General Ramcke nor your own bravery can change this decision. Brest cannot be compared to the mountain city of Cassino. Brest is like the harbor towns of Cherbourg and Saint-Malo. There, the defenders realized that holding out was useless. Brest is now encircled by land, sea, and air and has been written off by the German High Command. Brest is lost.

BUT YOU ARE NOT!

The large-scale attack on Brest is in progress. Nevertheless, American troops been have ordered to spare the life of every German soldier who surrenders. You still have the opportunity to get home to your families.

THE TIME FOR HESITATION IS PAST

M D E 200

BREST IST VERLOREN!

Es ist nur noch eine Zeitfrage bis Brest unter der Macht der alliierten Materialsüberlegenheit fallen muss. An dieser Entscheidung kann weder General Ramcke noch Eure eigene Tapferkeit irgendetwas ändern. Brest kann nicht mit der Gebirgsstadt Cassino verglichen werden. Brest gleicht der Lage von den Hafenstädten Cherbourg und Saint-Malo. Dort sahen die Verteidiger ein dass Aushalten nutzlos ist.

Brest ist jetzt auch zu Land, Luft und See eingekesselt und vom OKW abgeschrieben worden. Brest ist verloren–

ABER IHR NICHT!

Der Grossangriff auf Brest ist im Gang. Die amerikanischen Truppen haben jedoch den Befehl das Leben eines jeden deutschen Soldaten zu verschonen der sich ergibt. Noch habt ihr die Gelegenheit Eure Heimat und Eure Familien wiederzusehen

DIE ZEIT DES ZÖGERNS IST VORBEI

Propaganda leaflets such as these were used to get the Germans to surrender. They were either dropped by aircraft, or stuffed into special propaganda shells fired by the artillery. Middleton also had Ramcke's refusal to surrender printed up as a propaganda leaflet, as well as distributed to every unit in the VIIIth Corps.
(National Archives)

SIEBEN TATSACHEN DIE JEDER WISSEN MUSS

1 WIE IST DIE BEHANDLUNG? Kriegsgefangene in amerikanischen Händen erhalten die *faire* Behandlung, die ihnen als Soldaten zusteht. Alle Gerüchte, dass Gefangene erschossen werden, sind falsch und werden von Seiten Eurer Führung verbreitet, um Euch zum sinnlosen Weiterkämpfen zu zwingen. Wie Ihr wisst, ist der Begriff der *Fairness* ein typisch amerikanischer, und liegt tief in unserem Nationalcharakter.

2 WOHIN GEHT ES? Kriegsgefangene werden unverzüglich aus der Kampfzone entfernt und in Sicherheit gebracht.

3 WIE IST DAS ESSEN? Wie allgemein bekannt, ist die amerikanische Armee die best ernährte der Welt. Kriegsgefangene erhalten bei uns dieselbe Verpflegung wie unsere eigenen Soldaten. Dreimal am Tage gibt es warme Mahlzeiten.

4 UND DIE BESOLDUNG? Die Besoldung geht weiter, wie in der deutschen Armee. Ausserdem wird für freiwillige Arbeit extra bezahlt.

5 WIE IST DIE MÖGLICHKEIT DER WEITERBILDUNG? Bildungs- und Lehrkurse in Wissenschaft, Handwerk und Technik werden in allen Lagern abgehalten. Daneben ist Gelegenheit zu Sport und Spiel und zu künstlerischen Darbietungen geboten. Zeitungen in deutscher und englischer Sprache, sowie Radioapparate stehen zur Verfügung.

6 BESTEHT POSTVERBINDUNG? Jawohl. Drei Briefe und vier Postkarten können monatlich geschrieben werden. Sie werden auf dem Wege über das Rote Kreuz in Genf schnell und zuverlässig befördert.

7 WANN GEHT'S NACH HAUSE? Unmittelbar nach Kriegsende, bei erster Gelegenheit.

DIESE BESTIMMUNGEN GELTEN FÜR ALLE ANGEHÖRIGEN DER WEHRMACHT UND KRIEGSMARINE, EINSCHLIESSLICH DER LUFTWAFFEFELDDIVISIONEN, WAFFEN-SS, FALLSCHIRMJÄGER, OSTBATAILLONE UND ARBEITSORGANISATIONEN.

M D 200

SEVEN FACTS WHICH EVERYONE MUST KNOW

1 HOW IS THE TREATMENT? Prisoners of war in American hands receive the *fair* treatment which is due them as soldiers. All rumors that prisoners will be shot are false and are being spread by your leaders to force you to fight on needlessly. You know that the concept of *fairness* is typically American. It is a national characteristic.

2 WHERE ARE YOU TAKEN? Prisoners of war are immediately removed from the combat zone and are taken to safety.

3 HOW IS THE FOOD? It is generally known that the American Army is the best fed in the world. Prisoners of war receive the same food as our own soldiers. There are three warm meals a day.

4 AND THE PAY? Pay continues as in the German Army. In addition, all voluntary labor is paid for extra.

5 WHAT ARE THE POSSIBILITIES FOR VOCATIONAL TRAINING? Training courses in Science, Crafts and Technical Subjects exist in all camps. There are also opportunities for sports, games and theatrical performances. Newspapers in German and English as well as radios are available.

6 IS THERE MAIL SERVICE? Yes. Three letters and four postal cards may be written a month. They are safely forwarded via the Red Cross in Geneva.

7 WHEN WILL YOU GET HOME? At the first opportunity, immediately after the end of the war.

THESE REGULATIONS APPLY TO ALL MEMBERS OF THE ARMY AND NAVY INCLUDING AIR FORCE FIELD DIVISIONS, WAFFEN-SS, PARATROOPERS EASTERN BATALLIONS AND LABOR ORGANISATIONS

injury to his right knee forced him out of the 45th and into the hospital.

Eisenhower asked for Middleton to command a corps in England, but was told of his bad knee. In his biography Ike recalled saying, "*I don't give a damn about his knees; I want his head and his heart. I'll take him into battle on a litter if we have to.*" When it was suggested to George Marshall that Middleton be sent back to the States for his injury, Marshall said, "*I would rather have a man with arthritis in the knee than one with arthritis in the head. Keep Middleton.*"

Middleton was given command of VIIIth Corps, at the request of George Patton, in March 1944. His corps began landing in France in mid-June and took part in the hedgerow fighting down the Cotentin Peninsula. Although his staff had worked out a number of different plans for breaking out into Brittany, Middleton later recalled that the plan used had been made up on the spot in reaction to the German situation at the time. He did ask for landing craft so he could assault some of the Brest positions from the sea, but was turned down by the Navy. After the capture of Brest Gen-

GERMAN UNITS AT BREST

Due to the destruction of records at the fall of Brest, the conversion of support troops to combat units, and inter-mixing of units, a complete German order of battle would be almost impossible to achieve. This is the list of German units from which POWs were taken by the VIIIth Corps during 15-17 Sept. It provides a good listing of the major units involved.

2ND FJ DIV

Division HQ	1 officer
2nd FJ Regt.	100
7th FJ Regt.	41
Service troops	190

343rd INFANTRY DIVISION

Division Staff	4
851st Inf. Regt.	32
852nd Inf. Regt.	133
Service troops	172
898th Infantry Regt.	391
899th Infantry Regt.	7
266th Division	
Service Troops	172
Russian Units	168
Fortress Base Company XXV	109
Security Regt. 56	20
Security Regt. 195	1
Home Guard Unit 13/19	99

7th Army Service Troops	37
KG Flamia	35
Telegraph Construction Co.	1
Funkness Bn. 1/3	10
4th Smoke Co.	5
Feuerschutz unit	35
Zollgrenzschutz Co.	26
Feldkommandantur 665	6
Gendarmerie 266	1
Feldschallabteilung Paris	1
Butcher Co. 743	65
559th Supply Bn.	3
Kreiskommandantur	2
Festungskabel Platoon 220	2
Festungskabel Platoon 114	26
Fernkabel Platoon	2
Pigeon Platoon	2
Italian soldiers	21
Organization Todt	12
Misc.	11

ARMY ARTILLERY UNITS

343rd Artillery Regt.	159
1161st GHQ Artillery Bn.	83
1162st GHQ Artillery Bn.	68

NAVY UNITS

Navy Artillery units	
3rd Navy A.A. Brigade HQ	12
231st Navy A.A. Bn.	133
803rd Navy A.A. Bn.	140
805th Navy A.A. Bn.	32
811th Navy A.A. Bn.	4

804th Navy A.A. Bn.	155
262nd Naval Artillery Bn.	75
Naval Kommandantur Brest	9
Naval Kommandantur Lorient	10
1st U Boat Flotilla	2
9th U Boat Flotilla	58
7th Vorposten Flotilla	11
Harbor Protection Flotilla	27
Harbor Protection Co.	37
6th Minesweeper	40
Harbor Einsatz Co.	54
Marine Arsenal Brest	65
2nd Navy Luftschutz Co.	28
Navy Civilian workers	43
Seenotdienst	43
20 Minensucher	40
Misc. naval units	51

LUFTWAFFE UNITS

Signal Unit 9/54	5
Signal Unit 8/54	8
Signal Unit 13/W Fr	15
Signal unit 304/11	7
AA Unit 4/207	17
AA Unit 5/102	6
Misc. Luftwaffe	5

MISCELLANEOUS

1274th Küsten Batterie	21
Civilians	10
Dutch civilians	3
Total	**3,369**

Colonel Kroh was considered by Ramcke to be one of the finest commanders he had ever known. Originally the commander of the 2nd FJ Regiment, he was promoted to command the 2 FJ Division at Brest when Ramcke became the commander of Fortress Brest. Kroh had earned the Knight's Cross during the paratroop invasion on Crete. The Oakleaves were awarded for combat in Russia. He would also be awarded the Swords for his defense of Brest. Kroh returned to the German Army after the war, and eventually retired as a major general. *(Courtesy Ramcke family)*

Top. **This rare photo shows Ramcke as an Oberleutnant of Marine Infantry. He served in the German Navy before World War 1, and earned a battlefield commission in July 1918 while fighting with the German Marines in the trenches of Flanders. His service as a common soldier allowed him to understand the needs of the enlisted men, and contributed to his nickname of "Papa Ramcke."** *(Courtesy Ramcke family)*

Top right. **General Ramcke, in fur coat, while serving in Russia during early 1944. While there he felt that the Wehrmacht was placing his Luftwaffe paratroopers in overly precarious positions, to try and eliminate them as a ground force. He felt his highly-trained men should be used for airborne missions, not just for defending a section of the front lines. Ramcke was quite outspoken, which may have hampered his promotions, but in combat he was a superb leader of men.** *(Courtesy Ramcke family)*

eral Patton awarded Middleton an Oak Leaf Cluster for his Distinguished Service Medal. Confusion over orders given to the 6th Armored Division in Brittany appeared to have resulted in some cooling in the friendship between Patton and Middleton. After Brittany Middleton's VIIIth Corps moved to the Ardennes, where his headquarters was in Bastogne. Learning the region as divisions were rotated in and out of his corps area, it was Middleton who made the decision to hold onto Bastogne when the Germans attacked in December. He later said, "*I knew the Germans had to have the road net focusing at Bastogne, I decided to deny it to them.*" He had wanted to stay in Bastogne running the defense, but was ordered out at the last minute by his superior, General Hodges.

It is said that he spent more time in combat than any other American general in WW2. Troy Middleton continued to command the VIIIth Corps for the rest of the war, then retired to return to administrative positions at Louisiana State University. In 1950 he was made president of the school and oversaw a great expansion of the institution. After he retired from LSU he served in an important position on the State's commission on racial relations during the very tumultuous 1960s.

General der Fallschirmtruppe Hermann Bernard Ramcke

Hermann Bernhard Ramcke was born on 24 January 1889. His family had traditionally been farmers, but he left his home to enlist in the German Navy. Trained on the sailing ship *S.M.S. Stosch*, Ramcke transferred to the naval infantry during WW1 and served in Marine Assault Battalion Flanders. He was awarded both the Iron Cross 2nd and 1st class.

Ramcke was also awarded the Military Cross for Merit in gold and, given the class structure of the Germans at the time, it was remarkable when he was promoted to the rank of ensign. He transferred to the army in 1919 and fought with the Freikorps in the Baltics. There he was wounded for the fifth time since the beginning of the war, which earned him the wound badge in gold. It is even more impressive that he continued to serve in the tiny postwar army, when there was room only for the very best.

He was promoted to captain in 1927, major in 1934 and lt. colonel in 1937. To his great dismay he was attached to the command staff only as an observer during the Polish campaign. His disappointment

continued when he spent the French campaign running a training camp. He was concerned about his career as he saw other officers getting combat commands and being awarded decorations. Having served through the lean Reichswehr years he knew how important this was for promotion in any army.

It seems that General Student, the father of the German paratroopers, had served in the same regiment as Ramcke and was an old friend of his. Desperate to get into a unit where he could command troops in combat. Ramcke, with the help of Student, transferred to the Luftwaffe (who controlled the paratroops) in July 1940. In tribute to his physical condition he went through the very rigorous jump school at the age of 51. He was then assigned to oversee the training of a paratroop replacement battalion, but took part in the planning for the airborne assault on Crete. On 21 May he was chosen to jump into Crete as the replacement for the wounded Col. Meindl. So quickly had the decision been made to send Ramcke into Crete that he made the jump wearing standard officer's cavalry boots; he had not even had time to change.

Ramcke was very successful at Crete. In August 1941 he was promoted to major general and awarded the Knight's Cross for his command of the 1st Parachute Assault Regiment on Crete. He then helped organize the Italian Folgore Parachute Division in 1942, before forming "Paratroop Brigade Ramcke" destined to be sent to North Africa.

Under command of General Rommel's Afrika Korps, Ramcke and the "Ramcke Brigade" fought at El Alamein. In October 1942 his unit was cut off during a British attack, but Ramcke refused to give up. He successfully marched his men across the desert back to their own lines. Along the way he captured a British supply column and used these vehicles and supplies to get his men to safety. For this action he was awarded the Oak Leaves to his Knight's Cross.

Having been an enlisted man he understood what it was like to be on the front line. Always protective of, but demanding of, his men he earned the affectionate nickname "Papa Ramcke." He was known as being very tough and disciplined, but also charismatic and likeable. Back in Germany he was given command of the 2nd FJ

ORDER OF BATTLE OF THE GERMAN 2. FALLSCHIRMJAGER-DIVISION IN BRITTANY

(units actually committed in Brest are underlined)

Division Staff
(General Hermann Ramcke. After 13 Aug. 44: Oberst Hans Kroh.
Adjutant: Major Paul)

Fallschirmjäger-Regiment 2
(Oberst Hans Kroh. After 8 aug 44: Major Karl Tannert)
● 1st Bn. (Not at Brest- at St. Malo)
● 2nd Bn. (Major Werner Ewald)
5, 6, 7, 8. Kompanie
● 3rd Bn. (Major Karl Tannert. After 11 Aug 44 : Hauptmann Herbert Kirsten)
9, 10, 11, 12. Kompanie

13. Kompanie- Mortars
14. Kompanie- Panzerjäger
15. Kompanie- Engineers
16. Kompanie - Reconnaissance

Fallschirmjäger-Regiment 6
(Oberst Von Der Heydte) (In Normandy- not at Brest)

Fallschirmjäger-Regiment 7
(Oberstleutant Erich Pietzonka)
● 1st Bn. (Reino Hamer)
1, 2, 3, 4. Kompanie
● 2nd Bn. (Major Fritz Becker. After 4 Sept 44: Hauptman Max Herbach)
5, 6, 7, 8. Kompanie
● 3rd Bn (not at Brest-in St Malo)
13. Kompanie- Mortars
14. Kompanie- Panzerjäger
15. Kompanie- Engineers

Fallschirm-Artillerie-Regiment 2 (Oberst Winkler)
● 1st Artillery Bn.
1, 2 , 3. Batterie
2nd and 3rd Bn not at Brest

● Fallschirm-Nachtrichten Bn. 2 (Major Ernst Mehler)
1 and 2. Kompanie
● Fallschirm-sanitäs Bn. 2 (Oberstabsarzt Muller)
1 and 2. Kompanie
● Fallschirm-Pionier Bn. 2 (Major Siegfried Gerstner)
1, 2, 3, 4.Kompanie
● Fallschirm-Panzerjäger-Abteilung 2 (Hauptmann Kemmitz)
1, 2, 3. Kompanie
● Division Nachschuß (Trains) (Major Schitterer)
● Fallschirm-Flak-Abteilung 2 (Hauptmann Hochmuth)

POWS CAPTURED ON THE CROZON PENINSULA (from 17-19 September 1944)	
343rd Infantry Div.	693
343rd Artillery Regt.	442
898th Infantry Regt.	497
Russian units	643
Fortress Base Co. XXV	122
56th Security Regt	120
KG Krueger	105
KG Naugoks	40
Luftwaffe Signal Regt. Westfrankreich	19
Dock Emplacement Co.	103
804th Navy AA Bn.	543
262nd Navy AA Bn.	255
Misc. Naval	100
1162 GHQ Artillery Bn.	12
1274 Army Coastal Btry.	91
Military Hospital Le Fret	201
Roscanvel PW enclosure	128
Misc. personnel	53
Total	**4,167**

Above.
In one of the rare photos taken of Ramcke in Brittany he is seen with some of his staff officers discussing the situation. His previous exploits in North Africa, where he marched his men many miles across enemy-held territory, caused the Americans to worry he might try and break out from Brest to disrupt Allied supply lines.
(Courtesy Ramcke family)

Left.
Paratrooper, Fallschirmjäger-Regiment 2
This Fallschirmjäger Unteroffizier is armed with the MP-40 submachine gun.
A pouch for extra clips is worn on his left, and a leather map case hangs from the other side. He wears the blue-gray "Fliegerbluse:" a short wool jacket worn by Luftwaffe personnel. The yellow insignia was worn by both aircraft crew and paratroopers. The tan canvas over-trousers are a nonregulation item worn to protect the blue-gray trousers underneath. He also wears a nonregulation neckerchief, and has picked up a pair of American binoculars during the withdrawal to Brest. The steel helmet is the special pattern for paratroopers.
(Reconstruction by Militaria Magazine)

General Ramcke had this photograph taken while at Camp Clinton, Mississippi in 1945. Although of poor quality, careful examination reveals he is wearing an American khaki shirt with his Knight's Cross, Oak Leaves, Swords, and Diamonds. The Swords and Diamonds were awarded him for his defense of Brest, and were presented to him through the Red Cross while a prisoner in England. According to the Ramcke family, once home after the war he never again wore a uniform, so this may be the only photograph showing him with his final awards.
(Courtesy Ramcke family)

Division. In Italy an Allied fighter forced his car off the road, and Ramcke temporarily relinquished command of his unit while recovering in a Dresden hospital.

In mid-June 1944 Ramcke and his 2nd FJ Div. were sent to Brittany. They entered Brest on 8 August. The division's 8th FJ Regt. was already in Normandy, and it would take part in the fighting there.

To ensure the safety of the local population Ramcke ordered the French civilians out of Brest on 21 Aug. 1944.

The two regiments of Ramcke's 2nd FJ Division in Brittany were not at full strength. Records indicate that while the 2nd and 7th FJ Regiments were at Brest, the 1st Battalion of the 2nd FJ Regiment was elsewhere being used as the cadre of a new unit. The 3rd Battalion of the 7th FJ Regiment was trapped at Saint-Malo, where it took part in the fighting for that city.

While at Brest Ramcke issued a statement to his troops explaining the importance of their continued fight. A translation reads, "*Faithful to the oath we have sworn to the Führer, the peo-ple and the Fatherland and safe guarding the traditional honor of the German soldier, we are going to defend this Fortress Brest to the last grenade committing our very lives and shall cede this important military port to the enemy only as a pile of ruins.*

Through our tenacity we are tying down considerable enemy forces. So far already strong armed forces and several infantry divisions have been committed against us. Besides, an American air fleet is being used to subdue us.

These forces cannot be used against our menaced West Wall. Every shell and every grenade which we are drawing on us - every American soldier marching against us is one threat less against the home. This explains convincingly the meaning of our endurance.

Should we, however, after heroic resistance, have to surrender to the numerical superiority of the enemy, it must be done in an honorable way. Many of us will have fallen during the heroic struggle. Many other wounded and not wounded will have to endure the sad fate of a POW. This fate we shall shoulder as true German soldiers."

For his defense of Brest he was awarded both the Swords and Diamonds to his Knight's Cross. He was only the twentieth German soldier to receive this high honor. On 16 Sept., when it became inevitable

The German paratroops were not only well-trained and highly motivated, but they had some special equipment that set them apart from regular German units. The FG-42, seen here being examined by an American ordnanceman, was a state of the art assault rifle which allowed for semi or fully automatic fire. The light weight and high fire power made it a perfect weapon for either hedgerow or city fighting. Although a relatively scarce item, a number have been found in Brittany since the war, indicating that they had been issued to the 2nd FJ Division.
(National Archives)

that Brest would fall Ramcke was ordered to leave his men and move to the Crozon Peninsula. Ramcke turned over command of Fortress Brest to von der Mosel and left for the Crozon. There, in a situation curiously parallel to Douglas MacArthur on Corregidor, the high command planned to rescue him with a torpedo boat and bring him back to Germany as a hero. Unfortunately, no torpedo boats were available for this mission. An attempt was made to find a seaplane to evacuate him, but none were available and Ramcke finally surrendered to the Americans on 19 Sept. While a prisoner in England he was presented with the Swords and Diamonds to his Knight's Cross via the Swiss Red Cross. Ramcke was pressured to cooperate with the Allies and provide information on the German paratroops and his defense of Brest. He politely refused and explained that his country was still at war and it was his duty to keep quiet. He used as an example the captured American General Jonathan Wainwright who had surrendered to the Japanese in the Philippines. Ramcke told his captives that the Americans would expect Wainwright to not cooperate with his captors, much in the same way the German Army would expect him to act.

During his captivity he was sent to a POW camp in Mississippi. When the war ended and the Americans discovered the poor treatment their own men had received in German POW camps, privileges of German POWs were cut. Ramcke, understanding their rights under the Geneva Convention, escaped from his camp one night and traveled to Jackson, Mississippi. There he bought postage stamps and mailed a letter of complaint to an American Congressman. Ramcke then returned to the camp with the guards never knowing he had left. When the uncensored letter reached Congress there was an uproar as to how it could have been mailed, but the end result was fair treatment was restored to the Germans.

Ramcke was turned over to the British who eventually handed him over to the French. He was imprisoned in France pending investigation of war crimes allegedly committed by his men. After almost five years passed without a formal charge Ramcke escaped to Germany to draw attention to his plight, and that of other German prisoners in France. He returned voluntarily when he was assured of a speedy trial, and was soon after sentenced to five years with hard labor. Allowing for the time already spent in prison, he served the remaining three months of the sentence before being released in July 1951.

Until his retirement Ramcke worked as a sales executive for a major supplier of raw materials important in the rebuilding of Germany. Before his death in 1968 his former soldiers frequently came to visit him and talk about old times. It is unfortunate that some historians have concluded that Ramcke must have been a fanatical Nazi for him to hold out at Brest for so long. He was, in fact, not even a member of the Nazi party. He considered himself a professional soldier, willing to do whatever he was ordered to the best of his abilities.

Ramcke could have easily spent the war safe at home running training centers, but like professional soldiers in every army he knew that promotions went to those in combat commands. His decision to transfer to the paratroops at age 51 shows just how far he was willing to go for his military career.

Ramcke and Middleton

When asked about Ramcke, Middleton said, "*He was a pretty decent sort,*" and "*No matter how ruthless, he was nevertheless a soldier.*" While Ramcke was being tried in France, Colonel Kroh wrote to General Middleton asking for help with the case. Middleton quickly responded that he had no idea as to what the French could hold against Ramcke, because as far as he had seen Ramcke had always conducted himself according to the rules of war.

Over the course of the Brest siege a number of messages would be sent back and forth across the lines. One of the first was sent to General Grow of the 6th Armored Division. Ramcke complained that some of his men who had been captured by the Americans had been turned over to FFI guards. The French, Ramcke said, had stripped the Germans of their possessions and threatened to shoot them. Ramcke asked that the conditions of the Geneva Convention be followed and that German POWs not be handed over to the FFI. In reply Grow explained that he would do what he could, but that it was very hard to control the large number of Frenchmen that had picked up guns on the battlefield.

On 27 Aug. Ramcke returned a group of American medical personnel stating that his fortress was so well-staffed that they were not needed. He also indicated that he had turned the area one kilometer around the village of Le Fret into a hospital and POW camp and asked it be spared from bombardment. He also sent detailed maps which pointed out where German aid stations and hospitals were and request-

VIIIth CORPS UNITS AS OF 14 SEPT. 1944
(unit code names where known)

VIII CORPS (MONARCH) Combat Units	Task Force A		(Review)
	● Hq/Hq Co, 1st TD Brigade	● 559th FA Bn. (155G) (*Munition Red*)	● 3042nd QM Graves Registration Co. (*Daisey*)
2nd Infantry Division (*Ivanhoe*)	● Hq/Hq Co., 6th Group 705th TD Bn. (SP) (Co. B)	● 578th FA Bn. (8"H) (*Munition Blue*)	● 3200th QM Service Co.
● 612th TD Bn. (T) (*Vertex*)	● Hq/Hq Troop, 15th Cavalry Group	● Hq/Hq Btry. 113th AAA Group (*Montana*)	● 3326th QM Truck Company (*Daily*)
● Co. D, 709th Tank Bn. (L) (*Healthy*)	● 15th Cavalry Recon Sq.	● 635th AAA (AW) Bn. (*Mayfair 635*)	● 3598th QM Truck Company (*Dairymaid*)
● Co. C, 86th Chemical Mortar Bn.	● 17th Cavalry Recon Sq.	● Hq/Hq Co. 1102nd Engineer Combat Group	● 3806th QM Truck Co.
● Co. B, 705th TD Bn. (SP)	● 35th Engineer Combat Bn. (*Handsome*)	(*Muscle*)	● 2nd Platoon 122nd QM Car Company .
	VIIIth Corps Troops	● 44th Engineer Combat Bn. (*Muscle-Able*)	● Hq/Hq Det, 64th Medical Group (*Dahlia*)
29th Infantry Division (*Latitude*)	● Hq/Hq Btry VIII Corps Artillery (*Mogul*)	● 511th Engineer Light Pontoon Co. (*Muscle-Dog*)	Hq/Hq Det, 170th Medical Bn.
● 821st TD Bn. (T)	● 12th FA Observation Bn. (*Mystery*)	● 628th Engineer Light Equip Co. (*Muscle-Easy*)	● 439th Medical Collecting Company
● Co. A, 709th Tank Bn.	● Hq/Hq Btry. 174th FA Group (*Munition*)	● Hq/Hq Co. 1107th Engineer Combat Group	(- Amb Platoon) (*Cosmic*)
● Cos. A&B, 86th Chem. Mortar Bn.	● Btry. A, 243rd FA Bn. (8"G) (*Hillock*)	(*Lurdan*)	● 590th Medical Ambulance Company
● Co. A, 644th TD Bn (SP) (*Hazard*)	● Btry. B, 740th FA Bn. (8"H) (*Hightime*)	● 168th Engineer Combat Bn. (*Hinder*)	(*Damsel*)
● 141st Regt. RAC (*the Buffs*)	● 2nd FA Bn. (155H) (*Hemstitch*)	● 202nd Engineer Combat Bn. (*Happy*)	● 623rd Medical Clearing Company (*Daphne*)
	● Btry A, 83rd Arm FA Bn. (105H) (*Cocaine*)	● 665th Engineer Topographic Co. (*Myopia*)	● Hq/Hq Det, 420th Medical Bn.
8th Infantry Division (*Granite*)	● 561st FA Bn. (155G) (*Munition White*)	● 969th Engineer Maintenance Co.	● 462nd Medical Collecting Company
● 445th AAA (AW) Bn. (*Mulberry*)	● 16th FA Obsn Bn. (Btry. A) (*Hillman*)	(*Muscle-Fox*)	● 580th Medical Ambulance Company
● 644th TD Bn. (SP) (-Co. A) (*Hazard*)	● Hq/Hq Btry. 333rd FA Group (*Monster*)	● 2nd Platoon, Co. A, 602nd Engineer Camouflage Bn. (*January*)	(*Data*)
● Co. D, 86th Chemical Mortar Bn.	● 333rd FA Bn. (155H) (*Monster Red*)	● 59th Signal Bn. (*Modulate*)	● 581st Medical Ambulance Company (*Davenport*)
Hq/Hq Btry 34th FA Brigade (*Heartless*)	● 557th FA Bn. (155G-SP) (*Varnish*)	● Det. 51 166th Signal Photo Co.	● 666th Medical Clearing Company
● 687th FA Bn. (105H) (*Lowbred*)	● 771st FA Bn (4.5"G) (*Lowpass*)	● 6th Platoon, 187th Signal Replacement Co. (*Monogram*)	● 595th Medical Ambulance Company (*Corkscrew*)
● 969th FA Bn. (155H) (*Monster White*)	● Hq/Hq Btry. 196th FA Group (*Lustful*)	● Co. A, 511th Military Police Bn.	● 53rd Field Hospital
● Hq/Hq Btry. 402nd FA Group (*Logslate*)	● 174th FA Bn. (155G-SP) (*Mallory Blue*)	● Hq/Hq Co. 7th TD Group (*Morbid*)	● 100th Evacuation Hosp.
● 256th FA Bn. (8"G) - Btry. C (*Highcap*)	● 965th FA Bn. (155H) (*Loiter*)	● Hq/Hq Det. 86th Chemical Mortar Bn.	● 102nd Evacuation Hospital (*Headlong*)
● 265th FA Bn. (240 H) (-Btry. C) (*Lulubelle*)	● Btry. C, 256th FA Bn. (8" G) (*Highcap*)	● 2nd Ranger Bn. (*Veteran*)	● 107th Evacuation Hospital (*Heathen*)
● 740th FA Bn. (8" H) (Btry. B) (*Hightime*)	● Btry. C, 265th FA Bn. (240H) (*Lulubelle*)	● 5th Ranger Bn. (*Vat*)	● 108th Evacuation Hosp.
● 770th FA Bn. (4.5" G) (*Lower*)	● Hq/Hq Btry. 202nd FA Group (*Lockman*)		● Advance Section, 33rd Medical Dep. Co.
● 83rd Armored FA Bn. (105H) (-Btry A) (*Cocaine*)	● 243rd FA Bn. (8"G) (*Hillock*)	**VIIIth Corps Service Units**	● 48th Replacement Bn. (*Monotone*)
● Btry. A, 16th FA Observation Bn (*Hillman*)	● 269th FA Bn. (240H) (*Cockpit*)	● Hq/Hq Det, 80th QM Bn. (M) (*Hawkville*)	● 13th Military Records Unit
		● 131st QM Truck Co.	● 577th Army Postal Unit
			● 599th Army Postal Unit
			● 63rd Finance Distribution Section

Headquarters VIII Corps
U.S. Army
12 September 1944

Lieutenant General Ramcke
Commanding German Forces at Brest and on Crozon Peninsula

"Sir:
There comes a time in war when the situation reaches a point where a commander is no longer justified in expending the lives and destroying the health of the men who have bravely carried out his orders in combat.
I have discussed with your officers and men, who have served you well and are now prisoners of war, the situation confronting the German Garrison at Brest. These men are of the belief that the situation is hopeless and that there is nothing to be gained by prolonging the struggle. I therefore feel that the German garrison at Brest and on the Crozon Peninsula no longer has a justifiable reason for continuing the fight.
Your men have fought well. Approximately 16,000 of them from this area are now prisoners of war. Your command has suffered casualties. You have lost much of the necessary implements of war and your men are encircled in a small, congested area. Therefore, it is the consensus of all that you and your command have fulfilled your obligation to your country.
In consideration of the preceding, I am calling upon you, as one professional soldier to another, to cease the struggle now in progress.
In accepting the terms of the surrender of Brest, I desire that your men lay down their arms and be assembled in proper military formation and marched under command of appropriate commanders to locations agreed upon by you and my representative who has handed you this communication. At the designated point, transport will convey the officers and men to the prisoner of war assembly point. For you and such members of you staff as you may designate, proper transportation will call at such a place as you may select.
I am sure that you realize the futility of continuing the battle. I am also of the opinion that you would prefer to surrender to the Americans who opposed you in this siege. And that, by doing so, save the remnants of your command who have served you so well. Furthermore, you must now realize that the Port of Brest has lost its significance since so many ports are now in Allied hands.
I trust, as a professional soldier who has served well and who has already fulfilled his obligation, you will give this request your favorable consideration".

Troy H. Middleton
Major General, U.S. Army
Commanding

After the fall of Brest Middleton is seen here talking to General Eisenhower. Ike had a great deal of confidence in Middleton's ability as a commander and requested him over many other potential corps commanders. Middleton would later play a major role in the Battle of the Bulge by being the one to decide to hold the vital crossroads at Bastogne. Although personally ordered out of Bastogne at the last moment by his Army commander, it was Middleton who first realized the importance of the town.
(National Archives)

ed that Middleton not shell them. He stated that ships painted white and marked with a red cross passing from Brest to the Crozon were for transport of wounded only (both German and American) and Ramcke promised not to misuse them.

Of course, Middleton realized that Ramcke had cleverly positioned some of his medical centers next to legitimate targets like ammunition dumps. It was a good try, but Middleton called his bluff and let Ramcke know that if there was a real target someplace it was going to get

shelled. It would be up to Ramcke to make sure that his hospitals were far from any military target. As Middleton replied, "*I note the hospital installations are so widely dispersed that I feel it would be an impossibility to prevent endangering some of them with unobserved artillery fire and by bombing from aircraft, both day and night. If such should happen, it would be entirely unintentional. The installations now so widely dispersed might be placed in more compact areas.*" Middleton went on to comment how with the large amount of air and artillery at the disposal of the Americans it was possible that accidents might occur. He concluded "*I, therefore, suggest that where possible, these installations be placed where accidents may not occur.*"

On 13 Sept. Middleton hoped to spare his men the bloody fighting that was certain to take place if he had to assault the old city. He sent his intelligence officer, Colonel Reeves, along with two officers and an enlisted translator into Brest under a white flag. His offer to end the fighting was refused by Ramcke with the simple statement, "*I must decline your offer.*" Middleton ordered that a copy of his surrender offer, accompanied by the reply, be distributed to every soldier under his command. He wanted to show that Ramcke had been given a fair chance to surrender, but had insisted on continuing the battle. He added to the exchange, "*General Ramcke has been given an opportunity to surrender. Since he has declined what is believed to be a humane and reasonable request, it now remains for the VIII Corps to make him sorry for his refusal. Therefore, I ask the combat soldiers of this command to enter the fray with renewed vigor – let's take them apart – and get the job finished.*"

Lt. General Simpson, commander of the Ninth Amy, took control of the VIIIth corps on 5 September. Not wanting to distract Middleton from the fighting at Brest, Simpson took direct command of the Corps units not in the Brest area. Simpson is seen here while inspecting the captured German guns of the Graf Spee Battery.
(National Archives)

SIMPSON'S NINTH ARMY

On 5 Sept.1944 command of the VIIIth Corps passed from Patton's Third Army to Lt. Gen. William H. Simpson's newly formed Ninth Army. At the time Patton and the bulk of his forces were hundreds of miles to the east. It only made sense to transfer the single corps in Brittany to the command of someone who was closer to the fighting. So as not to distract Middleton from the Brest area Simpson took over direct command of the 83rd Infantry and 6th Armored Divisions.

One of the reasons that this made sense was that according to the American doctrine, a corps was supposed to be only a combat headquarters, and not involved with logistical support. All units dealing with supply and logistics were kept at an army level. Each division went directly to an army level quartermaster unit for their supplies. Thus in the case of the Third Army it became very difficult to support divisions both on the German border and hundreds of miles to the west in Brittany. The activation of the Ninth Army allowed the Third Army support troops to focus on only one sector.

Chapter 9

THE ARTILLERY WAR

Above.
The largest artillery piece used by the Americans at Brest was the 240mm howitzer. This 27 foot long gun could fire a 360 pound shell over 25,000 yards. It took a crew of 35 men for each howitzer, which could fire an average of one shell a minute.
(National Archives)

Below.
There were six 81mm mortars in each infantry heavy weapons company. The 81mm had a range of 3,300 yards, so they could cover their entire battalion area. The mortars seen here are far enough behind the lines at Brest that the crews felt comfortable not digging them in.
(National Archives)

Artillery played a major role in the battle for Brest. When an enemy is dug in, like the Germans were, one of the best ways to deal with them is with artillery. Middleton knew this and as soon as Saint-Malo had fallen he moved the corps artillery units up to Brest. American artillery used at Brest ranged from the 105mm and 155mm howitzers, which were an integral part of each infantry division, to the larger 8" and 240mm howitzers.

Most of the Allied naval vessels had been sent to the Mediterranean to take part in the Southern France landings so there was little naval gunfire support in Brittany. The *H.M.S. Warspite* did fire a few rounds at various targets before she too was sent to the Mediterranean.

American intelligence estimated that the German defense at Brest included over 550 artillery and antiaircraft guns; the equivalent of more than 86 artillery battalions. After the capture of the city it was discovered that the Germans only had approximately 80 battalions of artillery, but a vastly greater number of light antiaircraft guns (roughly 315 20mm, 40mm, and 75mm) which had proved very effective in ground combat. Captured German officers later claimed that they did not have enough artillery to adequately defend the city, however it was only due to a concentrated counter-battery effort that the Americans were able to reduce the German threat.

The greatest German artillery threat was the 280mm guns of the Graf Spee Battery at Lochrist. These guns not only commanded the sea lanes off Brittany, but regularly shelled the American troops outside Brest. The fixed guns were often erroneously referred to as railway guns by the Americans. The three landward firing Graf Spee guns were put out of commission by air and artillery, but at least one gun was being repaired when the position was finally captured by the 2nd Rangers.

One of the main problems the German artillery had was that many of their guns were captured foreign models so they had a very limited ammunition supply. The battery commanders were issued with all the ammo that was available, told to ration it as they saw fit, then destroy their guns when they ran out. Another problem was that many of the naval and flak gun crews had not been trained in unobserved fire. Coupled with the lack of aerial observation and artillery observation units, the Germans had difficulty targeting behind the American lines.

American artillery

In every American infantry division there were four artillery battalions: three 105mm battalions and a fourth 155mm battalion. The 105's were normally in direct support of one of the three infantry regiments of the division, while the heavier 155mm could fire into the sector of any of the regiments. Additionally each infantry regiment had a cannon company consisting of six short barreled 105mm howitzers. The corps artillery units were composed of guns 155mm or heavier. These had the range to reach targets in areas outside a divisional boundary.

The 57mm gun was the standard antitank weapon of the infantry. Each infantry regiment had 18 of them. They were small enough to be pushed into position by hand, but large enough to penetrate most light armor. With the special British-produced discarding sabot ammunition they could penetrate most German tanks. *(National Archives)*

Below.
Six of these short barreled M3 105mm howitzers made up the cannon company found in each infantry regiment. The original idea behind these units was to provide an artillery unit that would operate right up on the front lines with direct fire against enemy strongpoints. In practice these tasks were performed by self-propelled guns and tank destroyers. The cannon companies were generally used as an additional artillery battery for indirect fire. *(National Archives)*

Heavy artillery at Brest consisted of 4.5" guns, 8" guns and howitzers, and the super heavy 240mm howitzers. Guns fired with a fairly direct trajectory, while the howitzers were better used for indirect fire due to the higher arc their rounds were fired at. These heavy artillery pieces were transported to their firing positions in sections and assembled on site. They had a slower rate of fire than the smaller guns, but the larger shells packed a tremendous punch.

At times self-propelled tank destroyers and assault guns were used alongside the artillery for indirect fire. The tanks would park with their treads perpendicular to the line of fire so the recoil would not knock them off target. Each of the three infantry divisions was also sent an experimental battery of 4.5" rocket launchers. For the most part these experimental devices proved unsatisfactory and were quickly returned to the ordnance corps for more work.

Due to the tight lines around Brest the artillery was concerned about accidentally firing into American units. Artillery units monitored a corps radio net on the SCR193 radio in case the code word "Axle" was broadcast. If the correct authentication word for the day was transmitted followed by "Axle," it indicated that a unit was receiving artillery fire from a friendly unit. When an Axle transmission occurred each battery scrambled to make sure it was not firing into American troops.

To the American artillery counter-battery fire was the top priority. They knew once the German guns were destroyed they could fire with impunity. An extensive effort was put into locating and destroying the German artillery positions. By the end of the campaign 262 different German artillery positions had been located and assigned a concentration number. Some of the more troublesome German batteries kept their guns under cover until they were needed, then wheeled them out

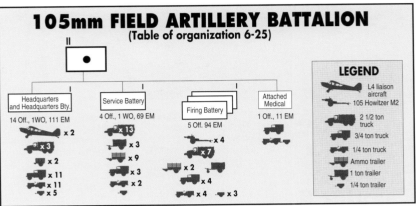

Towed tank destroyer battalions were equipped with 3" antitank guns. These were powerful weapons against German armor, but had limited mobility due to their size. Normally they were placed behind the lines to prevent a breakthrough by German tanks. This gun is positioned near Avranches, ready to stop a German breakthrough at Mortain.
(National Archives)

Below.
The M2 105mm howitzer was considered the standard artillery piece of the American Army. A single 105mm battalion of 12 howitzers was normally assigned to support each infantry regiment. The 105mm had a range of 12,000 yards and fired a 33 pound shell.
(National Archives)

to fire. The Americans gave code names to these positions, and when an observer spotted one of these difficult targets in action the code name was sent out over the radio net. Immediately the artillery unit assigned to that target would fire on the position in hopes of damaging the guns while they were in the open. This technique is credited with knocking out many German guns.

After counter-battery fire American artillery made flak (or antiaircraft fire) neutralization their second priority. When air raids were planned the artillery would fire a few volleys at known flak positions to drive the gun crews to cover, then continue to fire intermittently while Allied aircraft were in the area. If an antiaircraft gun did open up it was subjected to intense fire. Aerial observation for flak positions was always planned when air raids were taking place. A specially trained aircraft flying overhead was in the best position of spotting and directing fire on firing antiaircraft positions.

The light spotter aircraft normally used for aerial observation were of limited value over the city of Brest. There were so many antiaircraft positions that the slow moving liaison planes were easy targets. The 10th Photo Reconnaissance Group was called in to observe from faster aircraft. Later on this role was taken over by the 363rd Tactical Recon Group. These planes flew in from an airfield near Paris, so they were generally briefed on their mission while they were in the air, and had only 40 minutes of fuel over the city. The high performance aircraft

were very effective at spotting. In over 900 missions only one was shot down over Brest. The lighter artillery spotter planes were used outside the city and given a safety line they were not to cross.

One of the other problems the observation planes ran into was a shortage of film to take reconnaissance photos with. The troops were in desperate need of up-to-date photos of the areas they were fighting in (particularly in the city when each day the landscape could change as buildings were destroyed). The advances of the Allies in the east needed vast amounts of photographic film and the troops at Brittany had a hard time getting their share. To spot the German gun emplacements from the ground both the 12th and 16th Field Artillery Observation Battalions were used. These two units were able to cover the entire corps area with both flash and sound ranging equipment. When positions were established on the Daoulas Peninsula, the city of Brest was under observation from both the front and rear.

There were four main sound ranging bases: two outside Brest, one on the Daoulas Peninsula, and one covering the Lochrist area (it would move to the Crozon after Lochrist was captured). These units had sensitive equipment that, when used in conjunction with spotters looking for the flashes of artillery pieces, could pin down the location of enemy batteries. Normally such units are forced to work along a straight front line, but with the semicircular coverage they had around Brest, German guns were quickly located as soon as they fired.

Opposite page, centre.
A French civilian helps unload artillery ammunition in Brittany. Although the U.S. Army had regulations on how to hire local help and what to pay them, many American units found it easier to get extra hands by offering the local population food instead of money.
(National Archives)

Opposite page, bottom.
One of the gun crew communicates by phone line to the battery headquarters. He relays firing instructions to each gun. Their elaborate communication system allowed the American artillery to focus massive amounts of firepower on specific targets faster than any other nation during the war.
(National Archives)

155mm Howitzer FIELD ARTILLERY BATTALION
(Table of organization 6-335)

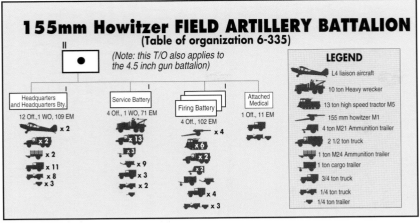

(Note: this T/O also applies to the 4.5 inch gun battalion)

Headquarters and Headquarters Bty.	Service Battery	Firing Battery	Attached Medical
12 Off.,1 WO, 109 EM	4 Off., 1 WO, 71 EM	4 Off., 102 EM	1 Off., 11 EM

Headquarters and Headquarters Bty.: x 2, x 2, x 2, x 11, x 8, x 3

Service Battery: x 13, x 3, x 9, x 3, x 2

Firing Battery: x 4, x 6, x 2, x 2, x 4, x 3

LEGEND

- L4 liaison aircraft
- 10 ton Heavy wrecker
- 13 ton high speed tractor M5
- 155 mm howitzer M1
- 4 ton M21 Ammunition trailer
- 2 1/2 ton truck
- 1 ton M24 Ammunition trailer
- 1 ton cargo trailer
- 3/4 ton truck
- 1/4 ton truck
- 1/4 ton trailer

Communication is what allowed all the various artillery and observation points to work together so well. Unfortunately, there was a severe shortage of field telephone wire at the time. Captured German wire was tried, but it was so poorly made that it had to quickly be replaced with the more durable American wire. Telephone wire was in such short supply that only one line could be laid to each battery, making the job of maintaining communications very difficult for the wire crews. The VIIIth Corps artillery laid over 140 miles of wire and by the end of the fighting was maintaining 235 miles of it.

On 3 Sept. an observer from the 8th Infantry Division worked his way in front of the lines to where he could see the Pontanezen Barracks. While he was adjusting the fire, a white phosphorus round (used so he could spot the smoke from the burning phosphorus where it had fallen) from the 559th Field Artillery started a fire. This provided good illumination at night and the rest of the battalion began to shell the barracks. After a brief pause the shelling resumed and caught many of the Germans who had left their shelters to fight the fires. On 7 Sept. the Americans shelled the main food supply point for Brest and German morale was lowered when rations were then cut in half.

Three of the only nine black artillery battalions in the (then segregated) U.S. Army served at Brest: the 333rd FA Bn. (155mm), the 969th FA Bn. (155mm), and the 578th FA Bn. (8" gun). Out of four black artillery group headquarters in the army only one, the 333rd FA Group was at Brest. A post action report on mixing black and white artillery units in the same artillery group found only one problem. Some white soldiers in the battalions assigned to the 333rd Group resented having only black chaplains for their use. The situation resolved itself as one of the black chaplains became ill and was replaced by a white officer. Otherwise the battalions and groups worked together fine. The black artillerymen became known for a chant they used while passing ammunition to the guns. Starting as *"Rommel, count your men!"* in Normandy, it soon changed to *"Ramcke, count your men!"* in Brittany. After the gun fired they'd ask, *"How many you got now, Ramcke?"*

Other guns

The Germans had no aircraft flying at Brest so the American anti-aircraft units were used in their secondary role, against ground targets. One battery of 90mm guns of the 407th AA Bn. was sent to the Daoulas Peninsula to fire at targets of opportunity in Brest. After one mission it was heavily shelled by the Germans in retaliation and had to be withdrawn. The rest of the unit was used to support the 2nd Infantry Division's advance, until it was withdrawn on 4 Sept.

One of the antiaircraft guns was set up on the tip of the Daoulas Peninsula, under radar control, to fire at the German ships passing back and forth from Brest to the Crozon.

The results were not considered good and the 407th was withdrawn from Brittany and sent east on 4 Sept. One unanticipated problem arose

AMERICAN AMMUNITION EXPENDITURE AT BREST

	# guns	Total rounds
105mm H	138	270,493
155mm H	84	91,547
155mm G	24	18,618
155mm SP	24	9,955
90mm G	16	2,248
3" G	108	40,870
4.5" G	24	14,861
8" H	24	11,528
240mm H	12	3,153
8" G	12	1,608
76mm G	12	13,747

H=Howitzer, G=Gun, SP= self-propelled

The 8" guns were transported in two sections. A crane was needed to place the barrel and muzzle assembly in place on the carriage. This meant that the heavy artillery units were slow to set up or move, but their long range and the greater damage caused by their larger shells made them worthwhile. This gun is from the 256th FA Bn.
(National Archives)

with its departure. No one had ever expected a corps to operate without any antiaircraft units. All the meteorological teams in a corps were part of these units. This left the VIIIth Corps without any weather men to record the data that was needed for accurate artillery fire. A meteorological team had to be detached from an antiaircraft unit to provide this data to the corps until the end of the siege.

With no real danger of a German tank attack at Brest, the two battalions of towed 3" antitank guns at Brest were not needed in their normal role. However, it was found that while supplies of artillery ammunition were short, there were plenty of rounds for these guns. The towed 3" guns were used at times to support attacks by firing at specific targets, but were mainly turned into additional indirect fire artillery units. The 821st TD Bn. (towed) supported the 29th Infantry Division while the 612th TD Bn. (towed) was assigned to the 2nd Infantry Division.

In August the 612th set up a four-gun battery to fire only indirect missions. In that month 3,250 rounds were fired by these four guns. Starting in September the number of antitank guns dedicated to indirect missions was raised to eight. These eight guns fired 3,883 rounds that month. One of the guns of the 612th had the unique honor of destroying an American M-8 armored car that had been captured and put to use by the Germans.

The M7 105mm and M12 155mm self-propelled guns had been designed to allow artillery to keep up with a rapid armored advance. At Brest they proved valuable for direct fire against German emplacements. Even if the shell did not penetrate the concrete bunker, the concussion inside the structure was enough to lower the morale of the most dedicated defenders. By the end of the battle all available M12's were working roughly 500 yards from the front lines in a direct fire role. At times the M12's would fire at targets no more than 25 yards away.

240mm Howitzer FIELD ARTILLERY BATTALION
(Table of organization 6-395)

One problem with the M12 was that only ten rounds could be carried in the vehicle. To ensure an adequate supply of ammunition each self-propelled gun was assigned its own tracked and armored cargo carrier. Depending upon the model these cargo carriers could transport from 40-100 rounds of the 155mm ammunition.

The Ammo Shortage

The capture of Brest took as long as it did partially due to a severe shortage of artillery ammunition. The supply shortages

An M1 155mm gun (different from the 155mm howitzer) is seen here being towed through Brittany. The 155mm could be towed by either a truck or a high-speed tractor. The 155mm gun (range 25,000 yards) had a longer barrel than the 155mm howitzer (range 16,000 yards) and twice the muzzle velocity for a flatter trajectory.
(National Archives)

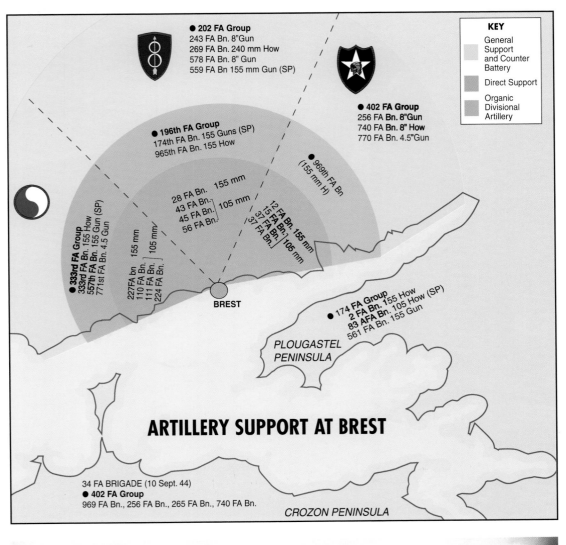

ARTILLERY SUPPORT AT BREST

● 202 FA Group
243 FA Bn. 8"Gun
269 FA Bn. 240 mm How
578 FA Bn. 8" Gun
559 FA Bn 155 mm Gun (SP)

● 402 FA Group
256 FA Bn. 8"Gun
740 FA Bn. 8" How
770 FA Bn. 4.5"Gun

● 196th FA Group
174th FA Bn. 155 Guns (SP)
965th FA Bn. 155 How

969th FA Bn
(155 mm H)

28 FA Bn.   155 mm
43 FA Bn.
45 FA Bn.   105 mm
56 FA Bn.

12 FA Bn. 155 mm
15 FA Bn.
37 FA Bn. 105 mm
37 FA Bn.

● 333rd FA Group
333rd FA Bn. 155 How
557th FA Bn. 155 Gun (SP)
771st FA Bn. 4.5 Gun

227FA bn   155 mm
110 FA Bn.
111 FA Bn.   105 mm
224 FA Bn.

BREST

● 174 FA Group
2 FA Bn. 155 How
83 AFA Bn. 105 How (SP)
561 FA Bn. 155 Gun

PLOUGASTEL PENINSULA

34 FA BRIGADE (10 Sept. 44)
● 402 FA Group
969 FA Bn., 256 FA Bn., 265 FA Bn., 740 FA Bn.

CROZON PENINSULA

KEY
General Support and Counter Battery
Direct Support
Organic Divisional Artillery

TOTAL OF ARTILLERY UNITS AT BREST

● 5 FA Group HQ
● 1 FA Obv. Bn.
● 1 Bn. 240mm Howitzer
● 2 Bn. 8" Gun
● 2 Bn. 8" Howitzer
● 2 Bn. 155 SP M12
● 2 Bn. 155 M1A1
● 4 Bn. 155 Howitzer
● 1 Bn. 105 Howitzer armored
● 1 Bn. 105 Howitzer
● plus the 12 batteries from the three divisions.
(After the attack started 2 Bn. 4.5" guns, 1 Bn. 240mm, 1 FA Obv/ Bn. and 1 FA Brig. HQ added)

The concussion of the 8" gun raised a lot of dust in dry areas. This could be spotted by enemy observers. When possible, the gun crews would wet down the area to minimize the dust. (Think of what a concussion strong enough to raise this much dust must do to the crewmen's ears. There are few artillerymen today who do not need a hearing aid).
(National Archives)

81

Some of the 8" artillery shells weighed well over 200 pounds. A large crew was needed to put the shell into the breech and ram it in. This was the moment when the enemy hoped to shell an artillery battery: when the ammunition was exposed near the gun and the crew was bunched together.
(National Archives)

Left.
A crane nicknamed "Swingshift Mazie" is being used to assemble a 240mm gun named "Hitler's Headache." This was one of the heaviest guns used by the U.S. Army in France. It was too heavy to be transported fully assembled; the barrel was carried separately when on the move.
(National Archives)

8 inch Howitzer FIELD ARTILLERY BATTALION
(Table of Organization 6-365)

Headquarters and Headquarters Bty.	Service Battery	Firing Battery	Attached Medical
11 Off., 1 WO, 93 EM	2 Off., 1 WO, 31 EM	4 Off., 135 EM	1 Off., 11 EM

LEGEND

L4 liaison aircraft
10-ton Heavy wrecker
8-ton Ammunition trailer M23
8 inch Howitzer M1
18-ton high speed tractor M4
M10 Ammunition trailer
2 1/2-ton truck
1-ton cargo trailer
3/4-ton truck
Command car
1/4-ton truck
1/4-ton trailer

feared by the Americans because of the lack of port facilities caused quartermasters to become very careful about issuing ammunition. There had been a serious ammunition shortage in Normandy due to the storm in late July, so the Army was careful to issue only what was needed. Artillery ammunition had started to become scarce at Saint-Malo, so after that battle the artillery units made sure to keep anything they had not used and brought it out to Brittany with them.

When Brest was assigned to the VIIIth Corps objective, the corps artillery officers used the actual ammunition expenditure at Saint-Malo for the basis of their supply requests. They figured that the expenditure of an army in combat against a German fortress would provide a better estimate than the charts and tables made up years ago without such combat experience. They asked for 8,700 tons to start, followed by 11,600 tons for the following three days. The Third Army ordnance officers did not believe they actually needed that much and only gave them 500 tons total. The VIIIth Corps was told that the majority of supply trucks were needed to haul material to the east and none were available to bring ammo to Brittany. The request for more ammo was sent directly to England, but again the Third Army stopped it. Patton felt that Brest should fall with a minimum of problems and wanted to keep the main focus of the Third Army attack to the east. Middleton felt he had not even been given the bare minimum so he went directly to Bradley to plead for more. He was given another 8,000 tons, and based on this promised supply Middleton ordered an attack on 25 Aug. The ammunition, however, did not arrive. Middleton was forced to suspend the attack because of the artillery ammunition shortage.

On 25 Aug. the distance between the VIIIth Corps and the Third Army was over 270 miles, so the region's supply functions were transferred to the newly formed Brittany Base Section of the Communications Zone. This new support unit immediately called for more ammunition for Brest, but not enough was available. Finally, on 27 Aug. the new stocks of artillery shells began to arrive in Brittany. Some came in on railway shipments to Ammo Supply Point 13 at Landivisiau. LSTs brought 2,500 tons ashore at Saint-Michel-en-Grève. So critical did the shortage become that 32 tons were airlifted from England into Brittany, much to irritation of the Air Force who did not like to be used for transporting artillery shells.

The worst of the ammo shortages started around 2 Sept. The three-

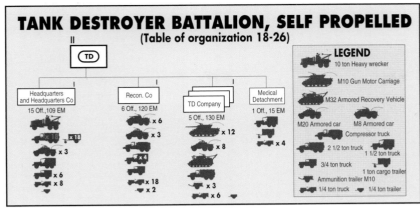

TANK DESTROYER BATTALION, SELF PROPELLED
(Table of organization 18-26)

LEGEND
- 10 ton Heavy wrecker
- M10 Gun Motor Carriage
- M32 Armored Recovery Vehicle
- M20 Armored car
- M8 Armored car
- Compressor truck
- 2 1/2 ton truck
- 1 1/2 ton truck
- 3/4 ton truck
- 1 ton cargo trailer
- Ammunition trailer M10
- 1/4 ton truck
- 1/4 ton trailer

Headquarters and Headquarters Co — 15 Off., 109 EM
Recon. Co — 6 Off., 120 EM
TD Company — 5 Off., 130 EM
Medical Detachment — 1 Off., 15 EM

TANK DESTROYER UNITS ATTACHED TO DIVISIONS AT BREST

- **2nd Infantry Division**
  — 612th TD Bn. (Towed)
  — B/705th TD Bn.
  (Self-Propelled)
- **29th Infantry Division**
  — 821st TD Bn. (Towed)
  — A/644th TD Bn.
  (Self-Propelled)
- **8th Infantry Division**
  — 644th TD Bn.
  (Self-Propelled) (less Company A)
- **Task Force Alpha**
  — 705th TD Bn.
  (Self-Propelled) (less Company B)
- **Task Force Baker**
  — A/603rd TD Bn.
  (Self-Propelled)
- **4th Armored Division**
  none
- **6th Armored Division**
  — 603rd TD Bn.
  (Self-propelled)

"Big Gee" is an M-18 belonging to one of the tank destroyer battalions at Brest. Unfortunately its unit can not be identified. There is some evidence that it may be from Company B/705th TD Bn., but that cannot be confirmed. Generally tank nicknames were given so that the first letter was the same as its company. The storage of personal baggage outside the turret was quite common because the crew had very little space inside. A bag getting in the way of loading the gun could mean the difference between life or death. *(National Archives)*

This overhead view shows the open turret of the M-18. Originally designed this way to provide the crew better visibility, it meant the vehicle was vulnerable to artillery and mortar fire. A few units welded makeshift armor to cover the turret, but this was only on a trial basis and never caught on. The 76mm gun of the M-18 was roughly as powerful as the 3" gun in the M-10, but it was smaller and lighter, making a smaller and faster moving vehicle. *(National Archives)*

against the dug in German positions, there was never enough of this type of shell during the Brittany fighting. It would later be estimated that 22,500 tons of artillery ammunition were actually used at Brest.

Brest was used in many ways as an experimental lab for the artillery units. Here was a chance for the Americans to practice the destruction of German defensive positions, much as they expected to find on the German border. A new fuse, the CP-T105, was tried out for its ability to penetrate concrete. What the Americans found was that it worked well against concrete structures, but they generally had to expend prodigious amounts of high explosive shells against such positions to blow away the dirt heaped around the concrete walls. This use of artillery to clear away the dirt (which absorbed much of the impact) became known as "agricultural shooting."

In the last days of the siege the Germans were subjected to a terrific 60 hour bombardment designed to keep them in their shelters and weaken morale. The city could have been captured slowly by fighting street by street, but the extensive use of artillery allowed Middleton to conserve the lives of his men. Now that the ammo shortage had ended the artillerymen found a new supply problem: they were running short of many of the parts they needed to maintain their guns. Local ordnance troops had to make replacement firing pins in their field shops, but many units just had to compensate for their worn out parts. Part of the problem was that back in July and August the Third Army ordnance units had most of their supplies transferred to support First Army units. It would take some time for the shortages to be made up in shipments from the States.

The massive artillery bombardment of Brest kept the defending Germans pinned in their shelters. Most American artillery battalions fired at a rate of one shell per minute: slow enough to keep the guns from overheating, but enough to drive the defenders to despair. Carrying parties with food, water, or ammunition were prevented from moving above ground. The constant pounding of the artillery shells ripped apart the last shreds of morale the Germans had. Even if they were safe in a deep concrete shelter, the constant pounding drummed into their heads.

Tank Destroyers at Brest

Perhaps the most influential weapon in the fight for Brittany was the tank destroyer. These open topped tanks played a number of different roles throughout the campaign. In the early years of the war a small 37mm gun was thought to be all that was needed for antitank use. The M-8 "Greyhound" armored car was originally designed as a tank destroyer, before the Army decided it was underpowered and moved the vehicle to a reconnaissance role. The 57mm gun was a more powerful weapon, and in Brittany each infantry regiment had 18 of them. These were generally positioned behind the front lines in areas the Germans might try and use tanks. The 57mm gun was still considered too small to be an effective weapon against German armor, but they did knock out a number of German tanks. These guns were also often used to fire at specific targets such as pillboxes or observation posts.

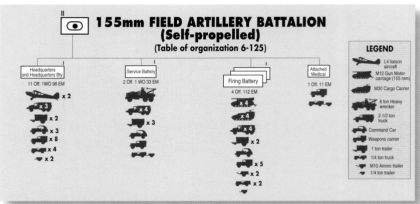

The 155mm gun of a self-propelled M-12 is seen here in full recoil. This vehicle is from the 557th Field Artillery Battalion, one of the two units with the M-12 in Brittany. The other being the 174th FA Bn. The black cardboard tubes in the foreground were used to transport the artillery shells *.(Courtesy Bruno Stadnicki)*

division attack scheduled for 4 Sept. had to be canceled for lack of artillery support. A steady flow of ammo finally began to arrive at Brest on 6 Sept., but it was not until the next day that Middleton felt comfortable enough with his stocks to resume the attack. On 10 Sept. Bradley ordered that the VIIIth Corps should have top priority in getting all that they needed. Only then, a few days before the fall of the city, did Middleton have enough artillery ammunition to fight the way he wanted. Although white phosphorous rounds were considered the best to use

THE AIR WAR

Throughout the fighting in Brittany heavy use was made of tactical air power. The XIXth Tactical Air Command under General Pete Weyland was responsible for the bulk of air operations at Brest. Aside from a handful of heavy and medium bomber missions, most of the aircraft assisting the VIIIth Corps was either P-47 Thunderbolts or P-38 Lightings. These fighters had the capability to drop a small bomb load and were therefore known as fighter-bombers.

Over 3,200 fighter-bomber sorties were flown in Brittany. Four aircraft were on air alert every day per division or task force. These planes would carry a mixture of high explosive bombs and jellied gasoline. An additional four aircraft were on call armed with rockets. Being on air alert meant that a flight of four aircraft was patrolling the area around the division and could be called in by the tactical air controller (normally located at division headquarters) to attack targets as they appeared.

Preplanned missions were not liked by the ground troops, since frequently when the planes got there the target had already been captured by the infantry. This resulted in a scrubbed mission, or in the ground troops being attacked by their own aircraft. In the 29th Infantry Division it was estimated that the average amount of time between a call for aircraft on alert and the actual bomb strike was generally 30-45 minutes. A preplanned air strike could take hours or even days to set up. A side benefit to keeping planes in the air over the German lines was that the Germans never knew if the aircraft were targeting them or observing for American artillery. When an Allied plane was in the air the Germans generally kept in their shelters.

The air alert missions generally worked like this. The front line units called division headquarters with targets. At headquarters the priority of the various missions was worked out and the targets assigned to an aircraft. The air support officer would then have an artillery unit fire a colored (generally red or green) smoke round onto the target to help orient the pilot. The air support officer would then, using a set of aerial photos of the area, provide information to the pilot. This allowed the ground based officer to see what the target area looked like from the air.

Most of the ground troops felt the fighter-bombers were most useful in striking German strongpoints at least 1,000 yards beyond their lines. All it took was one misplaced bomb, or a few rounds of machine gun fire from a friendly plane, and the unit became reluctant to call for air support. Unfortunately, American aircraft accidentally attacked their own men more often than seems to have been reported. The official 9th Air Force report on Brittany claims no friendly casualties in Brittany, but there are numerous stories of bombs dropped behind the lines. Perhaps one of the largest such accidental bombings was at Telgruc when seven men of the 15th Cavalry and 35th Engineers were killed and 24 were wounded. The heavy (B-17) and medium (B-26) attacks on Brest were not considered very helpful by the ground troops. They may have lowered German morale, but did little to effect the final outcome of the battle. The Air Force agreed that the heavy bombing missions did not play a major role, but blamed poor cooperation from the ground troops in supplying them with good targets and information so they could select the correct fuses.

The air support officer for the 2nd Infantry Division uses the hood of his jeep to prepare an air strike. This officer would be in radio contact with the aircraft during the mission. He would normally have aerial photographs of the area in hand, to be able to direct the pilot to the target. *(National Archives)*

Inset.
The tactical air support at Brest was under the command of the 9th Air Force. This version of their shoulder patch is a silk screened version produced in England. It was supplied to the Americans under the reverse lend-lease program.

Below
The most commonly seen Allied aircraft at Brest was the P-47 Thunderbolt. The damaged P-47 seen here is being towed off an airfield in France by an M2 seven ton tractor. This fighter-bomber could carry three bombs, with the maximum capacity being two 1,000 pounders and one 500 pound bomb.
(National Archives)

The standard tank destroyer battalion consisted of 3" towed guns. These could knock out most German tanks, but were difficult to move into position. They were towed behind trucks and were too large to be easily moved by hand. A self-propelled tank destroyer was made by placing the same 3" gun in an open topped turret, on the chassis of a Sherman tank. This vehicle was called the M-10, and allowed a high powered gun to be driven up to the front lines and put into action without exposing the crew to small arms fire. One drawback was the open turret. It had been designed that way for better observation for the vehicle commander, but made the M-10 vulnerable to mortar and artillery fire.

By the fall of 1944 a few of the self-propelled tank destroyer battalions had been reequipped with a newer vehicle. The M18 "Hellcat" was similar to the M-10 in that it had an open turret, but it mounted a 76mm gun on a smaller chassis. The new gun had about the same power as the 3", but was lighter. By the end of the war many of the M10s were given a heavier 90mm gun and renamed the M36, but none of these saw combat in Brittany. Brit-

tany was one of the first operations where the M18 was used and crews gave it a good evaluation.

Both the M10 and M18 tank destroyers are frequently mentioned in after action reports from Brittany. Each infantry division or task force had TDs assigned to it and they seemed to be in near constant use. Aside from a handful of self-propelled guns and captured American vehicles, the Germans in Brest had no tanks. Without needing to defend against German tanks, the American TDs were used to support the infantry. In practice they were used much as the German army used their own assault guns. The TDs proved well-suited to hitting such targets as pillbox openings or machine gun nests. Their antitank rounds were used to penetrate steel reinforced concrete bunkers. At times the towed 57mm and 3" guns were used in much the same way, although being self-propelled made the TDs faster and more flexible in the front lines.

Officially, the Army referred to its self-propelled guns as "gun motor carriages." The same term was used for the M7 and M12 self-propelled artillery vehicles. There was a third type of gun motor carriage found in American armored units. Both the M8 (75mm) and the 105mm howitzer gun motor carriages were essentially artillery pieces placed into tank turrets. They were designed to provide highly mobile support to the fast moving tank columns. Technically they were assault guns, and were assigned to "assault gun platoons." They were used for both direct and indirect fire missions. Unlike the TDs with high-powered armor piercing guns, the M8 and 105mm howitzer assault guns tended to fire a lower velocity high explosive shell. Often forgotten amidst the more glamorous tanks and TDs, the assault guns added an extra punch to American armored units.

THE 8th INFANTRY DIVISION IN BRITTANY

Chapter 10

The 8th Infantry Division landed in France on 4 July 1944. They then took part in the advance down the Cotentin Peninsula from La Haye-du-Puits. After the breakout the 13th Infantry Regiment was the first part of the division to enter Brittany. On 30 July the 13th was put onto trucks and assigned to follow the 4th Armored Division south to Rennes.

Above.
Pvt. Riley and other soldiers from the 8th Division take a closer look at the German defenses on Hill 88. The tangled mess of iron and wire held a camouflage cover that concealed the gun until it was ready to open fire. When used against ground targets these guns were positioned very low, allowing only a small section to be exposed.
(Courtesy Frank Orville Gray)

The 13th wanted a day to organize for the attack on Rennes, but was ordered directly into the assault on the afternoon of 3 Aug. The Americans moved forward a few hundred yards that night and discovered the Germans had already withdrawn. On the morning of 4 Aug. the 13th Infantry moved into Rennes welcomed by cheering Frenchmen. Although attached to the 4th Armored Division at the time, the 13th Infantry was the first unit to enter the city. For the next eight days the 13th Infantry occupied Rennes and prepared for a possible German counterattack. I/13th was sent south to defend the vital bridge at Messac.

The remainder of the 8th Division moved to Rennes and prepared to defend the city. Various companies of the 28th Infantry were sent out to establish roadblocks to the south and east. According to the plans made back in England, Rennes should have been the site of one of the largest battles in France, but due to the Allied breakout the situation had changed and the city was left to the Americans.

Scattered fighting

On 8 Aug. the 1/28th was attached to the 6th Armored Division and sent to Landivisiau. The guide from the 6th Armored did not arrive to meet them at Huelgoat, so the battalion commander decided to use a local Frenchman to help find a safe route. The Germans had moved back to occupy the main road, so the 1/28th traveled by smaller side roads until it reached Saint-Thégonnec. There contact was made with the 6th Armored and the battalion moved up to Brest to provide an infantry force for the tankers.

The 1/28th attacked, under the direction of the 6th Armored Division, in the area around the Guipavas airport. At first the unit was able to push into the German lines, taking most of the airport and its surrounding defenses. Strong German counterattacks

86

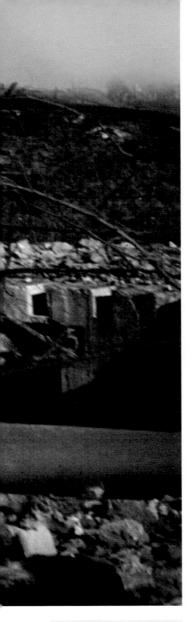

CAP FREHEL TASK FORCE

- 3/28th Infantry Regiment
- One company 644th TD Battalion
- One platoon 709th Tank Battalion.
- One battery 45th FA Battalion.
- D/86th Chemical Mortar Battalion.
- One platoon Antitank Company.
- One platoon 12th Eng. Combat Battalion.
- Detachment, 8th Medical Battalion.
- Detachment, 8th Division Signal Company.

were directed at the small infantry force and it was finally ordered to pull back. The armored commander realized he did not have the troop strength to guard the flanks and the 1/28th was in danger of being cut off. Later, when the 2nd Infantry Division arrived at Brest they would have to fight for some of the same ground that the 1/28th was forced to give up.

The 121st was split from the division and attached to the 83rd Infantry Division for the attack on Saint-Malo. After heavy fighting, the 3rd Battalion was surrounded for four days and would become known as the "Lost Battalion of Dinard." On 15 Aug., after Saint-Malo had fallen, the 121st was sent by truck to rejoin the 8th Division at Brest. On 14 Aug. a small task force was formed from elements of the 28th Infantry. They were sent north to Cap Fréhel to clear a pocket of roughly 300 Germans. A contingent of the FFI had pinned the Germans in their positions, but were not strong enough to capture them.

After the artillery and mortars started an initial barrage the German commander decided to surrender to the Americans. Soon afterwards the entire 28th Infantry was sent to Landerneau to join up for the siege of Brest.

Hill 88

The main portion of the 8th Division reached Brest on the night of 17-18 Aug. It relieved the 6th Armored Division which moved south to Lorient. The 8th Division started to develop the situation by sending out patrols to locate the German defensive lines. On 20 Aug. the 2nd Infantry Division moved in on the left flank. Soon afterwards the 29th Infantry Division arrived to take up a position on the right flank.

While setting up their positions one of the battalion surgeons and nine of his medics wandered too far into German territory and were captured. They were taken to a chateau in Brest where they claimed they were wined and dined to show how well the Germans in the city lived. However, the men all developed a severe case of diarrhea from the food. They were returned to American lines with General Ramcke's compliments, and his comment that he was so well-equipped he did not need the additional medical assistance.

On 21 Aug. the 8th stopped their screening activity outside the city and prepared for the assault. A few small-scale attacks were made to test the German defenses and move forward to better positions. For the most part this fighting was very similar to the hedgerow combat of Normandy, except here the Germans had plenty of time to survey the terrain and dig in. The Germans knew the land very well and could drop their mortars on any suspected American position with deadly accuracy. The veterans of this fight all recalled the kettledrum sound of the German mortars firing. Every major terrain feature, or hedgerow corner, was zeroed in on by the German mortars.

With patrols operating on both sides, there was always a possibility of running into the enemy behind your own lines. Walking back to his company one day, Lt. John O. Gawne was suddenly confronted by a German with an MP40. The German opened fire and, as the machine pistol sprayed back and forth, the bullets miraculously passed to both sides of the American officer who was able to rush his enemy and knock the gun from his hands.

On the night of 24 Aug. both the 13th and 28th Infantry Regiments attempted to infiltrate through the German outposts in preparation for an attack the next day. They were to move up to the creek that runs just south of Gouesnou. The main attack planned for 24 Aug. had been postponed 24 hours due to the shortage of artillery ammunition. At 1300 hrs. on 25 Aug. the attack began and was supported by heavy artillery, plus shelling from the *HMS Warspite* which fired six missions of 50 rounds each. Four fighter-bombers were on alert per division and 32 battalions of artillery supported the whole American line. Even with all this support the Germans were able to hold their positions against the 2nd and 8th Divisions. In the 13th Infantry sector 1/13th on the right was engaged in a bitter fight for the town of Bohars, while 2/13th was caught up in a fight for Hill 88. Both of these areas were stubbornly defended by German paratroopers.

Hill 88, named by the GIs for the number of 88mm guns located there, is just northeast of Keranchosen. It probably didn't have any actual 88's there, but it did have four 105mm antiaircraft guns that were just as deadly against ground targets. The hill looks out over the Penfeld River, which is more the size of a stream at this point. The Americans had to cross 600 yards of open ground, against heavy machine

gun and mortar fire, to get to the German positions. On top of the steep slopes the Germans were well dug in. The fight for Hill 88 took more than 30 hours, during which time the troops of both sides became intermingled and, at times, some of the companies were cut off.

At first both the 1&2/13th were pinned down trying to cross the open ground. One company was unable to get 200 yards past their line of departure. About 1730 that night one platoon was able to cross the Penfeld. They were able to take some of the pressure off their comrades and the rest of the Americans were able to get to the hill about dusk. The left flank of the hill was exposed to German machine gun fire so American casualties could not be evacuated. The entire position was covered with German trenches and emplacements, and the fight for the Hill 88 resembled the trench fighting of the First World War. Grenades were the main weapon;

soldiers were forced to keep hauling sandbags filled with 60 pounds of grenades across the open area and up the hill to keep their comrades supplied.

The first squad to get to the top of the hill was led by S/Sgt. Needham Morris. After numerous German counterattacks Hill 88 was finally in American hands by the night of 26 Aug. On 27 Aug. all of the objectives in the 13th Infantry sector had been captured and the men were told to dig in and hold while the rest of the line moved up. The artillery ammunition shortage prevented another major assault, so until the end of August the men essentially held their ground while sending out numerous combat patrols into no man's land. The 12th Engineers moved up behind the front lines and built a bridge across the Penfeld River so tanks and TDs could be brought up in support.

On 26 Aug. a curious incident was reported by the 13th Infantry. Previously, there had been numerous reports of Germans attempting to enter the American lines dressed as GIs. On this day the 13th Infantry claimed to have killed four Germans dressed in American uniforms. Warnings were sent out to all Allied units in the Brest area to be on their guard. Sightings of Germans in American uniforms increased over the next few weeks, but an official investigation by the 8th Infantry Division Adjutant General's office was unable to find any evidence that this was happening. Curiously, no more mention is made of the supposed four dead Germans and it may be that they were in reality Americans, possibly from a different unit, killed trying to reenter their own lines.

On the left the 2&3/28th Infantry had made slow progress pushing through the hedgerows. On 25 Aug. the 28th was able to move 200 yards past the Penfeld River, and another few hundred yards the next day. The 3/28th had suffered a great

THE GENERAL'S SON

A sad incident occurred while the 8th Division was at Brest. The commanding general's son, Major Harry R. Stroh, was a pilot in the 378th Fighter Squadron flying P-47 fighter-bombers. His unit was one of those assigned to support the fighting at Brest. On 27 August 1944 Major Stroh was flying mission number 206 in the 8th Division area. According to the Stroh family, the assigned target had been hit and the planes still had some ordnance left. They radioed to their ground controller asking if there were any targets of opportunity in the area they could drop their remaining munitions on. General Don Stroh was present and directed the aircraft to strike a small wooded area that one unit had been having some problems with.

The actual facts may never be known. Some feel young Stroh's plane was shot down by German antiaircraft fire from the woods, while his squadron reported that they thought he had flown too low and been struck by a friendly artillery shell. Whatever the cause, Harry Stroh's aircraft was hit and he crashed near Gouesnou. It was not until a few days later that General Stroh was to find out that the plane he directed to that target was flown by his son. A few months later, while fighting in the Hürtgen Forest, the strain would prove too much for Stroh and he would be relieved of command. The official reason given was that he was worn out and needed a rest, but it was clear that he must have been under enormous stress resulting from the loss of his son. Sent home for a rest, his superiors realized what he had been through and allowed him to return to Europe in February 1945 to take command of the 106th Infantry Division.

(Courtesy Stroh family)

89

many casualties, mainly from German artillery and mortar fire, so all three battalions of the 28th were committed to the attack on 27 Aug. in an attempt to make some headway.

Perhaps the most memorable incident to happen to the 8th Division at Brest took place when the 28th Infantry Regiment was trying to push forward to straighten the division lines. According to the regimental history, upon which most other historians have relied, a truce was held in front of the 28th Infantry lines to allow both sides to pull out their wounded and dead. According to the story, the Germans took advantage of this truce to infiltrate some paratroopers behind the American lines. The Americans were supposedly cut off and forced to surrender. Examining the battalion records, and questioning veterans who were there, shows this is not what happened.

The rifle companies of 2/28th were at roughly 2/3 strength when they were ordered to attack south from the Gouesnou-Saint-Renan highway on 25 Aug. The attack that afternoon was stopped

by the German 7th FJR supported by heavy artillery fire. After dark the Americans reorganized and prepared for another attack the next morning. Due to the artillery shortage they would have no artillery support and would be forced to use their 81mm mortars sparingly. On the morning of 26 Aug. companies E&G attacked four separate times, but were pinned down by machine guns firing from Kergroas on their left flank.

By the end of the morning no ground had been gained and the battalion commander was relieved from command. The new commander immediately ordered a fifth attack, supported by a section of three tanks from B/709th Tank Bn. After one tank was knocked out the attack was halted. A sixth attempt was made with the promise of a smoke screen, but due to the ammunition shortage only six smoke rounds were available, and of these only two landed in the correct area. This final attack of the day was also a failure.

On 27 Aug. another attempt was made to push forward, sup-

Above.
Trucks were used to bring the men of the 8th most of the way to Brest, but the infantry was always left with a few miles more to march. Here the 28th Infantry Regiment makes its way past a knocked out German 88mm gun. To most GIs every high velocity German gun was called "an 88."
(National Archives)

Left.
An 8th Infantry Division aid station in a house somewhere north of Brest. The battalion aid station was the first stop for a casualty on their way to a field hospital. An 8th Division patch can be seen on the casualty in the foreground. A paper casualty tag indicating his injury and treatment has been tied to his jacket.
(Courtesy: Strob Family.)

ported by the remaining two Sherman tanks. Under the cover of a heavy morning fog the men started to advance. Suddenly, the lead tank was hit in the turret by a panzerfaust and the crew bailed out. In what would have serious repercussions later on, the Germans were able to retrieve the Sherman and drive it back into their lines.

That afternoon another attack was ordered, under the promise of a heavy artillery barrage. Again, only two rounds impacted in the area, but the order was still given to attack. The attempt was half-hearted and no progress was made. The decision was made to try a night attack. The men had noticed that the Germans kept their emplacements to the sides of the fields next to the hedgerows, generally in the corners. A plan was developed to move two full infantry companies through the center of a field during a dark night. They planned to capture an area to the south of Kergroas, which would deny the Germans observation of the regimental area.

About 0200 hrs. on 29 Aug. both Company E, commanded by Captain Charles Tisdale, and Company G, Commanded by Captain Burke, began to move in single file right down the center of a large field. Captain Burke had just joined the company the day before so he told Lieutenant Rossini, who had previously been commanding the company, to continue to run things while he got acclimated. The men were ordered to keep their rifle safeties on and to use only the bayonet until day-

light. Each man was to pin a patch of white cloth to his back so he could be easily followed in the dark. Both companies were to move to their objectives behind the German lines and dig in for an all-around defense. Company F would follow them later at dawn to clear any Germans that had been bypassed.

During the briefing Lt. Rossini informed the battalion commander that all of the bazookas in Company E had been lost. Captain Tisdale pointed out that he had only two bazookas with six rounds total in Company G. A request to transfer bazookas and ammo from Company F (in reserve) was refused. At this time all of the 28th Infantry rifle companies were on the line, except for F/28th which served as the regimental reserve. The 3rd Battalion was to the left and the 1st Battalion was on the right flank. These other battalions were to also attempt night attacks.

Both E&G Companies infiltrated to their positions with only one casualty. At 0215 hrs. a German machine gun fired out across the field wounding one man. He did not cry out, and the infiltration continued until all were in position. A gentle rain helped mask the sounds of their movement. About half way to their objective a group of three Germans walked into a man from Company G. Five shots were fired resulting in two Germans killed and one wounded. By this time the fighting to the left and right of the area, caused by the attacks of the 1st and 3rd Battalions,

MAJOR GENERAL DONALD STROH

The commander of the 8th Infantry Division graduated from Michigan Agricultural College in 1915 and was commissioned in the Army in 1917. He served with the 17th Cavalry in Arizona and Hawaii, then transferred to the infantry in 1920. At the start of WW2 he was an intelligence officer and attended the British Army Intelligence School. In 1942 he was made the assistant division commander of the 9th Infantry Division and served with that unit in Tunisia and Sicily.

Later, in France, the 8th Division did not make an impressive entry into combat and within a few days many of the senior commanders were replaced. Stroh assumed command on 11 July 1944, and led the division until he was sent home for

a rest in December 1944. Normally, being sent back to the States was the end of an officer's career, but Stroh was soon returned to Europe where he was given command of the 106th Infantry Division and helped rebuild this unit that had been shattered in the Ardennes.

Commander of the 8th Infantry Division Donald Stroh was promoted to major general outside Brest on 30 August 1944. General Troy Middleton is shown here pinning on the second stars. In Stroh's personal photo album he modestly captioned this photo: *"You only have to live long enough..."*
(National Archives)

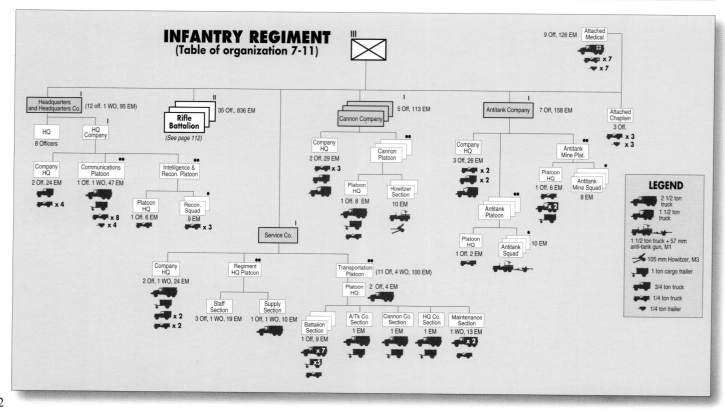

Above.
Two mademoiselles observe a group of soldiers getting directions in late August 1944. A censor has tried to obscure the patch on the MP at right, but it is clearly an 8th Division patch on his M43 field jacket. The GI with his back to the camera carries a private purchase hunting knife on his belt, as well as a captured German Luger holster.
(National Archives)

Left.
At a typical Breton crossroads, Lt. Frank Orville Gray is shown with his camera hanging from his belt. Lt. Gray documented 2/28th with his photographs, many in color, from Northern Ireland through Brittany. At Brest he commanded Company F, but was unable to break through and relieve the surrounded E&G companies at Kergroas.
(Courtesy Frank Orville Gray)

was drawing the attention of the German defenders.

At 0545 hrs. G Company called in on their SCR-300 radio saying they were in position. At 0630 Company E also reported they were ready. About this time four more Germans wandered into the G Company area and started to speak to one of the Americans digging in. Once they realized they were talking to Americans a furious grenade battle began. This quickly escalated as more Germans arrived on the scene. By 0800 hrs. three separate German attacks had been repulsed, but the Americans discovered that one of their bazookas, and two rounds for it, had been lost.

The area that E&G were in was relatively small and the men were dug in in small groups. The two company command posts were on opposite sides of a hedgerow, so that when Lt. Rossini's radio went out he was close enough to yell directions for

Below.
Sgt. Maurice Tidball, the communications sergeant of F/28th, is seen here with the main communications equipment used in a rifle company. He holds the handset of the battery operated EE-8 field telephone (in leather case). In front of him is a DR-8 reel of telephone wire with a sound powered telephone (the TS-10 handset) clipped to the reel.
(Courtesy Frank Orville Gray)

artillery support over to Captain Tisdale, who relayed them on his set. About 08 30hrs. the Germans turned three armored vehicles (including the one captured the day before) against the cut off Americans. No artillery support was available, but a few American tank destroyers were able to fire on the area. The German tanks were concealed by heavy foliage, but Rossini and Tisdale were able to relay instructions over the sole working radio to direct their fire. After 11 rounds two of the German tanks were knocked out, leaving only the captured Sherman.

Suddenly the two officers were told that they could get no more support from the tank destroyers, as it was considered wasteful of their ammo to fire at unobserved targets.

This message was sent in the clear (uncoded) so nearby German radiomen listening in discovered the cut off Americans would get no more help. Later on, after being taken prisoner, Tisdale personally witnessed the Germans listening to American transmissions at their command post.

The captured Sherman then entered the American position. The remaining four bazooka rockets were fired at the tank. Two missed, while the other two were glancing hits that drove the tank from the field. When Captain Tisdale informed the battalion of the tank, they asked over the radio how many rounds of bazooka ammunition he had left. His answer, "zero," was also intercepted by the German radiomen, and the Germans brought the Sherman back into the American position.

A few men tried to knock out the captured Sherman. Pfc. Willard Jones and Sgt. Walker jumped out of their foxholes and climbed onto the tank. Jones pounded on the hatches with a grenade trying to find a way to toss one inside, until German machine gun fire sprayed the tank and wounded him. Walker actually shimmied out on the tank barrel to stuff a grenade down the muzzle. Just as he got near the end of the tube the main gun fired and the concussion stunned him and knocked him off.

A report from 2nd Battalion HQ claimed that a patrol from

Members of the 8th Division MP platoon receive instructions from the Division Provost Marshal. The bands on their helmets would have been painted yellow to indicate divisional level MPs. In the jeep can be seen a Thompson sub machinegun with magazines taped together for quick reloading.
(National Archives)

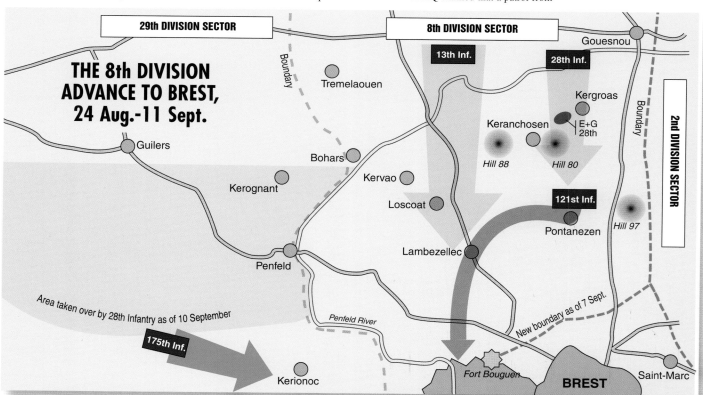

THE 8th DIVISION ADVANCE TO BREST, 24 Aug.-11 Sept.

29th DIVISION SECTOR

8th DIVISION SECTOR

2nd DIVISION SECTOR

Gouesnou

Boundary

13th Inf.

28th Inf.

Tremelaouen

Kergroas

Keranchosen

E+G 28th

Boundary

Hill 88

Hill 80

Guilers

Bohars

Kervao

121st Inf.

Kerognant

Loscoat

Hill 97

Pontanezen

Lambezellec

Area taken over by 28th Infantry as of 10 September

Penfeld

Penfeld River

New boundary as of 7 Sept.

175th Inf.

Kerionoc

Fort Bouguen

BREST

Saint-Marc

This infantryman of the 8th Infantry Division wears his M41 field jacket inside out because the inner dark wool lining provides far better concealment than the light colored cotton outside. He carries the standard equipment of the GI: ammo belt, M-28 haversack, canteen, and entrenching tool. A first aid pouch containing a bandage and sulfanilamide powder (to prevent the wound from becoming infected) would be on the back of his belt. A dark green (olive drab shade number 7) gas mask carrier is slung on his left hip. This darker color was adopted by the U.S. Army in 1943 and began to show up in the front lines by September 1944. The gas mask would often be thrown away or left with the unit baggage, and the bag used to carry personnel items. He also wears a blue civilian neckerchief to keep the wool collar from chafing against his neck.
(Reconstruction by Militaria Magazine)

An antiaircraft emplacement near Bohars known as Battery de Rochglas. This position was manned by the 4th battery of the German 805th Naval Antiaircraft Artillery Bn. with 75mm guns, this was typical of the antiaircraft positions around Brest, the emplacement was eventually captured by 13th Infantry.
(National Archives)

Company F with bazookas had been sent to assist, but it was over 1,000 yards away. The remnants of Company G were pulled back to join Company E in another field. Just as a frantic request for artillery support was made, a German squad armed with machine pistols surprised the combined command post and captured the two officers and only the working radio. It was now about 1200 hrs., and the requested artillery fire began to land in the area. By chance, the concentration of 155mm rounds landed 75 yards short and heavily damaged the German command post that had been intercepting the American transmissions.

At 1218 hrs. battalion headquarters reported that they had lost radio contact with both of the companies. As the Americans were herded together, Pfc. Jones turned to Tisdale with tears streaking down his face and said, *"I tried Captain, I really tried, but I just could not knock out that tank."* Both Sgt. Walker and Pfc. Jones would later be awarded the Silver Star for their efforts.

At 1245 hrs. men from the 28th Regimental Intelligence and Reconnaissance Platoon reported that they could see a large group of Americans being marched down the road towards Brest. An artillery observer reported this on the corps radio net so that no artillery units in the area would mistake them for Germans and start shelling. The loss of the two companies left a weak spot in the American lines and the Germans attempted to break through it. Every soldier from the 2nd Battalion, including the cooks, was called up to man the defenses. With assistance from A/28th and the 2nd Battalion A&P Platoon the lines were held and the German attack was driven off. The lost companies were soon reconstituted from 247 rushed up green replacements. The few experienced officers and NCOs remaining in the 2nd Battalion were shuffled around to try and get a mix of experienced men in all companies.

For cutting off the American penetration and capturing what was claimed to be close to 500 Americans, Major Reino Hamer, commander of the First Battalion, 7th FJ Regiment, would receive the Knight's Cross. There are claims that the Germans purposely hid in their foxholes, allowing the Americans to pass them by, then cut them off. The evidence does not support this, and both veterans' memories and official records support the fact that the Americans had successfully infiltrated the German lines at night and were cut off when Company F was not allowed to put its full strength into the follow-up. The problem was that Company F, under command of Captain Frank Gray, was the only company the entire regiment had in reserve. Captain Gray was only allowed to move forward with his 3rd platoon, commanded by Lt. Jonekait, which became stuck in the town of Kergroas. The Germans were defending in buildings with thick stone walls, with deep trenches around them. Afterwards, Gray stated that if he had been allowed to use his entire company he would have been able to break through.

The story of the truce actually comes from the 3rd Battalion sector. On the same night as the 2nd Battalion infiltration, the 3rd Battalion had also been attempting a night attack, but ran into a minefield. After the first man tripped a mine the Germans were alerted and opened up. The 3/28th was driven back, leaving a number of wounded and dead in front of the German lines. At roughly 1015 hrs. the commander of K/28th, Capt. Clarence Hollingsworth, called back to battalion headquarters saying that two German medics had come forward, accompanied by a wounded American, to say that there were a number of casualties lying between the lines. They asked for a truce to allow both sides to remove the dead and wounded. The offer was accepted by the battalion commander and the three aid men attached to K/28th, went out to recover their wounded. They reported that the German medics were helpful in pointing out where the Americans lay.

The terms of the truce were that there was to be no firing in the battalion area. At 1105 hrs. a few small German mortars from outside the area began to shell Company K. His aid men were still working between the lines, so Hollingsworth sent one of the German medics to stop the mortars. As soon as the German reached the mortar position the firing stopped. Before the truce ended the German medics returned to say they had been ordered to bring back the American casualty that had

THE FATE OF CAPTAIN TISDALE

The story of Captain Tisdale and the two rifle companies did not end with their capture. They were marched through Brest and taken by boat to a small fishing village on the Crozon Peninsula. Although the village of Le Fou was supposed to be where casualties and POWs were held, period documents claim the men were actually held at nearby Rostellac. Food was terrible there and consisted mainly of horsemeat, sugar beet tops, and rough brown bread. As much as the men complained about it, it was the same food the Germans ate. In the POW camp a French barber was allowed to visit the Americans to cut their hair. Security was lax and the barber agreed, for the right amount of money, to help a few men get back to the American lines.

The records of the 174th Field Artillery Group on the Daoulas Peninsula report that one boatload of four escaped Americans arrived on 13 Sept. A second boat arrived the next day and two boatloads on the 15th. These men were able to provide some valuable intelligence about the locations of German supply routes and an ammo dump on the Ile Longue.

The Germans sent a few English speaking naval officers to interrogate the Americans in the POW camp. At first they tried to subtly find out where the men had been before Brest by asking how the region compared to various parts of England. Finally one of the German officers broke down and asked in desperation, "*Where did you hide your parachutes?*" Since no German outposts had spotted such a large number of men moving through their positions, it had been assumed they had to be paratroops dropped behind the lines.

In the final stages of the fighting on the Crozon, the elderly guards at the POW camp (some of them armed with WW1 French caval-

These maps of the incident south of Kergroas on 29 Aug. 1944 were drawn just after the war by captain Tisdale.

ry carbines) fled the area. Nearby was a small peninsula holding a well-fortified position (thought to be the Ile Longue) which held a few coastal artillery guns and seemed well-defended. The lax security allowed a few of the American POWs to wander up to it. They were sent back by the German commandant with orders to "*send up their CO.*" Captain Tisdale walked up to the fort and was accosted by the English speaking German officer who wanted know "*what the hell was he doing, sending men up there without weapons.*" Tisdale immediately realized the officer thought they were the advance party of the American forces fighting up the Crozon. Tisdale asked the German if he was ready to surrender his position, and the German told him that they were well-supplied and prepared to hold out for a while longer.

The fort had been bombed the day before with jellied gasoline. Noticing that the German officer was injured and quite leery of some American aircraft in the sky, Tisdale looked at his watch and said, "*Well, if you're not going to give up you'd better get back under cover.*" The thought of another air attack was too much for the German, who then agreed to give up. He took his men back into the fort, destroyed their weapons, and marched his men out to surrender.

At the same time Col. Rudder and the 2nd Ranger Bn. was moving up to assault the position. The Rangers, prepared for a tough fight, were greeted by their opponents lined up and already marching out as prisoners. Captain Burke spotted Rudder, broke into a run, and tackled him with a big bear hug. They had been roommates at Texas A&M University before the war. Back at the 28th Regiment E&G Companies had already been reformed, so Captain Tisdale and some of his men were sent to Company L, which had taken a beating in the Crozon fighting and was in desperate need of officers and men.

8th INFANTRY DIVISION "PATHFINDERS"

The 8th Division arrived too late in France to see combat in WW1. The arrow on the patch denotes the compass used by early explorers of America. After training in Northern Ireland the 8th arrived in France on 4 July 1944.

Taking part in the breakout, it crossed the Ay River and moved south to Rennes, then out to Brest. After a brief period in Luxembourg the 8th fought in the Hürtgen Forest and crossed the Roer River in February 1945.

Reaching the Rhine in March, the 8th helped clear the Ruhr pocket, then crossed the Elbe to end the war at Schwerin.

8th Infantry Division (*Granite*)
● 13th Infantry Regt. (*Greyhound*)
● 28th Infantry Regt (*Grasshopper*)
● 121st Infantry Regt (*Grapefruit*)

Division Artillery (*Grindstone*)
● 28th Field Artillery Bn. (*Gunshot*)
● 43rd Field Artillery Bn. (*Gopher*)

● 45th Field Artillery Bn. (*Greenback*)
● 56th Field Artillery Bn. (*Goldenrod*)

8th Division Special Troops
● 8th Recon Troop (*Gypsy*)
● 8th Medical Bn. (*Guillotine*)
● 8th Quartermaster Bn. (*Gobbler*)
● 8th Signal Co. (*Goat*)
● 12th Engineer Combat Bn. (*Gondola*)
● 708th Ordnance Co. (*Govener*)

Attached
● 709th Tank Bn. (*Healthy*)
● 644th Tank Destroyer Bn. (*Hazard*)
● 445th AAA Bn. (*Mayfair 445*)

come with them, as he was technically their prisoner. Hollingsworth refused.

A few minor attempts by the Germans to take advantage of the truce were noted. Two Germans removed some ammunition from a nearby knocked out American tank. Another German soldier left his dugout and retrieved a machine gun that had been dropped in the open. A German naval officer walked out between the lines, probably to examine the terrain. There is no evidence in the battalion or regimental records that this truce was used by the Germans to capture E&G/28th.

The only effect the truce may have had on the fate of the two companies was that it prevented the 3rd Battalion from attacking in support of them. However, in the 3rd Battalion records there is no mention of any request for such help, or that they felt under pressure to come to the aid of the two companies. It was the 1st Battalion, on the right, that had attacked forward towards E&G, but had been stopped by strong German defenses. The regimental records state, *"Conflicting reports regarding enemy patrols and infiltrations were received throughout the day, none of them were confirmed."* Most of these were probably Germans attempting to move into the vacated E&G company positions.

A 3/4 ton truck from the 8th Division Signal Company lays telephone wire through Gouesnou. The "caution, left hand drive" painted on the rear of the truck is a reminder of the unit's time spent in Northern Ireland, before the invasion, where traffic drove on the left side of the road. The sign at left indicates the main supply route (MSR) of the 8th Division.
(National Archives)

Below, left.
The Company F, 28th Infantry Regiment command post somewhere in France. It shows a typical CP set up in a hurry, wherever a convenient location could be found. All that made it special was a few maps, some bedrolls, and a 5-gallon can of water. If the unit was going to stay in the area then foxholes would be dug and a telephone line run to the battalion HQ.
(Courtesy Frank Orville Gray)

PFC. ERNEST W. PRUSSMAN, MEDAL OF HONOR CITATION

13th Infantry Regiment, 8th Infantry Division
"For conspicuous gallantry and intrepidity at risk of life above and beyond the call of duty on 8 September 1944, near Les Coates, Brittany, France. When the advance of the flank companies of 2 battalions was halted by intense enemy mortar, machine gun, and sniper fire from a fortified position on his left, Pfc. Prussman maneuvered his squad to assault the enemy fortifications. Hurdling a hedgerow, he came upon 2 enemy riflemen whom he disarmed. After leading his squad across an open field to the next hedgerow, he advanced to a machine gun position, destroyed the gun, and captured its crew and 2 riflemen. Again advancing ahead of his squad in the assault, he was mortally wounded by an enemy rifleman, but as he fell to the ground he threw a hand grenade, killing his opponent. His superb leadership and heroic action at the cost of his life so demoralized the enemy that resistance at this point collapsed, permitting the two battalions to continue their advance."

The American Army always had problems with French and Breton names. Although the official citation places Prussman's actions at Les Coates, it was in fact at Loscoat, which is just north of Lambezellec.

In the division command post the S-2 (intelligence) officer Lt. Col. Joseph Gibson, points out the German positions on the situation map to General Stroh. Behind Stroh is the division artillery commander, General Pickering. The 8th Division chief of staff Col. Tom Cross observes from left (in raincoat).
(National Archives)

Bottom.
The 8th Division command post, somewhere in Normandy, with the divisional switchboard set up under a camouflage net. Col. Tom Cross (Division Chief of Staff - seated right) goes over the situation. Col. Cross took command of the 121st Infantry Regiment later in the Hürtgen Forest.
(National Archives)

Bottom right.
At an observation post north of Brest Pvt. M. Von Nes, of the 1/13th Infantry, entertains his headquarters over the radio. The soldier at right wears a commonly seen variation of the 8th Division patch with the top cut straight across rather than curved.
(National Archives)

For some reason the truce would be used to explain how two companies could be captured. An order was issued from the division commander that no more truces would be allowed unless he approved them. It was probably easier to blame the capture on Germans using a truce, than on the failure of the rest of the regiment to break through to them, or the lack of artillery support.

Col. Bailey, the 2nd Battalion commander, was relieved that morning. He was replaced by Col. Buckley. The next day the 28th Infantry Regiment commander, Col. K.S. Anderson was replaced by Col. Merrit E. Olmstead. It should also be noted that Captain Hollingsworth was considered a superb officer and would rise to the rank of lt. col. before being killed near the end of the war. He would not have fallen for a German ruse.

It was not until November 1944 that the official Adjutant General's report on the matter would conclude that the truce had no bearing on the capture of the two companies.

Although the official document requests that the unit records be corrected to reflect this, it was never done and the incorrect story was entered in the history books.

In front of Brest

On 1 Sept. the 121st Infantry launched a limited attack on the Fourneuf Ridge. This was in conjunction with an attack on the left flank by the 2nd Infantry Division. The town of Kergroas was shelled with 600 rounds of 81mm mortars, 1,600 rounds from 60mm mortars, and 400 rounds of white phosphorus from 4.2" mortars. Afterwards I/121st was able to occupy what was left of Kergroas without much trouble.

Supporting fire from the 13th Infantry enabled the 121st to make a moderate advance, but two hills (80 and 97) remained in German hands, preventing further advances. The next day both the 121st and the 9th Infantry (2nd Division) again worked as a team to force their way onto Hill 80 which dominated the 121st sector. The 121st recaptured an American Sherman tank that the Germans were using, possibly the one involved with the capture of E&G/28th. When the German crew was pulled from the tank one of them was wearing an American uniform. Later in the day another captured American tank was discovered as the division moved forward. Five men were injured when they set off a booby trap hidden inside.

At another point Sgt. Floyd Taylor was severely wounded while trying to cross

a gap in a hedgerow. He had been trying to find a better position to set up his gun, but it had been shot out of his hands. Rather than move back to find an aid man, Taylor crawled up to the German position with a handful of fragmentation grenades and knocked out the German machine gun nest that was holding up his unit, and that had wounded him. Taylor would later be awarded the DSC for this action. It was this kind of individual effort that allowed the Americans to move forward.

By noon the 121st had again moved on Hill 80, but were soon driven off by heavy artillery fire. On the night of 2-3 Sept. the Americans discovered the Germans had withdrawn to a new defensive line. A patrol, led by Lt. Joe Stalcup, took up positions on Hill 80. At daybreak they found themselves about to be attacked by American fighter-bombers who had not been told of the advance. They pulled off their shirts and waved furiously to get the attention of the aircraft, which broke off the attack at the last minute. Taking this hill allowed the 9th Infantry on the left flank to move their line up even with the 121st. Due to the shortage in artillery ammunition, continuing the attack was out of the question. The division sat in place for the next four days, but continued to send out patrols to determine where the new German lines were.

The new German position was on the Lambezellec Ridge line running parallel to the front. Patrols indicated the ridge line was heavily defended by the Germans. In front of the ridge was a small stream that the Americans would have to cross, and it was assumed that the Germans had the area covered with heavy machine gun and mortar fire. The cannon company of the 13th Infantry was given an eight tube rocket launcher to test, but the results were not very good and the rockets were returned to an ordnance unit. Loudspeakers were set up in the area to broadcast propaganda material to the Germans, but the effort did not result in many surrenders.

On 5 Sept. the 13th Infantry was strafed by American P–38's. There were claims that another unit behind them had put out their aerial recognition panels, confusing the pilots as to the actual front line. This happened a number of times in the battle. Units that had been attacked by their own aircraft became so afraid of it happening again they put out their marker panels, not realizing that the pilots would assume they were marking the front line and anyone to their front was the enemy.

The best area for the 8th Division to attack was in the 121st sector, so plans were made to once again work in conjunction with the 2nd Division on their left flank. An attack was made on 8 Sept. to capture the towns of Mesmerrien and Pontanezen. It was hoped that with these two towns in American hands the 8th Division could turn to the west and move down the Lambezellec Ridge, without having to attack straight into the German defenses in front of the 13th Infantry. On the right the 13th Infantry advanced a short ways to the last high ground before the ridge. This would allow it to support the 121st when that regiment turned to the west.

The two regiments jumped off in the morning and, after a twenty minute artillery bombardment, initially made good progress. The 38th Infantry on the left flank also attacked to add more pressure to the German lines. The 13th Infantry captured its initial objective in only 12 minutes. Heavy mortar fire delayed the 1/13th until the mortars of 2/13th came to their aid. In the afternoon 1/121st captured the Pontanezen Barracks. This was an odd kind of homecoming, as the 121st had been stationed at these barracks back in Sept. 1918.

By evening both battalions of the 13th Infantry had taken their objectives. The 121st advanced slowly, using flamethrowers to knock out strongpoints. In the 1st Battalion sector one soldier had pounded on the side of a tank with a rock to get the crew's attention, then directed them to fire upon the positions holding up his men. Under cover of a smoke screen the 121st moved forward and by midnight had captured their objective on the ridge. The 2nd Division was still slightly behind the 121st

to the left flank, so General Stroh (CG 8th Division) placed the 1/121st in the gap between the two divisions. They would cover the flank until the 2nd Division moved up, and make sure the Germans did not try to push into the divisional boundary.

On 9 Sept. the 13th Infantry attempted to pin down the Germans on the ridge, as the 121st started to roll up their flank. Again using smoke to cover the assault the 121st moved west to Lambezellec in only two hours. As the 121st continued to press the attack the 13th Infantry moved forward to within only a few hundred yards of the Penfeld River. The 8th was now in sight of the Brest city wall.

The next day, 10 Sept., the 13th Infantry moved forward clearing out all German positions in its sector. The 121st assaulted the city wall at Fort Bouguen with two battalions. By 1000 hrs. the 121st had advanced to the fortress moat, but were forced to withdraw under heavy artillery bombardment. Another assault against the fort was planned for the afternoon, but at the last minute was canceled because the officers realized they needed more support for such a mission.

Fort Bouguen was one of the old 17th century forts ringing Brest. The stone wall was between 25 and 35 feet thick. Outside the fort the moat was 20 feet deep. The western edge of the fort rested on the Penfeld River, with a steep cliff between the river and wall. The fort had only one small entrance which passed through two tunnels and over two bridges. A patrol from I/121st managed to get into the moat. However, for every grenade they tossed over the wall the Germans threw back four and the Americans were forced to withdraw.

Stroh knew that such a fortification could not be taken without strong engineer support, or by shelling the wall with heavy artillery. For this reason the assault was suspended until the artillery had time to target the fortress. Both 8" and 155mm guns fired directly on the wall and knocked enough rubble down into the moat to allow small parties of infantry to cross, but it was decided that assaulting the fort was not worthwhile and the attack was postponed until the Americans had a better advantage.

On the night of 10 Sept. the 28th Infantry (less 2/28th) was pulled from the reserve and sent to the right flank to relieve three battalions of the 29th Division. 2/28th remained behind as division reserve. Again, Stroh was being careful to make sure the boundary where his division tied into a neighbor's was firmly held. He thought Ramcke might attempt to split the Americans by attacking at the weak point where two divisions came together.

Back at Fort Bouguen the shelling by heavy artillery did little damage to the fortress walls. One GI later wrote, "*I watched the attack from atop Lambezellec Ridge. The artillery boys certainly showed guts on that day. They would move their pieces right into the open and fire away. They tossed in everything they had, but couldn't put a dent in the walls. The shells bounced off the walls like steel balls bouncing on a marble floor.*"

Middleton decided that he would hold the line in front of the fort and attempt to penetrate the city defenses to the east in the 2nd Division sector. On the night of 11-12 Sept. he withdrew most of the 8th Division from the front lines by shifting elements of the 2nd Division to the west. Both the 13th and 121st Regiments were relieved by the 9th Infantry (2nd Div.) and pulled back to a rest area at Plouvien to reorganize. The 28th Infantry was left holding their sector of the line until the 29th Division could advance. During the evening of 11 Sept. 2/28th was sent off to form a reserve for Task Force A on the Crozon. They were only to be committed to action in the event of an emergency, such as the Germans attempting to break out of the Crozon. Eventually the 29th Division advanced to the point where the rest of the 28th Infantry could be released, and all three regiments of the 8th Division were sent south to capture the Crozon Peninsula.

Pontanezen Barracks as they were found when captured by the 121st Infantry Regiment. In the years since WW1 the size of the barracks complex had drastically shrunk. Many of the buildings were destroyed during the siege, leaving only a fraction of what had been there in 1919. Note the aerial recognition panels laid out in the field to prevent attack by friendly aircraft. This view of the barracks shows the burnt buildings in the center, and the holes in the roofs from artillery shells. After WW1 the open area surrounding these buildings was covered with temporary wooden structures.
(National Archives)

Below.
On his initial inspection visit to Brest, General Simpson, the Ninth Army commander (at left) is seen checking the maps with General Troy Middleton (center) and General Donald Stroh (at right). This photo was taken on 6 Sept. 1944.
(National Archives)

Chapter 11

THE 29TH INFANTRY DIVISION

Men from the 29th Division take a break somewhere in the city of Brest. They all wear full M-1928 packs, which indicates that this was probably taken after the city was captured, but before the unit was pulled out to the countryside to rest and reorganize. Typically soldiers fighting in the city carried only what they needed, because they knew they would not move very far from their company supply point, and carrying heavy packs was particularly difficult in the debris clogged buildings.
(National Archives)

The 29th Infantry Division is best known for its bloody assault on Omaha Beach. After landing in Normandy the 29th moved south through thick hedgerow country to capture the vital road junction at Saint-Lô. In late August the division had been moved out to Brittany, where it would take on the challenge of holding the far right flank of the American lines outside Brest. By this time there were only a few veterans of D-day left in the unit, but casualties from the invasion and the early fighting in Normandy were starting to return from hospitals.

The 29th was put into the line outside Brest, roughly four miles north of the city, on 24 Aug. They took up a position along the railroad tracks which ran from just north of Bohars west to Saint-Renan. The right flank of the American VIIIth Corps, facing the Atlantic Ocean, would be wide open to German infiltration from Le Conquet until enough troops were available to tie it into the coastline. On the morning of 25 Aug. "Task Force Sugar" (TFS) was formed and given the mission

of guarding this right flank and reducing the German garrisons to the west. TFS, composed of units from the 29th Division, two Ranger battalions, and some corps troops, would operate as an independent unit until they had reached their objective.

Initially the 116th Infantry Regiment, which had been in the first waves of the Normandy landing, was assigned to the eastern half of the 29th line with the 115th Infantry to their west. The 175th was initially given the task of guarding the open right flank of the 29th Division and serving as the divisional reserve. On the afternoon of 25 Aug. the 115th and 116th moved forward into the German lines. Small pockets of German defenders were dug into carefully camouflaged positions and the advance was very slow. By the end of the first day the 115th was still in the vicinity of Tremelaouen and the 116th had advanced only to Kerionoc.

An emotional incident occurred on 26 Aug. in the 115th sector, just next to the Kerespern farm (in Bohars) when a patrol of 10 men from L/115th was cut down by machine gun fire as they were halfway across a field. Repeated attempts to get to the wounded men were repulsed by strong German fire. A sergeant dropped all of his equipment and put on a red cross armband, but was shot by the Germans when he ventured forth into the field. It seemed that further attempts to get to the casualties would only result in more men getting hit. Finally, one of the wounded men, Corporal George Clayton, shot himself

with his own weapon rather than see his friends get hit trying to rescue him. The bodies of the 10 men would lie in the field for days as a reminder that this was the edge of the German main line of resistance.

In the 116th sector the troops ran up against a strongpoint at Keriolet. A/116th, which had been the first unit of the division to land on Omaha Beach, was down to only 60 men. The 3rd platoon was composed of only nine men. This company was the closest to the strongpoint so they were given the task of attacking it. The company commander, Lt. Wilbur McCormick, took a look at the German emplacements and said, "*I'll try it.*"

Charging across the open fields many of the soldiers were cut down, but the 1st platoon, under command of Lt. Orman Kimborough, was able to move up to the fortifications and into a German communications trench. The defenders took to their bunkers and called in their own artillery to drive the Americans off. Kimborough was able to bring up the 2nd platoon and took 43 prisoners (all from the 6th Bn. 3rd Naval AA Brigade). Unfortunately, B&C/116th did not get the word to move up and remained in their starting positions.

By this time Company A was worn out, and consisted of only 12 men. Lt. McCormick had injured his knee and had to crawl back. His men pulled back to the American lines, leaving a gap in the 1st Battalion frontage. Major James Morris, the 1st Battalion commander, hastily put together a blocking force and called for artillery fire. Inside the strongpoint the situation had changed and Lt. Kimborough and seven men (six

Shown here with General Gerhardt is Lt. General William H. Simpson, commander of the Ninth Army. When the Ninth Army was activated, it took command of the VIIIth Corps. One of the first things Simpson did was make an inspection tour of all the units in his new command.
(*National Archives*)

A telephone switchboard has been placed in a deep trench for protection from the German artillery. American radios were good, but the majority of messages were sent along telephone lines. The naming of the soldier's rifle "Cry Baby" was relatively unusual in WW2. A number of men from the 115th Infantry had painted their weapons in this way while crossing the channel for D-day. It is possible that this is when this soldier painted his weapon.
(*National Archives*)

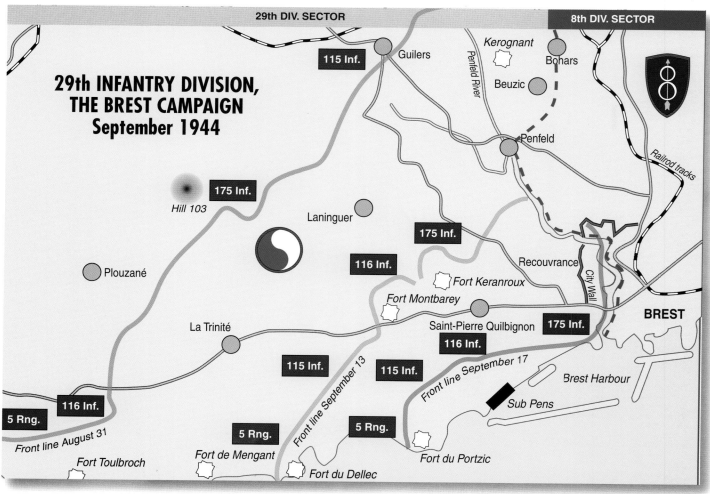

115 Inf.

Kerognant

Bohars

Beuzic

Penfeld River

29th INFANTRY DIVISION, THE BREST CAMPAIGN
September 1944

Penfeld

Railrod tracks

175 Inf.

Hill 103

Laninguer

175 Inf.

116 Inf.

Recouvrance

City Wall

Plouzané

Fort Keranroux

Fort Montbarey

La Trinité

Saint-Pierre Quilbignon

175 Inf.

BREST

116 Inf.

115 Inf.

115 Inf.

Front line September 17

Brest Harbour

116 Inf.

Front line September 13

Sub Pens

5 Rng.

5 Rng.

5 Rng.

Front line August 31

Fort du Portzic

Fort Toulbroch

Fort de Mengant

Fort du Dellec

104

Previous page, top. **After eating little else but K-rations continually from June through September, these soldiers have decided to take matters into their own hands and cook a bird for dinner. Officially this was frowned upon, but soldiers always tried to add some variety to their diet whenever possible. Note that these 29th men all wear their chin straps in the manner ordered by General Gerhardt.**
(National Archives)

Right. **Fort Penfeld was finally captured by the 1/115th.**

Inset. **One of the field expedients tried by the 29th was attaching a 60mm mortar shell to the base of a rifle grenade. The men liked this as it gave them much more firepower on the front lines, but the Ordnance corps was concerned that the mortar round could explode when fired.**
(National Archives)

Bottom. **The Keriolet strongpoint was initially captured by Company A of the 116th Infantry Regiment. Unfortunately, poor communication prevented the rest of the battalion from moving up to support them and the position was retaken by a German counterattack.**

SHERWOOD HALLMAN, MEDAL OF HONOR

S/Sgt. Sherwood H. Hallman
175th Infantry, 29th Infantry Division
Citation reads: "For conspicuous gallantry and intrepidity at risk of his life above and beyond the call of duty. On 13 September 1944, in Brittany, France, the 2nd Battalion in its attack on the fortified city of Brest was held up by a strongly defended enemy position which had prevented its advance despite repeated attacks extending over a 3-day period. Finally, Company F advanced to within several hundred yards of the enemy position, but was again halted by intense fire. Realizing that the position must be neutralized without delay, S/Sgt. Hallman ordered his squad to cover his movements with fire while he advanced alone to a point from which he could make the assault. Without hesitating, S/Sgt. Hallman leaped over a hedgerow into a sunken road, the central point of the German defenses which was known to contain an enemy machine gun position and at least 30 enemy

riflemen. Firing his carbine and hurling grenades, S/Sgt. Hallman, unassisted, killed or wounded four of the enemy, then ordered the remainder to surrender. Immediately, 12 of the enemy surrendered and the position was shortly secured by the remainder of his company. Seeing the surrender of this position, about 75 of the enemy in the vicinity surrendered, yielding a defensive organization which the battalion with heavy supporting fires had been unable to take. This single heroic act on the part of S/Sgt. Hallman resulted in the immediate advance of the entire battalion for a distance of 2,000 yards to a position from which Fort Keranroux was captured later the same day. S/Sgt. Hallman's fighting determination and intrepidity in battle exemplify the highest tradition of the U.S. Armed Forces."

According to veterans of the 29th Division and local French historian Yannick Creach, there are a few errors in the official Hallman citation. In fact, Hallman carried a BAR and not a carbine, and he performed his heroic actions a day earlier than stated in the citation, on 12 Sept. on the Ilioc Farm, midway between Hill 103 and Fort Keranroux. S/Sgt. Hallman was killed two days later on 14 Sept. 1944.

Top.
The Medal of Honor awarded to Staff Sergeant Hallman.

Right.
Pfc. Sherwood H. Hallman, F/175th Infantry, 2nd Platoon.

Left.
March 1943, Sherwood and Virginia Hallman at Fort Mc Clellan, Alabama. *(Courtesy Y. Creach)*

---

of them wounded) were captured. Kimborough and two of the men were able to escape from their guards during an artillery attack. They hid in French homes until finally making their way back to their own lines a few days later. During his captivity Kimborough learned there were 200 Germans in the strongpoint and another 200 just outside it. The following day the 116th was pulled out of the area and relieved by the 115th Infantry. The Americans were held up by the emplacement, which they had come so close to capturing, for another ten days.

Hill 103

The 175th was swung around the right flank on 26 Aug. in a move against the high ground of Hill 103. This hill provided an excellent view of the area west of Brest and control of it was considered essential to any attack on Brest from that direction. An aggressive assault of the 175th against Hill 103 was brought to a stop by German antiaircraft guns operating as artillery. The Germans were well dug in on Hill 103 with plenty of barbed wire entanglements, well-positioned emplacements, and foxholes. A stone quarry at the top of the hill provided a concealed area to protect the German troops.

On the morning of 27 Aug. the 2/175th captured the town of Plouzané, just to the west of Hill 103. Even with armor support from the 709th Tank Bn. their advance remained slow. The 29th continued to work forward field by field in the same type of hedgerow fighting they had learned in Normandy. The 175th inched forward until 29 Aug. when they had almost closed a ring around Hill 103. That night a patrol from A/175th blew

a hole in the barbed wire with pole charges. This allowed the 1/175th to advance the next morning onto the hill itself.

The Germans withdrew to positions on the eastern half of Hill 103 and the 175th continued to press forward foxhole by foxhole. Just before midnight on 30 Aug. the 16th Company of the 2nd FJ Regt. attempted to counterattack. The result was an intermingling of American and German units which limited American artillery support, out of fear of hitting their own men. The 175th found itself outnumbered by German troops on the hill, and for the next three days the positions remained fairly static. It was not until 3 Sept., after eight days of bitter fighting, that the German defenses on Hill 103 were finally broken.

The last attack was made by the 3/115th which moved up the eastern slope of the hill. Near the end of August this battalion had been pulled out of the line for intensive training in assaulting fortifications. It was commanded by Major Randolph Millholland, who had previously been in charge of the 29th Ranger Battalion. His men had been taught about flamethrowers, pole charges, and other demolitions used to attack fortifications. For the attack on Hill 103 the 3/115th was attached to the 175th Infantry. Their success at Hill 103 would earn Millholland his promotion to lt. colonel.

The 4.2" mortars of the 86th Chemical Mortar Battalion laid down a heavy barrage and the infantry followed closely behind. This final assault was actually made from the rear of the German defenses. Until this time the Germans had outnumbered

Opposite page, inset, top.
The remains of Fort Keranroux resemble little more than a pile of dirt and debris. There is not much left to indicate this was once a 19th century fortress. After a two-hour bombardment, the Americans stormed the fort under cover of a smoke screen and captured it in less than 15 minutes.
(National Archives)

Opposite page, inset, left and main pictures.
This aerial view of Fort Keranroux was taken from the west. The northern side of the fort (on the left) has been pulverized by American artillery. This was the side the 29th Division advanced on. After all the bombardments there was little remaining of the original defenses.
(National Archives)

(Continued on page 110)

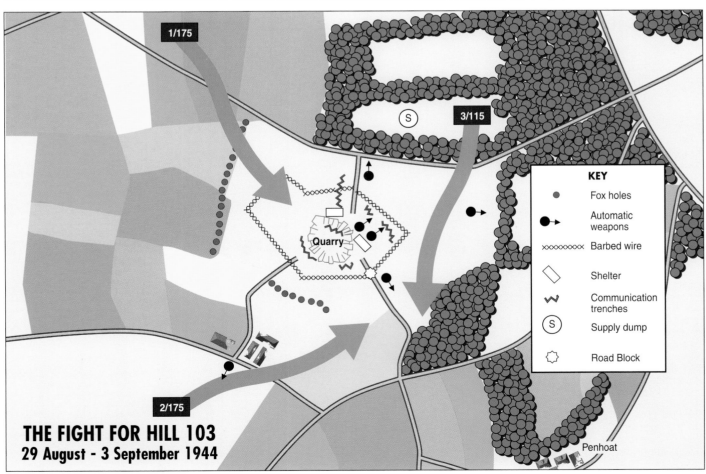

THE FIGHT FOR HILL 103
29 August - 3 September 1944

1/175

3/115

S

2/175

Quarry

Penhoat

KEY

●	Fox holes
●→	Automatic weapons
××××××	Barbed wire
▱	Shelter
ᨑ	Communication trenches
Ⓢ	Supply dump
⬡	Road Block

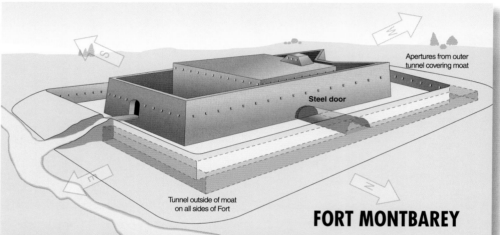

Apertures from outer
tunnel covering moat

Steel door

Tunnel outside of moat
on all sides of Fort

FORT MONTBAREY

Top.
This French Renault or Hotchkiss tank turret with 37mm gun was emplaced just to the west of Ft. Montbarey. Although the exact location has not been determined, it is thought to be just outside the antitank ditch. To the right of the turret can be seen what appears to be the entrance to a trench system.
(National Archives)

Above.
Fort Montbarey is seen here from the south. At the top right of the fort is the main entrance where the Germans constructed a stone barricade, after the wooden door had been burnt away. In the moat, on the right hand side, can be seen a tunnel leading from the main fort to positions in the moat wall. This is a duplicate of the tunnel on the other side which was used by the Americans to place explosives underneath the wall.
The main allied attack began in the area of the antitank ditches to the upper left.
(National Archives)

Left.
A closer view of the main building inside Fort Montbarey from the southeast. It was in the section of this building closest to the camera that the defenders discovered a storeroom filled with gas masks. Without this lucky find the smoke from the Crocodiles would have forced them to evacuate the complex.
(National Archives)

29th Division infantryman.
The 29th Division was one of the only American divisions to make a major effort for every man to have the unit insignia painted on his helmet. This soldier wears the standard wool shirt and trousers, and carries the basic web gear normally seen on most GIs. The large canvas bag slung on his side is the M1 ammunition bag, which could be used to carry anything from extra socks to bottles of Calvados, but was typically used to carry either hand or rifle grenades. The dark green M-43 combat jacket and combat boots with the buckled leather upper are still an unusual sight in the ETO. Both were just starting to show up on the front lines, but were in high demand by the troops. The jacket was warmer, provided better concealment, and had larger more useful pockets than the khaki colored M-41 field jacket. The combat boots were particularly popular as they could be worn without the cumbersome canvas leggings.
(Reconstruction by Militaria Magazine)

Above. US Navy officer Angus Thuermer was present when the British Crocodiles moved up. He snapped these rare photos showing the tank, and the special trailer filled with the flamethrower fuel, on their way to Fort Montbarey. This unit was lent to the Americans to test the effectiveness of flame throwing tanks against German fortifications. *(Courtesy Angus Thuermer)*

Below. A British Crocodile demonstrates the range of its flamethrower. It could shoot the flame an average of 80 yards. The trailer carries the flamethrower fuel, enough for 120 one-second shots. These tanks also had a standard 75mm gun mounted in the turret. *(National Archives)*

B SQUADRON, 141st REGIMENT ROYAL ARMOURED CORPS

- 2 command Churchill tanks- 75mm gun, HE and AP
- 2 'Gun' Churchills (95mm) HE only
- 5 troops of 3 Crocodiles each w/ 2-wheeled trailer

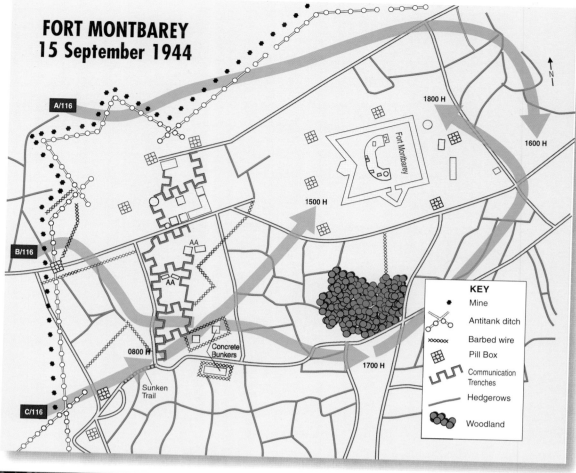

KEY

❋	Mine
	Antitank ditch
	Barbed wire
	Pill Box
	Communication Trenches
	Hedgerows
	Woodland

A/116

B/116

C/116

AA

AA

0800 H

1500 H

1600 H

1700 H

1800 H

Fort Montbarey

Concrete Bunkers

Sunken Trail

N

Bottom, right.
This is one of the only known photos of an M-10 tank destroyer at Brest. The M-10 was essentially a 3" gun in an open top turret, mounted on a Sherman hull. The nickname "Armored Ace" has been painted on the front. Because most of the other footage on this film reel showed 29th Division troops, it is probable that Armored Ace was from Company A, 644th Tank Destroyer Bn.
(National Archives)

resulted in a steady stream of casualties. Although the 115th line remained static the men were always on their toes for infiltrating Germans. Numerous interesting incidents were recorded during this period. One sergeant spotted a German walking on the other side of a hedgerow and hit him over the head with his rifle. A group of American soldiers rigged up a large slingshot so they could harass the Germans with rocks. One American was knocked out when a German hand grenade bounced off his head.

The 115th's Cannon Company was sent an experimental eight tubed 4.5" rocket launcher mounted on a truck. It proved to be very temperamental, but gave Major Miller of 2/115th an idea. He organized what he called the "Wienerschnitzel Battery" out of four bazooka teams. The group would sneak up to the front lines and fire the four bazookas simultaneously at a high angle. The effect seemed to demoralize the Germans, and eventually the battery would grow to eight bazookas firing at once. The troops also tried 60mm mortar shells fired off M1's on rifle grenade adapters, but the German foxholes were so

the Americans on the hill, but with the addition of the 3/115th Infantry the tide was turned and the Germans abandoned Hill 103. However, German prisoners later claimed that they had withdrawn from the vital position only due to a misinterpretation of orders. But Lt. Tollkein, commander of the 12th company/FJR 2 which defended Hill 103, claimed in his memoirs that they were simply not able to hold the position. He launched a last counterattack after the Americans captured the hill, but was unable to regain it.

Hill 103 now gave the 29th a marvelous view of the city of Brest, that would prove invaluable for American artillery observers. From this point the 29th could follow the advances on both Forts Keranroux and Montbarey and on the artificial hill constructed originally as a backstop for the French Navy gunnery range. The Americans promptly nicknamed this 50-foot mound "Sugar Loaf Hill." It was later found to have been an important German observation post.

In the last days of August the 29th Division had made little progress in its eastern sector. The 115th had extended east into the 116th sector, allowing that regiment to move around to the new right flank of the division. Until the 3/115th had been pulled back for their training all nine rifle companies were on the line, leaving no force in reserve. Constant patrolling along the front

Above.
These American helmet shell and liner have been found on the battlefield in Brittany, both bear the distinctive Blue and gray "ying-yang" insignia of the 29th Infantry Division.

close they normally passed over the German positions.

On 5 Sept. the 5th Rangers, officially attached to the 29th, captured Forts Toulbroch, Mengant, and Dellec on the Bay of Brest. That afternoon and into the next day the Air Force attacked Brest with both fighter-and heavy bombers. After this air attack the Germans decided to fall back to their second line of defense. Observation posts started to report German withdrawal all along the line. Combat patrols from the three regiments of the 29th attempted to follow on the heels of the retreating Germans to establish where the new line of defense would be. It was discovered only a few hundred yards closer to Brest.

The Kerrognant strongpoint

On 8 Sept. the 175th and 115th attacked the new German line. The 116th had sent its 3rd Bn. to assist Task Force Sugar and the remainder moved into division reserve. After a hard day of fighting the 115th had captured three German strongpoints. The first was an anti aircraft emplacement at Kerrognant. It had been organized as a strongpoint and is sometimes referred to in records as Fort Kergonant.

Like many of the strongpoints around Brest, Kerrognant was an antiaircraft (AA) position with concrete bunkers and reinforced weapons pits. Located on high ground with a commanding view of the area, the AA guns had been set up to fire against both air and ground targets and the zone around it had clear fields of fire. However, once the ridge to the north was captured by the 2/115th, they had a good view of the approaches to the German position. Previous air and artillery bombardment had put most of the AA guns out of action. The Kerrognant strongpoint was organized to hold out independent of support from Brest, and was thought to be the command point for all other German defensive positions in the area.

The 29th Division had taken a lot of casualties since D-day. In 2/115th it was estimated that at least 50% of all men were recent replacements received at the start of the Brest campaign. Most of the rifle companies were low in strength. In E/115th the three normal 41-man platoons consisted of 21, 31, and only 18 men in the 3rd platoon.

The attack began with some good luck for a patrol from G/115th that had been sent to reconnoiter the village of Le Beuzit, located just to the north of Kerrognant. They surprised a German machine gun crew who was eating lunch, shot two of them, and captured that position. The patrol leader, Sgt. Finder, who realized he had broken into the enemy lines immediately sent back word and the company moved up into the village without having to fight for it. Further patrols sent out were stopped by German guard dogs who sounded an alert.

These antitank obstacles are similar to the Belgian gates used in beach defenses. They are joined together here to create a barrier across the open area of the naval gunnery range to the west of Brest. In the background can be seen the large backstop for the range, known as "Sugar Loaf Hill" to the Americans.
(National Archives)

111

29th INFANTRY DIVISION
(*Latitude*)

Originally a National Guard unit from the Maryland/Virginia area, the shoulder patch denotes that units from the division fought on both sides of the American Civil War. The 29th fought in the Meuse-Argone in WW1. Arriving in England in October 1942, the 29th was one of the first units to land on Omaha beach on D-day. After fighting through to Saint-Lô and Vire, the 29th was sent west to help capture Brest. In November 1944 the 29th crossed the Roer. Attacking again in February 1945, they moved trough Jülich to Munchen-Gladbach and on to the Elbe. After the war ended, the division garrisoned the port of Bremen before returning home.

- 115th Infantry Regiment (*Lagoon*)
- 116th Infantry Regiment (*Lemon*)
- 175th Infantry Regiment (*Limestone*)

Division Artillery
- 110th Field Artillery Bn. (*Larkspur*)
- 111th Field Artillery Bn.
- 224th Field Artillery Bn.
- 227th Field Artillery Bn
- 121st Engineer Combat Bn.

29th Division Special Troops
- 104th Medical Bn.
- 729th Ordnance Co.
- 29th Quartermaster Bn.
- 29th Signal Co.

According to the battalion records the planned artillery barrage on 8 Sept., directed at the strongpoint, was off target and only three rounds hit the position. Instead, four Sherman tanks from A/709th fired at the German emplacements for 10 minutes. At 1010 hrs. Companies E&G/115, which were at roughly half their authorized strength, charged the position, firing their weapons from the hip and yelling the division battle cry "*29 - Let's Go!*" All available supporting weapons, including the heavy machine gun section from H/115, provided covering fire to keep the enemy down. As they reached the final hedge line they claimed to see some of the German defenders running away.

E/115th was then pinned down by machine gun fire and their advance stalled. G/115th, commanded by Lt. Robert Rideout, was also stopped momentarily. Hearing that E/115th was unable to advance Lt. Rideout got an engineer platoon to come forward and, in the next three hours, clear a path through the minefields. Then Rideout brought up one of the Shermans and guided it through.

About 1600 this first tank was knocked out by a Panzerfaust hit to the turret. Two of the crew clambered out and fell on the ground dazed. A small group of infantrymen close by realized that the Germans were going to machine-gun the tank crew survivors, so they broke cover and brought the two burnt and blinded men back to safety. As they were carrying back the tankers one died from his severe burns.

Most of E/115th remained pinned down, but by pushing his men forward Lt. Rideout was able to get G/115th

Men of the 29th Infantry Division move up during the siege of Brest. Although often captioned as the 115th Infantry Regiment, veterans have identified a number of men in the photo as coming from A/116th. This assault company took horrendous casualties on D-day. The first man in the left-hand column wears an M-41 field jacket inside out (the inside lining was darker and made the wearer less visible). He is followed by a BAR man wearing an M-43 combat jacket. Close examination of the photo shows a number of men with M-43 jackets, indicating that this garment was starting to make its way to the front line troops in September 1944.
(*National Archives*)

Opposite page, top.
This is what the inside of the submarine pens looked like when they were finally captured by the 29th Division. A small group of men from the 29th Division were held prisoner in the sub complex for the last few days of the siege. Before they surrendered German troops threw large amounts of equipment into the water to prevent it from being captured by the Americans.
(*National Archives*)

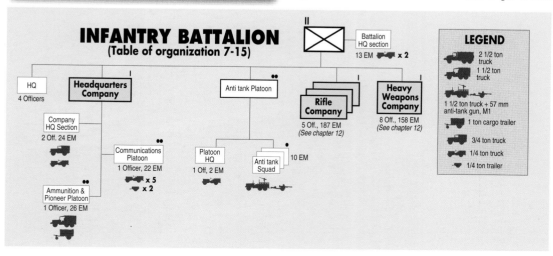

INFANTRY BATTALION
(Table of organization 7-15)

II

Battalion HQ section
13 EM ⬛ x 2

LEGEND
- 2 1/2 ton truck
- 1 1/2 ton truck
- 1 1/2 ton truck + 57 mm anti-tank gun, M1
- 1 ton cargo trailer
- 3/4 ton truck
- 1/4 ton truck
- 1/4 ton trailer

HQ
4 Officers

Headquarters Company

Company HQ Section
2 Off. 24 EM

Communications Platoon
1 Officer, 22 EM
⬛ x 5
⬛ x 2

Ammunition & Pioneer Platoon
1 Officer, 26 EM

Anti tank Platoon

Platoon HQ
1 Off, 2 EM

Anti tank Squad
10 EM

Rifle Company
5 Off., 187 EM
(*See chapter 12*)

Heavy Weapons Company
8 Off., 158 EM
(*See chapter 12*)

to move up to the German defenses. Sniper fire from the flank was stopped when a few GIs discovered a carefully camouflaged sniper platform in a tree.

At 1800 hrs. E&G were finally able to enter the center of the strongpoint, which had been reduced to rubble from previous bombs and shelling. By this time most of the Germans had fled south down a deep trench line and sunken road, leaving this key position to the Americans. With Kerrognant captured the 115th was able to move south to a chateau that had also been converted to a strongpoint. This position was only lightly held and the two companies were able to capture it without much of a fight. This brought the Americans to Fort Penfeld, an old fortification with earthen emplacements. Again air and artillery fire allowed the 115th to capture the position, which put the 29th Division right up to the fork in the Penfeld River.

To the west the 175th found few strong German defenses and advanced 500 yards. A German searchlight position, used in the air defense of Brest, was found undefended and the Americans swiftly occupied it. Again on 9 Sept. the 115th pushed forward, this time capturing the village of Penfeld, but the 175th made little progress. The 29th Division spent 10 Sept. reorganizing and preparing for a major assault the next day. Its 29th sector was shifted to the right and the 115th was relieved from the line by units of the 8th Infantry Division.

On 11 Sept. only small gains were made against the German defenses. A major problem for the division was the two forts of Keranroux and Montbarey. These lay directly in the path of the 29th and there was no way to advance around them. These two forts dominated the last ring of hills northwest of the city. The forts appeared to be mutually supporting, so an attack against one would result in the other providing defensive fire.

Fort Keranroux

On 12 Sept. a twelve-man patrol from F/175th surprised a German pillbox in front of Fort Keranroux and was able to knock the position out and take a number of prisoners. The main attack against the fort began on 13 Sept. when 2/175th moved forward. Supporting them were the 4.2" mortars of A/86th Chemical Mortar Bn.

All through the previous night the Americans had probed the defenses of the fort, and the attached artillery units had pounded the German position. After a two hour bombardment on the morning of 13 Sept. the 175th moved up for another attempt. At 1430 hrs. a smoke screen was put down by 4.2 inch and 81mm mortars. It took over 45 minutes to build an adequate smoke screen.

At 1430 hrs. Company E, commanded by 1st Lt. Carl A. Hobbs, and Company F, commanded by Captain Joe R. Stewart, crossed the open ground under cover of the smoke. In 15 minutes they had entered the fort. Company G in reserve moved into the fort to escape the German artillery. Only ten American casualties were suffered and 107 Germans were taken prisoner. By 1800 hrs. that night the fort was considered secure, but a hand-

ful of Germans continued to lurk in the area and had to be mopped up. By this time the area had been so heavily bombarded that it resembled the cratered surface of the moon.

Fort Montbarey

The capture of Fort Montbarey is probably one of the better known incidents at Brest due to the use of British flame throwing tanks. The old fort had earth filled masonry walls 40 feet thick and was surrounded by a 15 foot moat. The area to the north was protected by 20mm guns and dug in rifle positions. Barbed wire was strung along the front and minefields included 300 pound naval shells fused to detonate when stepped on. The fort had been used by the Germans as an equipment depot and signals station. Information on the German side of the struggle has been documented by one of the paratroopers that took part, Sgt. Ekkehard Priller of FJ Regiment 2. He maintains that Fort Montbarey was never intended to serve as a strongpoint in the German defensive line.

The fight for Fort Montbarey started on 11 Sept. when the 2/115th started to move just after midnight. It seemed there were no Germans defending the fort, but a heavy German artillery barrage drove the attackers back. At this time the Americans thought that a force of approximately 200 Germans had occupied the fort. According to Priller, the only Germans in the immediate area had been given orders to defend a nearby Organization Todt workers' camp. They had been told to hold for at least three days so that a new defensive line could be formed behind them. Both the 5th and 6th Companies of FJ Regiment 2 took up positions in the area and were subjected to a tremendous artillery attack.

On 12 Sept. an incident happened near the fort that may have influenced how the Germans would defend the area. The 2/115th halted to allow the 3/115th to move forward through it to attack Fort Montbarey. S/Sgt. Don Van Roosen, a heavy machine gun squad leader in H/115, walked along with the advancing battalion talking to friends. Finding himself a few hundred yards in front of his former position, he and a BAR man were heading back when, out of curiosity, they wandered over to a small berm. As they rounded the corner they stumbled upon a German soldier who was shaving beside the entrance to an underground bunker.

Quietly speaking in German, Van Roosen told the soldier to put down the razor. Leaving the BAR man as a guard, he went down into the bunker and told the Germans to get their belongings, leave their weapons, and prepare to move out. 60-70 German troops filed out and were sent on their way back to the American lines.

Apparently the two Americans had wandered between outposts guarding the area and taken the German bunker by surprise. They moved to other bunkers and repeated the performance two more times. A fourth bunker was much larger. As they started down the concrete stairway they saw movement from an armored firing point. With relief they realized the Germans were sticking out a pole with a white flag. Taking this last group back with them, the two men turned them over to battalion headquarters and went about their business. They had, purely by accident, cleared a gap in the German lines roughly 500 yards wide and taken over 200 prisoners.

SGT. VAN ROOSEN, Co. H/175th INFANTRY

On 13 Sept. Sgt. Donald Van Roosen's heavy machine gun section (H/115) was supporting an attack by G/115th. Their objective was a pillbox to the southwest of Fort Montbarey, numbered "19" on the maps. After taking one German position and the surrounding trench system the men were running out of ammunition. The platoon sergeant commanding the unit was killed and the group was on their own. There was no communication back to company or battalion so Van Roosen gathered up two wounded riflemen and led them back, past a concrete water tower, to the battalion aid station. He then found Major Miller, the 2/115th Battalion commander, and explained their need for reinforcements. After picking up more ammunition Van Roosen went back to his machine gun squad.

Above.
This bunker is part of the defensive line near Ft. Montbarey. It is thought to be one of the bunkers that Van Roosen captured; possibly even the same bunker as seen in the German photo below. The remains of camouflage netting can be seen stretched over the top of the bunker. When properly camouflaged, these bunkers were almost invisible from the air.

Left. Sgt. Donald Van Roosen of the 115th Infantry Regiment was captured by the Germans north of Brest, and held in the submarine pens for a few days until the German surrender. Only a few weeks later this photo was taken of him after receiving a battlefield commission. *(Courtesy Don Van Roosen)*

T/Sgt. Jack Lemmon came up to take over the rifle platoon, but was soon wounded by German mortar fire and evacuated. As night fell the group's casualties went back to the aid station, but no one was sent up to take their place. About 2200 hrs. one of the heavy machine guns in the section was damaged, so two men from the crew were sent back with instructions to get some more men sent up to the line.

By this time Van Roosen was suffering from blurred vision- the effects of a close 50mm mortar round. Without any warning a German soldier jammed a weapon into his back and said, "*Hände hoch.*" Realizing that German paratroopers had infiltrated the area, Van Roosen agreed to surrender and told the rest of the Americans down in a bunker to come out with their hands up. Moving from position to position, with a German lieutenant covering him, Van Roosen calmly told the rest of the Americans holding the overrun position to give up. Running short of ammunition, there was little else the small party could do. As he moved among his men he quietly told them to make sure they discarded any German souvenirs they might have on them.

The captured Americans were marched away to an underground bunker a few hundred yards away. At this time one of the men, Pfc. Joe Rockman, told Van Roosen that, being Jewish, he feared for his life. Van Roosen reassured him that everything would be all right and not to worry. The Americans were lined up in the bunker in two ranks to be inspected, with Rockman standing right behind Van Roosen for safety. A German officer walked past the first row and then down the next. As he got near the end he shouted out the name "*Rockman!*"

Rockman, surprised that this German knew his name, figured his number was up and almost fainted. However, in a remarkable coincidence it turned out that the German officer had actually lived in the States before the war, in the same neighborhood where Rockman was a policeman. The doctor had gone back to visit his family in Germany in 1939 and had been drafted into the army. He assured the shaken Rockman that he would be all right.

The American prisoners were then marched down to the city and into the submarine pens. After a short interrogation the POWs were put into a large windowless room somewhere in the same complex as the sub pens. Twice a day they were taken out to use a toilet in one of the submarine bays. There they noticed the Germans had been throwing weapons and equipment into the water. Soon they were joined in captivity by some men from the 8th Division (possibly from E&G/28th).

One night they were all led out to the sub pens and put on board a 60 foot motor launch. They were told they were being moved to a location where all the American POWs were being collected. Only two guards were sent with the boat. The Americans prisoners quietly decided they were going to overpower the guards, capture the boat, and sail it out to find one of the American ships blockading the bay. Before they could act on this plan the boat crew realized they had accidentally ran into a minefield, turned about, and went back to the sub pens.

The POWs stayed in the submarine pens until 18 Sept., when an American medical officer suddenly appeared at the door and told them they were free. But the story does not end there. The 13 men from H/115 were trucked to the 29th Division HQ without even a chance to clean up. Put before the entire division staff, General Gerhardt appeared and began to berate the former prisoners.

In an incident that would later be written up by historian S.L.A. Marshall, Gerhardt claimed that German soldiers had stated that this group of Americans had been captured because they had stopped fighting to hunt for souvenirs. Gerhardt was furious at this and was going to take steps to ensure that nothing like this would ever happen in his division again. With these statements the group of soldiers started to grow uneasy. Van Roosen told his men to settle down, and Gerhardt turned to him and said, "*Do you have something to say sergeant?*"

Van Roosen explained to the general that they had not been looking for souvenirs, but had held a position after having requested reinforcements for hours. He had surrendered only after being shaken by a near mortar blast and having a German stick a gun in his back. Gerhardt grew very quiet, muttered something about having been misinformed, and quickly left. Without any further comment on the event the men were sent back to their units. The next month, on 13 Oct. 1944, Van Roosen, who had landed on Omaha Beach on 6 June as a private, was given a battlefield commission and commanded a rifle platoon for the rest of the war.

This photo was taken from a German soldier captured by Don Van Roosen. It shows one of the numerous underground bunkers the 29th Division had to take before moving into Forts Montbarey and Keranroux. It appears to be one of the same bunkers that Van Roosen would capture on 12 Sept.

LIEUTENANT RIDEOUT AT KERROGNANT

For his heroic leadership at Kerrognant Lt. Rideout was awarded the Silver Star. Of the action he was quoted as saying:

"You have a plan. You have an objective. You have an organization and your men start out with that first objective in mind. But in the process of getting up there and taking up fire positions, disorganization sets in. The men look for cover and that scatters them. To get them going again an officer must expose himself to the point of suicide. The men do not want to go on because they have already taken great risks. The officers do not feel like taking extraordinary risks. They know the men will work well when well led. But they also know that if the leader is killed, that's the finish. So, the farther you go, the greater the difficulty. It is harder to get men to mop-up after a charge than to get them to charge."

Rideout was soon promoted to captain, but he was killed in November 1944.

For reasons unknown the 115th did not follow up on this lucky event. However, the capture of these men probably affected the German defense of the area. The 115th Infantry records for the day list 219 POWs as being captured, only six of whom were paratroopers. Most of the men captured by Van Roosen and his comrade were probably noncombatant troops sent into the front lines and only too glad to be out of the fight.

On 13 Sept. fire from the German paratroopers pushed the 115th out of the antitank ditch outside the fort. The 116th Infantry was brought in to relieve the 115th just after midnight. A series of local attacks pushed the Germans back until the fort was partially surrounded by 14 Sept. The main American forces attacking Fort Montbarey were the 1/116th Infantry, a platoon of engineers from the 121st Engineer Bn., one platoon of 4.2" mortars, and three tank destroyers from the 821st TD Bn. A British tank squadron was sent to assist the 29th Division at Montbarey. Their Churchill tanks were equipped with flamethrowers and had been nicknamed "Crocodiles."

B/141st of the Royal Armored Corps was under command of Major I.N. Rye. He had 15 Crocodile flamethrowing tanks, two gun tanks with 95mm guns, and two command tanks. The Crocodile tanks each had a 75mm gun, three machine guns, and the flamethrower. A two-wheeled trailer carried 400 gallons of the flamethrower fuel, which allowed each Crocodile 120 one-second shots of flame at a range of roughly 80 yards. One problem with the British tanks was that they did not have radios on the American frequencies, so the Americans could only communicate with the individual Crocodiles through the command tanks. American engineers welded hedgerow cutters on the front of the Crocodiles to help them move cross-country.

The Americans started their main drive on Fort Montbarey on 14 Sept. After time was spent allowing the American infantry to practice with the British tanks, the Crocodiles moved in. The Germans defending the area outside the fort had no antitank weapons, so were forced to pull back when attacked by armor. The smoke caused by the flame covered their movement and, according to Sgt. Priller, about 60 men fell back to the fort. They had no plans to defend the fort, but it seemed like a logical place to retreat to at the time. The company commander, Herzog, made the decision to move there on his own initiative. Once inside, the men began to barricade the main door with piles of stone rubble and steel barrels.

The Germans found the communications center had been totally destroyed and they were cut off from any help.

Fallschirmjäger NCO
This Oberjäger of Fallschirmjäger Regiment 2 wears the typical uniform and equipment of the German paratroopers in Brittany. The second type camouflage jump smock is worn with wool jump trousers and standard short boots. The cotton bandoleer of rifle ammunition around his neck is an item specifically issued to the paratroops. To keep it from flopping about, the back of the bandoleer attaches to the leather belt. Also on the belt is a bayonet attached to a tan colored web frog. Most German field gear was constructed from leather, but as the war went on a greater and greater amount was produced in cotton webbing.
(Reconstruction by Militaria Magazine)

There was no ammunition in the fort, but they did find a pile of packs from another German unit and a large number of gas masks. Water was in short supply because the fortress well was stagnant. The roughly 60 defenders had only the small arms, grenades, and three machine guns they had carried in with them.

From the American viewpoint the attack started at 1615 hrs. when engineers moved up to clear a path through a minefield. The mines were actually artillery shells fitted with pressure fuses. The engineers were covered by a smoke screen laid by the 4.2" mortars. Once the path was clear three Crocodiles moved up, closely followed by B/116th. The attached tank destroyers provided supporting fire on likely gun positions in the fort. The first tank, commanded by Lt. Herbert A. Ward, exhausted its flame against enemy emplacements, from the sunken road, then continued to support B/116th with the remaining guns. According to the British records, once Ward's tank had exhausted its flamethrower fuel it turned back and fell into an antitank ditch. The American history claims that Ward's tank was struck by a 20mm gun before it turned back and fell into a camouflaged pit. The second tank struck one of the mines and was disabled. The third tank made its way past the others and got close to the walls of the fort. It was unable to find an opening to flame the inside of the fort and finally withdrew. One of the command tanks in the area also hit a mine and was damaged. Two other Crocodiles moved up and one became stuck in a crater while the other fell victim to the antitank ditch.

The flame attack allowed the infantry of the 116th to move in close to the fort and eliminate all defenses but those inside the fort itself. The Germans in the fort were saved by only one factor: the supply of gas masks they had found. They had long before discarded their own masks, and when the thick black smoke of the Crocodiles flooded into the fort the only way to breathe was with the masks. The wooden main door was burned by the flame and this allowed the Americans a partial view into the fort. The Germans rebuilt the stone barricade in the doorway as best as they were able.

On the night of 14 Sept. the 3rd platoon from B/121st Engineers, under Lt. Shelton R. Clemer, went back into action and cleared another path for the tanks. Working in the dark by touch alone, they located five of the artillery shell mines and fixed a one pound charge of C-2 explosive to each. These were connected by primacord to charges placed in the

walls of the antitank trench. This was all finished by 0500 hrs. At 0830 everything was detonated to signal the start of a new attack by the infantry. The engineers moved up to construct a causeway across the antitank ditch with pick and shovel.

On 15 Sept. attacks by the 1/116th came close to encircling the fort, but a small corridor to the southeast was still held by the Germans. At 1030 hrs. the Crocodiles returned and flamed the moat and over the fortress wall until they had used up their fuel. During the attack the Germans pulled back from the walls and fled into whatever shelter they could find. Their gas masks once again protected them from suffocation in the thick smoke.

At one point an armored bulldozer was brought up to clear a path around one of the disabled tanks. Two Germans with scoped rifles fired at the vision slit in the front of the armor plate and the driver was killed. Inside the fort Lt. Floter gave the order to defend the fortress to the last

man. Without any heavy weapons the paratroopers were not too happy with that idea, so he changed his orders to "the last cartridge." That same day the Germans spotted a wounded American officer lying in the moat. They brought him inside the fort and sent a man, under a white flag, to ask the Americans to come and pick up the wounded. Suspecting a German trick, the Americans refused and demanded that the Germans carry the wounded to the American lines, then surrender. The Germans refused, but during the siege of the fort one German medic was wounded in the eyes. His officers sent him out under a white flag to seek medical attention from the Americans.

Sometime later a captured German paratrooper was sent out from the American lines, with a white flag, bringing a request from Major Tom Dallas, commander of the 1/116th, to surrender. The threat of more flamethrower attacks was made, but the Germans refused to give up. The captured paratrooper returned to the American lines, then came back a sec-

Top left.
This photo was taken by John Fowler of the 104th Medical Bn. It shows 29th soldiers escorting German POWs on Rue Jean Jaurès in Saint-Pierre. The GI is talking to two captured female prisoners, one of which is hiding her face from the camera.

Top right.
Another group of German POWs leaving for captivity. The column is led by a naval officer, but close examination of the original photograph reveals a number of German female auxiliaries in the group.
(Courtesy: John Fowler)

Left.
These steel pillboxes were used in the final line of German defense around the naval facilities. Clearly visible are the impacts of numerous hits by tank destroyers. The curved surface caused many of the rounds to ricochet rather than penetrate the 14 inch armor.
(National Archives)

FRENCH CROIX DE GUERRE
WITH SILVER-GILT STAR
AWARD TO 2nd BN, 175th IR

Citation reads:
"This battalion is animated by the finest military qualities. It was ordered to occupy Fort Keranroux, a key position defending the city of Brest, between 12 and 16 Sept. 1944. After five days of uninterrupted combat, including hand-to-hand fighting, it occupied the fort and was able to maintain its position, in spite of intense artillery fire."

MAJOR GENERAL CHARLES H. GERHARDT

The commander of the 29th Division gradu-ated from West Point in 1917 as a cavalry lieutenant. He went to France with the 3rd Cavalry Regiment, but was soon transferred to be the aide to the commander of the 89th Division. After the war he continued in caval-ry positions until the outbreak of WW2, when he was given command of the 91st Infantry Division. Later he was sent to England to assume command of the 29th Division, which he led throughout the war. Afterwards he served as military attaché to Brazil.

Gerhardt, or "Uncle Charlie" as some of his men called him, was well-known for his idiosyncracies. He insisted that his men keep their chin straps secured at all times. He pro-hibited the use of canvas vehicle tops in com-bat and demanded that vehicles be kept clean at all times. In reports he refused to allow the word "counterattack" to be used, insisting they be referred to as "German enthusiasms." Gerhardt made the 29th one of the only divi-sions in the Army to consistently require the divisional insignia be painted on every man's helmet. He also took great pains to provide his replacements with a refresher course in com-bat techniques before they entered combat, and was a pioneer in treating combat exhaus-tion.

General Charles H. Gerhardt, Commander of the 29th Infantry Division, and staff member Major William W. Bratton. Gerhardt is seen here wearing his helmet chin strap on the point of the chin. He felt that a man could not fight and hold onto his helmet at the same time, so demanded that chin straps be securely fastened in this manner at all times.
(National Archives)

ond time with the message that if they did not surrender the American commander would blow them all up. The Germans again refused.

On the morning of 16 Sept. the 1/116th was ready for a final all-out assault. At 1300 hrs. three Crocodiles attacked the fort, while one of the supporting TDs fired high explosive rounds at the main gate. Roughly 200 rounds were fired at a range of no more than 200 yards. The main effect of the flamethrowing Crocodiles was to drive the defenders away from the walls. With no anti-tank weapons there was no way the Germans could strike out at the tanks. After the TD had fired all its ammunition against the main door a second was brought up to take its place. The third TD was directed to fire at the con-crete top of a tunnel crossing under the moat, to the north of the fort. A small hole was made which allowed the Americans to enter the passageways underneath the fort.

The TDs did not have much of an effect upon the debris filled main doorway, so a short barreled 105mm howitzer was brought up from the cannon company. Placed in front of the door, the gun fired 15-20 rounds of high explosive which effec-tively destroyed the barricade. To prevent the Germans from firing at the gun crew two BARs and an infantry squad fired at anyone who dared show themselves in the fortress. One of the shells hit a supply of fuel inside the fort. The Amer-icans thought the resulting explosion was the fort's ammunition supply. Three more Crocodiles moved up and flamed the fort.

According to the American records three wounded Germans came out under a white flag asking that the Americans stop blasting the fort as the walls were about to collapse. Major Dallas recalled he replied to their request, "*What more can I ask*" (referring to his previous attempts to get the Germans to surrender). Dallas sent word back to the fort that since they would not surrender he was going to blow them all to hell. Sgt.

Priller has questioned all of his comrades he could find, but they do not recall this happening and have been unable to figure out who these men might have been.

When the 105mm howitzer ran out of ammo one of the British tanks took its place and continued firing into the main doorway. Three Crocodiles moved up and flamed everything but the northern side of the fort. This was the side the tunnel was on. B/116th Infantry took positions in that area to cover the engineers as they moved in to place explosives. An explosive charge of between 1,500-2,000 pounds of TNT was placed in the tunnel underneath the fortress wall. All this time heavy machine gun and rifle grenade fire kept the Germans from inter-fering with the engineers.

The explosive charge was ready in 20 min-utes and things were double-checked to make sure no Americans were left in the area. When they were ready to set it off a German POW offered to go back to the fort one more time to get a surrender. The engineers reported that Major Dallas replied, " *Fuck 'em, blow them all up!*" The charge was detonated and the entire side of the fort caved in.

The Germans had enough at this point and sent 1st Sgt. Rose outside with a white flag. The rest of the garrison destroyed their weapons and pre-pared to surrender. The Infantry of B/116th moved in over the ruined north wall and the Germans gave up. When questioned about the battle the Ger-mans claimed that the flamethrower tanks had played an important role in

117

getting them to give up. The flame was terrifying and they had no weapons to fight back with. Had it not been for the stock of gas masks in the fort they would have had to give up long before from the heavy smoke the flame made.

Inside the fort a wounded American officer was found and, to the relief of the Germans, he told his countrymen that he had been well-treated. Between 60 and 80 Germans were captured at Montbarey. The numbers shown in various reports differ, and some may have been stragglers taken from the outlying defensive positions.

Amazingly, Sgt. Priller claims that in all the fighting for the fortress no Germans were killed and only one was wounded (the German medic). Acting on their own and without communications, resupply, or firm orders, the small group of paratroopers held off a reinforced infantry battalion for a few days. To be fair, the Americans did not make a major infantry assault on the fort, but had tried to capture it without losing too many men.

Fort Montbarey was not as important as some of the other positions the 29th fought for, but due to the use of flamethrower tanks it was fairly well documented on the American side. The abundance of documentation has caused it to grow in importance in writings about the battle. After the capitulation of Fort Montbarey the Crocodile tanks were scheduled to be assigned to the Rangers for the assault on Fort Portzic, but Brest surrendered before it occurred.

Into Recouvrance

With Montbarey and Keranroux in American hands the 29th was positioned to move into the city of Recouvrance. The front lines had grown so close to the city outskirts by this time the 8th Infantry Division could be pulled out, leaving only a small gap that the 29th and 2nd Divisions could fill. The boundary between the 2nd and 29th Divisions was now the Penfeld River. With the area to the north now cleared of Germans, all three regiments were on the front line. The 116th was in the center, with the 115th to the right, and the 175th to the left. On the far right flank was the 5th Ranger Bn. working its way up the coastline.

On 14 Sept. Sugar Loaf Hill, the man-made backstop to the naval gunnery range, was captured by C/175. The company made their way to the south of the mound and captured it from the rear. This action denied the Germans their last good observation point west of Brest, and provided the Americans with an ideal location to direct the final shelling of the city.

On 16 Sept. the 29th shifted from hedgerow fighting to street fighting in the outskirts of Recouvrance. The front line ran from the outskirts of the city, past Sugar Loaf Hill, to Fort du Portzic on the Bay of Brest. Before the 115th could enter the city they had to fight their way through a final perimeter of German pillboxes. They jumped off at 1000 hrs. on 16 Sept., but were held up for the next few hours.

By slow and careful effort the 115th made its way closer to their final objective, the submarine pens.

The 116th moved south from Saint-Pierre into the city. Progress was slow as the remaining Germans attempted to hold on to every position. The 29th Division finally reached the old city wall on 16 Sept. and, in conjunction with the 2nd Infantry Division, was ready to make one last effort to finish the campaign.

Pvt. Patrick McDonald of the 29th Division Military Police platoon stands guard at division headquarters. He wears woven straw overshoes taken from German stocks. According to the divisional history this German sentry box was captured at Brest (below), brought along with the unit into Germany, and then taken back to the USA in 1945. Its current whereabouts remain a mystery.
(National Archives)

118

Chapter 12

THE 2ND INFANTRY DIVISION

T/Sgt. Johnny Yanak, a Texan in A/9th Infantry peers over a hedgerow at German positions north of Brest. He wears HBT fatigues and a heavily camouflaged helmet, and carries a Thompson submachine gun. The 2nd Infantry Division was one of the few units in which rifle companies were issued with Thompsons. This was to test their value in city fighting.
(National Archives)

The 2nd Infantry Division, nicknamed the "Indianhead" Division after their shoulder sleeve insignia, landed in France on 7 June 1944. The unit moved into their first attack on 9 June and continued to fight through the hedgerows on the drive inland. After brutal combat at Hill 192 outside Saint-Lô, they continued to move on to Vire. As part of the American breakout they seized the town of Tinchebray before being transferred on 19 August to Middleton's VIIIth Corps for the Brittany Campaign.

Above.
On the way to Brest these men from the 38th Infantry Regiment stop to get a drink of fresh milk from a local woman. The canvas covering on the jeep windshield was an issued item designed to prevent light from glinting off the glass and making the vehicle easier to spot by the enemy. This cover is often seen with a star inside a circle painted on it for aerial recognition purposes.
(Courtesy Jim Love)

Left.
Pvt. James Pearson, a 2nd Div. MP takes a break under a religious monument in Plabennec. Signal Corps wire teams took great pains to string their wire off the ground so no one would accidentally cut the lines by driving over them. It was also not uncommon for local farmers to cut phone lines on the ground, not realizing they were in use.
(National Archives)

Opposite page, far right.
This pillbox was captured by the 9th Infantry at the Guipavas airfield to the north of Brest. Most of the airfield had been originally taken by the 1/28th Infantry under the command of the 6th Armored Division, but the ground had to be relinquished because there were not enough men to hold the area against a German counterattack.
(National Archives)

The 2nd Infantry Division, under command of General Walter M. Robertson, was moved out to Brest in trucks of attached quartermaster units. The troops chalked the humorous slogan "Brest or Bust" on the vehicles. On 20 Aug. the 2nd began to relieve elements of both the 8th Infantry and 6th Armored Divisions on the far left flank around Brest. They would be responsible for the area bordering the Elorn River to the east and the 8th Division to the west.

To the south the Daoulas Peninsula provided a perfect site for the Germans to watch over the 2nd Division sector. As Robertson's men moved on Brest, the Germans would be able to use the Daoulas Peninsula to shell the Americans. It had to be taken from the Germans. Doing so would also give the

JOHN J. McVEIGH, MEDAL OF HONOR CITATION

23rd Infantry Regiment, 2nd Infantry Division
Citation reads: "For conspicuous gallantry and intrepidity at risk of his life above and beyond the call of duty near Brest, France, on 29 August 1944. Shortly after dusk an enemy counterattack of platoon strength was launched against one platoon of Company G, 23rd Infantry. Since the Company G platoon was not dug in and had just begun to assume defensive positions along a hedge, part of the line sagged momentarily under heavy fire from small arms and two flak guns, leaving a section of heavy machine guns holding a wide frontage without rifle protection.

The enemy drive moved so swiftly that German riflemen were soon almost on top of one machine gun position. Sgt. McVeigh, heedless of a tremendous amount of small arms and flak fire directed toward him, stood up in full view of the enemy and directed the fire of his squad on the attacking Germans until his position was almost overrun. He then drew his trench knife and single-handed charged several of the enemy. In a savage hand-to-hand struggle, Sgt. McVeigh killed one German with the knife, his only weapon, and was advancing on three more of the enemy when he was shot down and killed with small arms fire at point-blank range. Sgt. McVeigh's heroic act allowed the two remaining men in his squad to concentrate their machine gun fire on the attacking enemy and then turn their weapons on the three Germans in the road, killing all three. Fire from this machine gun and the other gun of the section was almost entirely responsible for stopping this enemy assault, and allowed the rifle platoon to which it was attached time to reorganize, assume positions on, and hold the high ground gained during the day."

At the end of August 1944,
Battery C of the 38th Field Artillery
Battalion fired its 50,000th shell
at the Germans. The large number
of rounds fired, coupled with a
shortage of spare parts in the Third
Army, posed a problem as many
artillery pieces began to suffer
extreme wear. Some components
had to be manufactured locally,
while others had to be specially
flown in.
(National Archives)

Americans a place for their artillery to shell the German defenses in Brest from the rear. The Germans understood the importance of the peninsula and had strongly garrisoned it.

Robertson formed a unit, named Task Force B (TFB), for the specific job of clearing the Daoulas peninsula. He gave command of TFB to his assistant division commander, General James Van Fleet. TFB was composed of General Earnest's Task Force A strengthened by a few elements of the 2nd Division. While Van Fleet was sent to capture the Daoulas peninsula, Robertson would concentrate on organizing the remainder of the division for the assault on Brest itself. The 2nd Recon Troop was given responsibility for maintaining contact between the bulk of the division and TFB to the south.

The Advance to the City

The terrain in front of the 2nd Division was typical hedgerow country. A few major German strongpoints had been positioned on the high ground, but it was thought that the 2nd would have an easy time moving forward. On 24 Aug. the troops prepared to attack. The division engineers ran a short course in the use of flamethrowers for the infantry regiments. The next day, 25 Aug., the 2nd Division jumped off at 1300 hrs. with the 9th Infantry on the right and the 23rd on the left. The main unit opposing the 9th Infantry was identified as the 2nd Battalion, 7th Fallschirmjäger-Regiment. The 2nd FJ Engineer Bn. was in front of the 23rd Infantry. Both German units were

supported by numerous other attachments from navy and anti-aircraft troops.

The initial 2nd Division line ran from Gouesnou through Guipavas to the Pyrotechnie de Saint-Nicolas. The plan of attack was for the 9th to first capture the village of Kervern and Hill 100. The 23rd was to take the villages of Lavallot and Toralan, as well as the nearby strongpoint of Hill 105. Then the 9th would drive south to the villages of Keraveloc and Le Rody. At first the division advanced slowly through fierce German resistance. The tank destroyers were used for direct fire against pillboxes and the divisional artillery fired over 700 rounds in support of the attack

The 9th Infantry soon found itself up against a strong German position centered on the town of Bourg-Neuf and the Fourneuf Ridge. In the 1/9th sector three tanks from D/709th were knocked out. One of them had slipped off a road and turned over, which trapped the crew inside. They were unable to escape because the Germans had set up a machine gun just outside their tank. Once a German patrol had even knocked on the tank in curiosity, unaware that the crew was still inside. The tankers stayed quiet until two days later when they heard American voices and obtained help getting out.

The attack continued and on 27 Aug. the 2nd ran into a series of fortified emplacements. Each in turn was subjected to aimed TD fire while an infantry unit attempted to flank the position. The determined resistance and mutually supporting positions of the Germans kept the advance at a slow pace. The 9th Infantry was finally able to move its command post into German bunkers at the Brest airport north of Guipavas.

A/9th ran into some difficulty when attacking the fortified village of Kervao. The majority of the men in the company were replacements, without experience on such weapons as Bangalore torpedoes or pole charges. Unable to find anyone in his company who knew how to operate a flamethrower, Captain Cameron A. Clough took it upon himself to charge a German emplacement with one. This allowed his company to

advance into Kervao, where it was counterattacked by an American tank the Germans had captured. With no antitank weapons available Clough and his men dragged a nearby German 37mm gun, which was missing its sight, into position and used it to drive back the Germans and their tank. During the engagement Clough was wounded and lost one eye. Temporarily blinded, the officer refused to be evacuated for medical treatment until he was sure his company was able to hold. He continued to command his unit in the defense of a second German counterattack and was awarded the DSC for his actions on that day.

Meanwhile, Lt. Col. H.K. Wesson, the 1st Battalion commander, moved forward to help rally B/9th. This company had lost its commander and was down to only 45 men. Wesson would earn a posthumous DSC for keeping the remains of the company in action. They too were attacked by a captured American tank painted with a swastika, probably the same one used against Captain Clough. Wesson personally led the company across an open field and was able to drive the exhausted men to capture the German positions that had been pinning them down. One of the more strongly defended positions commanded the approach to Hill 105. Known as the Battery Domaine, it contained a battery of 105mm antiaircraft guns in heavily constructed concrete emplacements. It was well-situated with good fields of fire to the north, west, and east. An air strike of two P-47's delivered direct hits on the gun emplacements, but the Germans stubbornly held on. Three times the 3/23rd attacked the position and were forced back. Only on the night of 28 Aug., when the nearby village of Keramo was captured and a fourth American assault succeeded in blowing holes in some of the concrete positions, did the Germans abandon the strongpoint.

There are a few different stories as to what next occurred. A few minutes after the Germans withdrew, six pillboxes loaded with munitions exploded and lit the night sky. Large chunks of concrete, some up to 2 feet in diameter, fell up to a thousand

Above.
A group of 2nd Division stretcher-bearers from the 9th Infantry Regiment move past a German roadblock outside Brest. Close examination reveals the casualty to be a German paratrooper. A great many Germans surrendered once they realized that the Americans provided good medical care to wounded German soldiers.
(National Archives)

Far left.
A 2d Division helmet liner found near Bourg Neuf-Fourneuf, in the 9th Infantry sector.

Left.
A helmet liner from the 2d Division Military Police platoon. The yellow band indicates an MP unit at divisional level.
(B. Cabioch, Musée Guerre 39-45, Roscoff)

UNIT CITATION- 3rd BATTALION, 23rd INFANTRY

General Order Number 15, 1945

"The 3rd Battalion, 23rd Infantry is cited for outstanding performance of duty against the enemy during the attack on Brest, France, between the dates 25 and 29 August 1944. This battalion was assigned the difficult task of breaking through a bitterly contested enemy fortified strongpoint commanding the only approach to Hill 105, the key terrain feature of that sector and part of the outer ring of defenses at Brest. The entire area was enclosed on three sides by a minefield 50-100 yards wide, with double apron barbed wire entanglements on each side. The fourth side of this bastion was a sunken road literally covered with antitank Teller mines and trip wire with extremely heavy machine gun support. Three different times the 3rd Battalion heroically charged the strongpoint, but each time they were driven back with heavy loss of life. During the evening of 28 August, night patrols went forward and succeeded in blasting four holes in the outer defense with pole charges. Thus the fourth attack, a savage assault on 29 August,

was successful and troops swept on through thick hedgerow, over the sunken road, and cut the fortification itself. The two assault platoons were well within the fortified position when the retreating enemy detonated heavy charges of explosives and 105mm ammunition which they had prepared in four bunkers. Although chunks of concrete 2 feet square were hurled as far as 250 yards and casualties were tremendous, the 3rd Battalion heroically pushed forward and drove the enemy from the strongpoint, thus opening the approach to the strategic point, Hill 105. The 3rd Battalion losses were five officers and 205 enlisted men wounded, 17 enlisted men killed, and two missing in action, out of a total of 22 officers and 691 enlisted men beginning the action. The courage and fighting determination exhibited by the officers and men of this battalion was a vital factor in the successful accomplishment of the mission. The loyalty, heroic effort, and devotion to duty exemplified by the 3rd Battalion, 23rd Infantry Regiment reflect great credit on the armed forces of the United States."

Opposite page, bottom.
Cannon company of the 9th Infantry Regiment shells Brest with an M3 105mm howitzer. This artillery piece was supposed to have been used for direct fire missions in the front lines, but at Brest the cannon companies typically were used as an extra artillery battery for indirect fire missions.
(National Archives)

yards away causing numerous casualties. 48 Americans were killed or wounded in this explosion. The commander of I/23rd had only 22 men that could still function after the massive concussion, but still pushed forward to the edge of Hill 105.

One story claims that the German garrison withdrew, leaving only an engineer detachment to light the fuses and then surrender to the Americans. Some sources claim this was done to deny the bunkers to the Americans. An officer on the scene claimed that the fuse delay was too long for this and could

only have been set in order to try and kill as many Americans as possible as they moved into the supposedly empty area. Another record claims the Germans detonated the explosion electrically from the next line of defense. The fact that 13 Germans surrendered to the Americans just prior to the explosion probably indicates that they had merely been ordered to destroy the bunkers, and had just not considered just how large the resulting explosion of the stockpiled 105mm antiaircraft rounds would be.

Colonel Chester J. Hirschfelder was the commander of the 9th Infantry Regiment at Brest. Seen here as a lt. col. in 1941, he was awarded the Distinguished Service Cross with two Oak Leaf clusters during the period he commanded the unit.
(National Archives)

Left.
The gunner of a heavy machine gun team runs forward carrying the heavy tripod of an M1917A1 machine gun. This was the easiest way to carry the tripod, with the cradle on the back and the tripod's two legs over the shoulders. Once the gun was put into place the assistant gunner would seat the machine gun onto the cradle, while the gunner would be already behind the tripod and ready to fire.
(National Archives)

Below.
Although the caption does not indicate the exact location of this photo, the concrete debris may indicate it was taken near the Batterie Domaine. The Germans destroyed the concrete positions there by exploding the remaining munitions. The resulting explosion killed a number of Americans and spread concrete rubble throughout the area.
(National Archives)

As the Americans fought on they realized it was the German paratroopers that caused them the most problems. The mixture of naval and assorted other troops, not generally used in ground combat, were frequently happy to give up and get out of the war. For this reason the German paratroopers had been ordered to prevent their less experienced comrades from surrendering and to serve as the strong backbone of the defenses. If an area was under attack the paratroopers would be sent to shore it up. Small groups of paratroopers were used to not only provide a cadre of combat experience and morale to the newly formed units, but also to help train and prepare them for ground combat. It is wrong to think of them as watching over their fellow Germans, from the rear, to prevent them from retreating or surrendering. The paras were used to lead the lesser trained Germans from the front and show the former sailors and airmen how to fight. If the paratroopers grew angry at their comrades' lack of desire to fight it was because they felt that every German soldier, no matter if a sailor or radio operator, should be willing to do their part. Experience in Russia had taught the paratroopers that if one group crumbled it put everyone else at risk.

While the German paratroopers proved themselves to be experts of hedgerow defense, the Americans used pole and satchel charges to blast holes through the barbed wire and hedgerows. Flamethrowers, normally not seen much in the ETO, were brought up and used to deal with some German positions. The Germans dug carefully, constructed their emplacements into the sides of the thick earthen hedgerows, and camouflaged them with great care. Frequently the Americans did not know where the Germans were until a machine gun opened up from the corner of a field, hitting a few men and pinning down the remainder of the squad. Rarely did the 2nd Division gain a yard of ground without having

to fight for it. If the Germans pulled back the Americans would suffer a few casualties in trying to locate the new German line.

The Americans used the handful of attached tanks and TDs to provide armored support when moving forward, but the close terrain made it very hazardous for any armored vehicle to get close to the German lines without a protective screen of infantry. Without such infantry support it was relatively easy for the Germans to wait for an American tank to move in close and knock it out with a single shot from a Panzerfaust. Fortunately for the Americans there was a critical shortage of Panzerfausts and Panzerschreck ammunition. There is some evidence that this was the only type of munitions that was airdropped into Brest by the Luftwaffe on one of its infrequent supply runs over Brittany.

On 29 Aug. the Americans paused momentarily to allow the units to reorganize, but by 1000 hrs. the attack was back on. That night another counterattack against the 1/9th Infantry lasted for two hours before the Germans were driven off. The 9th Infantry was facing impregnable positions outside the villages of Bourg Neuf and Fourneuf. On 30 Aug. the 3/9th, under Major William F Kernan, began an attack against this area which lasted four days. The battalion was awarded a Unit Citation for this action.

The principal defenders of the area were the 4th and 8th companies of the 7th Parachute Regiment. The 9th Infantry was forced to attack across an open field strewn with mines. One platoon of I/9th was wiped out in a single charge. Another platoon made five attempts before it was able to cross a single field. Hand to hand fighting erupted in Bourg Neuf; the Germans fought hard to defend every house. On the night of 1 Sept. the Germans began to withdraw from the area. A few counterattacks recovered some of the lost ground, but the main German defensive line in the sector was broken. The 9th Infantry, however, was worn out after the battle and was pulled back to division reserve. There it would rest, replacements would build back up its strength, and the men would train in the use of special weapons, such as flamethrowers and demolition charges, that would be needed in the coming street fighting.

At last it seemed the German defensive line was starting to crack. Over a thousand prisoners were taken. An entire unit of Armenians serving in the German Army surrendered. One German officer surrendered carrying a briefcase filled with underwear, towels, and other personal items. When questioned he claimed he always equipped himself this way when he went out on a patrol. One night a German car drove up to the American lines. Two men got out; one dressed as an officer, the other as a private. After surrendering it became known that they were both officer's orderlies and had decided to head off to captivity "in style."

On 30 Aug. the 38th Infantry Regiment was reassigned from Task Force B and brought back to the 2nd Division to replace the 9th Infantry. During an attack at Coataudon an unusual event occurred in one of the rifle platoons of E/38th. One of the squad leaders was badly hit by machine gun fire. Sgt. Frank Valentich was bleeding heavily when he was dragged into a nearby building. The platoon leader, Lt. Charles Curley, had heard Valentich previously say that as a Catholic he believed that since he had gone to nine consecutive First Friday Masses when he died there would be a priest present to give him the last rites. Just when it appeared that Valentich would die unabsolved a trap door in the empty house opened and miraculously out came two French priests. The building turned out to be a hostel for traveling priests and, true to the sergeant's belief, he was indeed given the last rites before he died from blood loss.

More and more noncombatant Germans surrendered as soon as they were able. A major propaganda campaign of German language programs broadcast by loudspeaker, in conjunction with leaflets promising good treatment, convinced many Germans to give up. Many Germans stated they would have surrendered sooner, except the paratroopers kept a careful eye on them. One German stated that, *Your propaganda leaflets may have accomplished a great deal, but the machine pistol of Oberleutnant Stortz (7th Para Regt.) is more powerful.*"

The fight for Hill 105

At the same time that the 9th was in its struggle, the 23rd Infantry was trying to capture the strongpoint at Hill 105. When General Grow of the 6th Armored Division had first arrived at Brest he had immediately recognized that Hill 105 was the key position to the east of Brest. To capture this important hill, companies A&C of the 5th Rangers were brought in to assist the 2nd Division. All three battalions of the 23rd took part in the fighting and by late evening the eastern slope was in American hands. A&C/5th Rangers held the center of the 23rd line.

Assisting in the fight for Hill 105 were the guns of "Ivory X" on the Daoulas Peninsula. Able to fire from the south upon the reverse slope of the hill, the .50 caliber machine gun fire from Ivory X neutralized German movement on the southern side of the hill. The gun and observation positions on the Daoulas Peninsula made life extremely difficult for the Germans, who were being fired upon from almost every angle.

On 1 Sept. the 2nd took part in a coordinated attack along with the 8th Infantry division on its right flank. Both Divisions working together were able to advance. The next day 2/23rd pushed forward 800 yards to the base of Hill 105. At noon 1&2/23rd were able to reach the crest of Hill 105, with 3/23rd moving up on the northeastern slope. These units fought through the German positions, which were strengthened by a handful of antiaircraft guns, for the remainder of the day. By nightfall elements of the 23rd Infantry had crossed the top of the hill and worked their way down the western slope. With Hill 105 nearly captured, and troops working around the sides, the remaining Germans withdrew to their next line of defense. This was centered on Hill 90, near Kermeur, the next high ground outside Brest. The attack on Hill 90 was directly supported by C/86th Chemical Mortar Bn., B/612th Tank Destroyer Bn. (towed), A&C/5th Ranger Bn., and a platoon from B/705th Tank Destroyer Bn.

The next day 3/9th occupied Fourneuf and the rest of the 9th Infantry moved into Kervern. A major air strike was planned against Brest on 3 Sept. so the front line troops were careful to lay out their aerial recognition panels. Even with this precaution several bombs fell in the 23rd Infantry sector. For a short period there was only weak German resistance as the

3rd BATTALION 9th INFANTRY UNIT CITATION

General Order Number 15, 1945

"The 3rd Battalion, 9th Infantry Regiment is cited for distinguished and extraordinary heroism against strong German forces in forcing the enemy defenses north of Brest, France, in a four day engagement beginning on 30 August 1944. The entire battle was fought at close range, sometimes from house to house and hand to hand, in rolling hedgerow country which the Germans had fortified with pillboxes, communications trenches, tunnels and cleverly camouflaged gun emplacements. The core of the enemy resistance defending these positions was a reinforced, full strength weapons company of a parachute regiment. With their arrogance, self assurance and high morale, these troops differed greatly from the demoralized disorganized German troops captured in great numbers in adjoining sectors. At a cost of 45 killed and 110 wounded, the 3rd Battalion captured two principal strongholds of the German main line of resistance at Bourg Neuf and Fourneuf, thereby denying the enemy positions of great tactical value; positions that formed the pivot of all the German ground and fire organizations in this sector. The enemy's line could no longer be held. The 3rd Battalion as well as the regiment on its right were able to advance 1,000 yards without major difficulty. The victory was a product of skillful leadership and relentless fighting. The highest personal bravery and self sacrifice were extracted of the troops, and the price was paid, in the case of one platoon to the extent of almost 100 percent casualties in a single bayonet assault. When the fighting ended on 1 Sept 1944, the bulk of enemy resistance had been crushed. That night the Germans made no attempt to reoccupy the positions from which they had been driven or to evacuate their dead. Dawn patrols revealed that all survivors had withdrawn. The ferocity and determination of the 3rd Battalion's repeated and relentless assaults dealt a lasting blow to the morale of the enemy who failed to make another comparable stand until they were within the heavily fortified lines at the old wall of the city of Brest. The loyalty, heroic effort and devotion to duty exemplified by the 3rd Battalion, 9th Infantry Regiment reflects highest credit on the armed forces of the United States".

2nd Division infantryman
Infantrymen did not normally carry Thompson submachine guns, but a small number were officially issued to the 2nd Division at Brest for use in the city fighting. This man wears the HBT fatigue jacket and trousers over a wool shirt. He also wears the standard U.S. Army service shoes and lace up canvas leggings.Under the camouflage net on his helmet he has placed a 2nd Infantry Division patch. Many of the original 2nd Division men landing in France had this insignia painted on their helmets. One soldier at Brest is seen in the photo on page 126 with a patch under his netting. This was an unusual practice, but may have resulted from a replacement wanting to fit in with the older men who had the insignia painted on their helmets.
(Reconstruction)

The approach to Brest from the east, the traditional hedgerows giving way to the built-up suburbs outside the old city. The Germans normally dug into the corners of the hedgerows for better fields of fire. Similarly, in the city they generally positioned their machine guns in corner buildings.

Above.
This sequence from a film shows men from Company A, 23rd Infantry Regiment, moving up to combat. The 2nd Division insignia on this helmet appears to be a shoulder patch placed under the netting. Helmet markings were not worn by every 2nd Division man at Brest. Possibly the painted helmets were only worn by the original soldiers, and the men without them are replacements. Although it is hard to see in this frame, the pole charges carried by the two men are constructed from recently cut branches still with their bark.
(National Archives)

Right.
The unit markings on the medical jeep (2/23 I) can clearly be seen. Curiously, the jeep has a piece of wood on the front to break any wires stretched across the road, instead of the typical metal bar. The medics have red cross armbands safety-pinned onto their jackets instead of being properly worn on the arm.
(National Archives)

Below.
Following the jeep is a group of men carrying various weapons used in city fighting. The first man has two sections of a Bangalore torpedo (a metal tube filled with explosives designed to blow gaps in barbed wire). Following him is a man carrying an M1A1 flamethrower wand and in the rear is a soldier with a pole charge.
(National Archives)

Americans advanced to the next German defensive line. Given time to prepare, German engineers had planted mines and booby traps liberally in the area. It was not unusual to find a booby trap with more than 200 pounds of explosives. Large naval artillery shells, torpedo warheads, and French 75mm shells were fitted with detonators. Two crossroads were discovered to have 2,000 pound charges buried beneath them. Houses were found with explosives attached to doorknobs, or mined and ready to detonate when an unsuspecting soldier tripped a wire. Teller mines, designed for anti tank use, were set to explode with only 65 pounds of pressure. Rumors of more insidious booby-traps, such as poisoned bottles of alcohol or booby trapped German pistols, circulated among the troops.

The closer they got to Brest the stronger the German defenses became. The shortage of artillery ammunition hampered the American advance, and the 2nd started to rotate the battalions in the front line so the men could take a break. On 4 and 5 Sept. the 2nd continued to press forward and keep pressure against the enemy with combat patrols. The 2nd Division artillery units took this time to displace forward to new positions for the final assault on Brest. The high ground captured on Hills 90 and 105 served as marvelous observation posts for both artillery and air strikes.

By now the men had learned to bring TDs and self-propelled 155mm guns right up to the front lines to fire point-

blank at German emplacements. The "Ivory X" units on the Daoulas Peninsula were pouring harassing fire into the rear of the German lines. Loudspeaker trucks continued to operate in the 2nd Division sector to induce the Germans to surrender. Propaganda flyers were dropped behind the lines by aircraft, while others were fired in specially designed artillery shells. German troops continued to surrender, but claimed that the explosive power of the American artillery and mortar fire were more persuasive than all of their propaganda techniques.

On 6 and 7 Sept. the 2nd Division artillery fired a bombardment to soften the German defenses for the next attack. Gen. Robertson planned to have the 23rd and 38th capture the area around Hill 90, Kervezennec, and Le Rody in the first phase. Then the 38th Infantry would move on to Hill 100 near Le Bot and the 23rd Infantry to Keraveloc and Le Rody.

The attack started off on the morning of 8 Sept. with 72 fighter-bombers striking German emplacements, and the division artillery firing 647 rounds at various designated targets. When the 23rd Infantry reached Saint-Marc, the largest town outside Brest still in German hands, they had their first real taste of street fighting. Progress was slow as the Americans made the transition from hedgerow to city fighting. The city water in the area was found to have been contaminated by the Germans as they fell back. By this time all electricity in the city was cut off, with the exception of the underground German bunkers and hospitals.

A large number of POWs were taken in the 23rd Regiment area on 8 Sept. 333 Germans were taken on this one day. Many of them claimed to have been ordered to fall back from Hill 90 into the city, but hid until able to give up to the Americans. At this point many of the German defenders had been pulled from noncombatant duties in Brest and sent into the front lines with little training or preparation. A large number had no idea to which ground unit they had been assigned, having previously been part of a naval unit. The prisoners also claimed that food was becoming scarce in the German lines. In fact, there were large stocks of food back in the city, but it was becoming very difficult to get it up to the front lines, thus causing even more discord among the combat troops.

At 1000 hrs. the 38th Infantry jumped off at Hill 100 and headed southwest. By the next day they had reached the hill just north of Le Bot. This was the last high ground to the east of Brest and it was strongly defended with antitank ditches and antiaircraft guns. It was A/38th and L/38th that led the drive over the hill, through Le Bot, and into the outskirts of Brest on the evening of 9 Sept. In the last 17 days the 2nd had reduced all German positions in their sector and captured 4,700 prisoners. Their own losses had been 312 killed, and 48 officers and 1,245 enlisted men wounded.

To the wall

At this point the Germans knew it was only a matter of time. All available manpower was rounded up and sent to the front lines. The 69 year old postmaster of the Brest military post office brought his men out to man defenses. The 30-man parachute regiment band and the parachute finance section were sent out as well. The main units by now had been scattered in combat or broken up to form the backbone of a new Kampfgruppe. This did not pose a great problem for the Germans, since the fighting was now house to house with little maneuvering. One experienced soldier could direct the actions

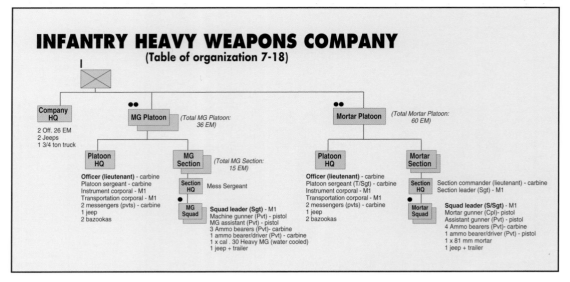

INFANTRY HEAVY WEAPONS COMPANY
(Table of organization 7-18)

Company HQ
2 Off. 26 EM
2 Jeeps
1 3/4 ton truck

MG Platoon *(Total MG Platoon: 36 EM)*

Platoon HQ
Officer (lieutenant) - carbine
Platoon sergeant - carbine
Instrument corporal - M1
Transportation corporal - M1
2 messengers (pvts) - carbine
1 jeep
2 bazookas

MG Section *(Total MG Section: 15 EM)*

Section HQ — Mess Sergeant

MG Squad — **Squad leader (Sgt)** - M1
Machine gunner (Pvt) - pistol
MG assistant (Pvt) - pistol
3 Ammo bearers (Pvt)- carbine
1 ammo bearer/driver (Pvt) - carbine
1 x cal . 30 Heavy MG (water cooled)
1 jeep + trailer

Mortar Platoon *(Total Mortar Platoon: 60 EM)*

Platoon HQ
Officer (lieutenant) - carbine
Platoon sergeant (T/Sgt) - carbine
Instrument corporal - M1
Transportation corporal - M1
2 messengers (pvts) - carbine
1 jeep
2 bazookas

Mortar Section

Section HQ — Section commander (lieutenant) - carbine
Section leader (Sgt) - M1

Mortar Squad — **Squad leader (S/Sgt)** - M1
Mortar gunner (Cpl)- pistol
Assistant gunner (Pvt) - pistol
4 Ammo bearers (Pvt)- carbine
1 ammo bearer/driver (Pvt) - pistol
1 x 81 mm mortar
1 jeep + trailer

Below.
A heavy, water-cooled machine gun tripod has been raised up onto a few crates and the barrel stuck through a hole in a wall. American soldiers could fire from behind stone walls like this and remain fairly safe. On the other hand, once a German machine gun crew exposed itself, a tank destroyer or self-propelled artillery piece would be brought up to demolish the wall.
(National Archives)

THE CAMOUFLAGE UNIFORM MYSTERY

A few photographs taken at Brest show one man, in the 2nd Division area, wearing a camouflage uniform. These uniforms were known to have been issued to a few American units back in Normandy, but they quickly fell out of favor. The standard tale is that men wearing camouflage were fired upon by their own countrymen because many soldiers in the ETO thought only the Germans wore camouflage. This story has never been confirmed.

It is interesting to note that the American Army had decided at the start of 1944 that no more supplies of camouflage uniforms would be sent overseas. This ruling was made after tests showed that the camouflage made the wearer more visible than a plain uniform when he was in motion.

There are unconfirmed reports that some men in the 2nd Division were issued 2-piece camouflage uniforms in Normandy. That some soldiers continued to wear these uniforms until Brest may be an indication that men stopped wearing them only when the fabric wore out from the strain of combat. If the soldiers had been concerned about being mistaken for Germans there is little chance that anyone would have held onto the uniform.
(National Archives)

of a group of men in a single building. As the Americans would soon learn, it did not take a highly trained and physically fit paratrooper to pull the trigger of a machine gun hidden inside a brick building.

On 9 Sept. the division artillery fired 6,700 rounds into the city during the day and almost 5,000 rounds that night. The next day both the 38th and 23rd Regiments attacked into the city. The artillery continued to shell Brest. Another 5,800 rounds were fired during daylight on 10 Sept., with continued harassing fire through the night.

On 11 Sept. the ground attack continued, but the 23rd Infantry was held up by strong enemy defenses. A/23rd was pinned down until noon by heavy machine gun fire. F/23rd to its right brought up tank destroyers from the 705th TD Bn. to knock out a particularly difficult pillbox. By midnight the 23rd Infantry had advanced roughly 800 yards from Saint-Marc into Brest.

Street fighting

The 38th Infantry now found itself fighting street by street. Demolition charges were used to blow holes between buildings so the troops could move forward under cover. TDs and bazookas were used to fire against hardened defensive positions. With no natural cover, smoke grenades became very important to conceal movement outside the buildings. At the end of the day the 38th had advanced only a few blocks and was still some distance from the city wall.

In the 2/23rd sector the advance ran into a large cemetery in the city surrounded by a high wall. The wall prevented supporting fire outside the cemetery from covering the advance through the tombstones. Several casualties were caused by flying rock splinters from the monuments. The cemetery was defended by a group of 200 paratroopers ordered to hold to the last man. To either side of the graveyard blocks of tall buildings were also strongly defended.

Attempts to move through the graveyard under smoke screens were unsuccessful. On 12 Sept. an effort was made to push around the flanks of the cemetery by blowing holes through the walls of the houses to either side, and attempting to rush past the defenders before they could react.

The 2/23rd Ammo and Pioneer (A&P) platoon was sent up to handle the explosives. Two of the A&P men were assigned to each infantry platoon. As quickly as the charges were set off, the men rushed into the next house in the block and prepared to set off another charge. This rapid advance took the Germans by surprise.

Once the buildings to each side of the cemetery were captured, riflemen were positioned to cover the Germans still defending the graveyard. Whenever a German attempted to shift positions he was immediately fired upon. Later in the day an American aid man was killed by a bullet which passed right through the red cross on his helmet. This angered the Americans and no attempt was made to allow the Germans in the area to surrender. A small group of Germans managed to hold out in the graveyard until the next morning.

On the night of 11 Sept. the 8th Infantry Division was pulled out of its position north of the city and sent south to the Crozon Peninsula. The 9th Infantry Regiment was brought forward from its rest and training area at Gouesnou to take over the 8th Division positions. With the left flank of the 2nd Division now fixed to the Elorn River, the 2nd Recon Troop was pulled back as the divisional reserve.

Over the next two days the 2nd Division advanced only a few hundred yards. Every possible weapon, including self-propelled 155's and towed 3" antitank guns, was used against the defenders. Division artillery continued to shell the city at an astounding rate, and fighter-bombers struck at any identifiable target within the old city. German snipers, most likely individual riflemen without any special training, posed a major problem to the Americans moving around behind the front lines. It was easy to let the Yanks bypass their position, then fire a few rounds and disappear into the debris to await another chance.

In the countryside the rifle companies had found it best to bring food and ammo up to the front line during the night. This kept the Germans from observing the activity. In the city the Americans had to alter their activities. They found out that there were so many obstacles in the city debris that it was almost impossible to move forward in the dark. Supply parties could move much faster and easier in the daylight and the ruined buildings concealed their activities. The men also discovered that their radios would not function in the city due to

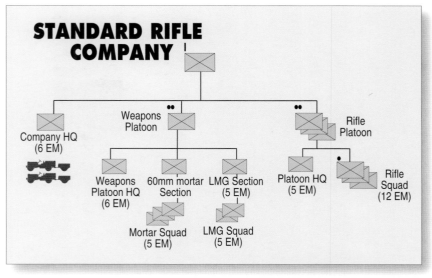

interference from the high walls. Communications were reduced to messenger or field telephone.

On 13 Sept. the 23rd Infantry advance was stopped by burning buildings. The Americans assumed that the Germans had started the fire to slow them down, but it was more likely to have been caused by the ceaseless shelling of the town. The fire allowed troops on both sides to have a chance to rest and reorganize before starting up the fight again. Not until late that night did the fires burn down enough to permit the advance to continue.

The use of flamethrowers in the city was limited, mainly because the burning buildings only held back the Americans. The only documented use was in the 23rd Infantry sector. Their advance was held up by a reinforced pillbox on a street corner with the embrasure no more than 10 inches from the ground. An assault team of two flamethrowers, two assistants, a bazooka team, and two BAR men was sent up. The team flanked the pillbox, smothered it with flame, and 13 Germans stumbled out to surrender.

Painfully slow progress was made until the night of 14 Sept. when most of the division was within a short distance of the old city wall. This posed the greatest obstacle in the 2nd Division area. It was a near impenetrable barrier to both armor and infantry alike. The ancient stone wall and moat had been upgraded by the Germans with modern weapon emplacements.

Above.
A group of GIs hug a building as they prepare to move into Saint-Marc. In the center can be seen a radioman carrying the SCR-300 on his back. This was the radio generally used to communicate from company headquarters up to battalion. Due to its range extra sets were frequently acquired and used by patrols.
(National Archives)

Right.
Trip wires were often used by the Germans to set off mines. This grappling hook was fixed to a rifle grenade body and fired into a minefield. Pulling the hook back by the attached cord would allow the men to detonate any such mines from behind cover. Demonstration movies show the technique worked, but the hooks were more often caught on an obstruction than on a trip wire.
(National Archives)

Fort Guelmeur was one of the few fortifications to the east of Brest.
Unlike the forts in the 29th sector, very little was written about
this one, and it seems the 2nd Division did not have
a hard time capturing it. Since the war it has been totally
demolished and houses built on the site.

All entrances had been sealed. Getting to the wall was hard enough, but scaling it under fire would be impossible. General Robertson ordered that, within the limits of the ammunition allowance, the artillery units including all three cannon companies were to execute 24-hour a day harassing fire on every known position along the wall.

The 2nd Division Artillery Commander, Brigadier General George P. Hays, directed that the artillery fire be continuously shifted at irregular intervals to maximize the psychological effects upon the defenders. 81mm mortars were to fire into the city at the rate of one round a minute. Whenever possible white phosphorus was to be used against known German strongpoints.

These rounds were known to terrorize the Germans and were specifically directed against ventilation ducts to the underground chambers. This constant stream of artillery fire directed at the center of the city began on 15 Sept.

On 16 Sept. the 2nd Infantry Division finally got to the city wall. After fighting through the hedgerow filled countryside, and then through the congested city of Brest, the Americans were now stopped by an obstacle more suited to a medieval siege than 20th century warfare. Only with the combined efforts of all units, and a small amount of luck, would the Americans break into the heart of Brest.

Deception at Brest- Task Forces X, Y& Z

The 23rd Special Troops was sent in late August to deceive the Germans at Brest as to the forces they faced outside the city. Three different task forces (X, Y, and Z) were set up to simulate two tank battalions of the 6th Armored (that had moved to Lorient) and a field artillery battalion. This operation lasted from 22 to 26 August and was a minor but important, aspect of the siege.

In preparation, the men of the 23rd Headquarters visited the 6th Armored Division on 18 August to make a detailed survey of how the unit marked their vehicles, painted signs, used code names, transmitted messages - everything that might tip

CAPTAIN DUCKWORTH'S COMPANY F

Company F of the 23rd Infantry Regiment was commanded by Captain George H. Duckworth at Brest. In a postwar study he recalled some of the unusual facts about his company that normally never make it into the history books. In Brittany he was the only officer of his company who had landed with the unit in France. Only 30% of his men had come ashore with him. This is not to say they were green troops, many had gained valuable combat experience fighting through Normandy. He also recalled that his unit was given a special issue of weapons for the assault on Brest. Each squad was issued with two Thompson SMGs and two BARs instead of the usual one. Although it was common for infantry squads to pick up additional BARs on their own, the issue of Thompsons to a rifle company was quite unusual. Unfortunately it is not clear when, or how, these weapons were provided, but one veteran recalls

the Thompsons were issued to the squad scouts. Other reports state that as early as July the 2nd Division had tried to get one Thompson in each squad, and had traded with the 1st Infantry Division for some. Duckworth also recalled that his company had found that the standard company issue of one SCR-300 radio, six SCR-536 Handi-talkies, and four sound powered phones was not enough to provide for adequate communications.

F/23rd (and it can be assumed than many other companies did likewise) acquired their own batch of gear including a German 8 line switchboard, 5 German field telephones, 12 sound powered phones, 2 SCR-300's and 6 SCR 536's. These were normally carried on one of the company jeeps when not in use. The company took care of the equipment and phone lines without assistance from the battalion communications section.

off an enemy intelligence officer that it was, in fact, the 6th Armored Division. During the operation the deception troops would use both real vehicles and rubber dummies painted with correct 6th Armored bumper markings and all men would wear 6th Armored Division patches.

Both the 15th and 69th Tank Bns. had left Brest and moved south down to Lorient, so a fake program of radio transmissions was supposed to be sent to indicate their return to Brest. Records indicate that this part of the operation was taken out of the hands of the 23rd and (supposedly) run by the 12th Army Group, much to the irritation of the 23rd signal officers. The evidence suggests that this part of the operation was never performed.

On 23 August Task Force X, under the command of Captain Oscar M. Seale, moved into position in the 2nd Infantry Division sector near Plabennec. His job was to make Company D of the 709th Tank Bn. appear to be the complete 15th Tank Bn. Starting with one sonic platoon, the appropriate sounds were played to simulate the approach of one tank. This increased over a period of 30 minutes until the sounds of a full tank company (18 tanks) were broadcast of them moving into an assembly area. Two other sonic cars also played similar

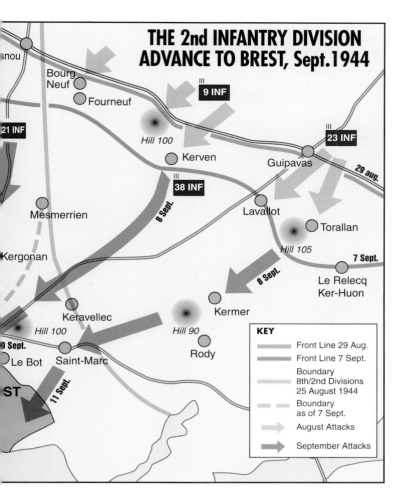

THE 2nd INFANTRY DIVISION ADVANCE TO BREST, Sept.1944

KEY

Front Line 29 Aug.	
Front Line 7 Sept.	
Boundary 8th/2nd Divisions 25 August 1944	
Boundary as of 7 Sept.	
August Attacks	
September Attacks	

sounds at distances 600 yards apart to simulate three full tank companies.

Meanwhile, an SCR-506 radio simulating the 15th Tank Bn. entered the 2nd Division radio net. Regular radio checks were made using the correct codes and frequencies of the 15th Tank, and a handful of coded messages were sent just as the real 15th Tank Battalion would have sent had it been there.

The effort was to make it look like the 15th had moved into an assembly area just behind the lines and was preparing for an assault. The first efforts by the sonic platoon were felt to be too far away from the Germans, so a closer position was selected only 500 yards behind the front line. This worked well and it was estimated that the tank sounds could be heard for more than 3,000 yards. A mile away the 2nd Division Engineers, who had not been informed of the deception, were convinced that a real tank unit had moved in.

That night the engineers erected 53 rubber dummies of medium tanks and jeeps. Because the Germans had no observation aircraft at Brest the dummies were set up so that observers on the ground could spot them from a distance. Guards kept everyone from getting within 200 yards of the dummies. The guards were dressed as men from the 6th Armored and everything possible was done to make the area look like it actually held a tank battalion from that unit. The 9th Infantry Regiment later estimated that between 20-50 additional German antitank guns were moved to the area after Task Force X had set up.

However, a heavy price was paid in this sector to teach the American Army to better coordinate their deception plans. Someone at a higher level had blundered and not realized that if Task Force X was successful this would not be the place for a real tank unit to attack, the Germans would be expecting them. On 25 Aug. D/709th Tank Bn. attacked in the very same area the Germans thought there was a full American tank battalion. As the light tanks moved forward the 2nd platoon leader's tank fell into a German emplacement and bogged down. Shortly afterwards the other three tanks in his platoon were knocked out. In the 1st platoon four of the five tanks bogged down and were unable to move. The platoon commander, Lt. Burnette, moved forward in his tank, but was soon hit by three Panzerfausts. The deception had worked, but the 709th Tank Bn. had paid a heavy price.

Task Force Z, under command of Lt. Col. Clifford Simonsen, set up a similar phony tank position in the 29th Division sector, turning Company A of the 709th Tank Bn. into the full 69th Tank Bn. They set up 40 rubber dummies one mile northwest of Millizac. A real tank was driven in the area to make tread marks on the ground. The real tanks of A/709th were set up along the road where passers-by would spot them. The rubber dummies were placed further away and also under a tight guard.

A failure in communication between the deception troops and the 29th Division almost led to another disaster. Just before the sonic deception portion of the operation was to start, Simonsen discovered that the local infantry commander had planned an attack to start 15 minutes after the tank noise was to begin. The plans were rapidly changed to start the tank noises at a later time. Had everything started as originally planned, the 29th Division Infantry would have attacked with the Germans at a full state of readiness.

The two deception operations were an attempt to draw off German antitank defences from the central attack in the 8th Division sector. Neither of the two notional tank units drew enemy fire, but the Americans were quite sure the Germans had been fooled. Prisoners taken in the area were convinced that they faced American tanks from the 6th Armored Division. When Col. Fürst was captured at Le Conquet, he was convinced the tanks were there as he had personally heard them moving up.

2nd INFANTRY DIVISION (*Ivanhoe*)

- 9th Infantry Regiment (*Index*)
- 23rd Infantry Regiment (*Inspire*)
- 38th Infantry Regiment (*Impressive*)
- 2nd Engineer Combat Bn. (*Impetuous*)

Division Artillery (*Ivory*)
- 12th Field Artillery Bn. (*Impact*)
- 15th Field Artillery Bn. (*Import*)
- 37th Field Artillery Bn. (*Impede*)
- 38th Field Artillery Bn. (*Imperial*)

Division Special Troops (*Indivisible*)
- 2nd Signal Co. (*Incredible*)
- 2nd QM Bn. (*Ipana*)
- 702nd Ordnance Co. (*Indigo*)
- 2nd Recon Troop (*Impudence*)
- 2nd Medical Bn. (*Immune*)
- 2nd Division MP platoon (*Insecure*)

Task Force Y, under command of Lt. Col. Mayo, was given a dual mission of simulating a field artillery battalion as well as seeing if they could fool the Germans into shelling a fake artillery position. Working with the 37th Field Artillery, this group set up three dummy artillery positions on a hill in the 2nd Division sector. These were 1,200 meters in front of a real 155mm artillery position of the 37th FA Bn.

Flash simulators powered by a 1/2 pint of black powder were used at night to trick the Germans into thinking the dummy guns had fired. In fact, these flashes were synchronized with the actual firing of the guns behind them. Less than 30 minutes after the first shots the Germans began counter-battery fire upon the phony positions. A number of times during the next two days the Germans fired at the simulated positions, and did not shell the real artillery unit behind them.

The 23rd Headquarters continued to perfect their deception techniques and performed a number of missions in the ETO. As more experience was gained, better coordination was developed between the deception troops and the combat units they worked alongside. The 23rd played a small but important part and their actions must be taken into account when assessing how the Germans reacted to the American advance in Northern Europe.

Above.
2nd Division MPs lead a group of POWs to the rear at the start of September 1944. A woman, wearing a white painted French helmet and red cross armband, is seen walking next to the officer in the lead. She is probably one of the local women who have volunteered to help the medics treat casualties. The white object she holds appears to be a cat.
(National Archives)

Opposite page.
The Intelligence & Reconnaissance Platoon of the 38th Infantry Regiment takes a break in captured German bombproof dugouts. These shelters were generally impregnable to Allied shells and bombs, but they could not protect the men against the psychological damage of being under constant bombardment.
(National Archives)

Down at the railroad yards, near the eastern edge of the port, an American gun crew fires on the last remaining German strongholds in the city of Brest. Most of the buildings are concealed in smoke from the many fires. Some of these were set by the Germans to form a barrier between them and the advancing Americans.
(National Archives)

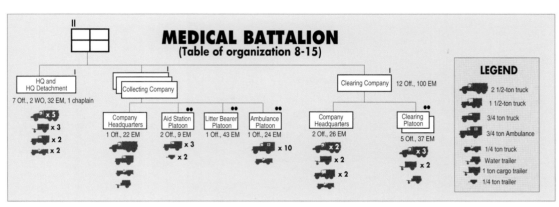

MEDICAL BATTALION
(Table of organization 8-15)

HQ and HQ Detachment
7 Off., 2 WO, 32 EM, 1 chaplain
x5 / x3 / x2 / x2

Collecting Company

Clearing Company — 12 Off., 100 EM

Company Headquarters
1 Off., 22 EM

Aid Station Platoon
2 Off., 9 EM
x3 / x2

Litter Bearer Platoon
1 Off., 43 EM

Ambulance Platoon
1 Off., 24 EM
x10

Company Headquarters
2 Off., 26 EM
x2 / x2

Clearing Platoon
5 Off., 37 EM
x3 / x2

LEGEND
- 2 1/2-ton truck
- 1 1/2-ton truck
- 3/4 ton truck
- 3/4 ton Ambulance
- 1/4 ton truck
- Water trailer
- 1 ton cargo trailer
- 1/4 ton trailer

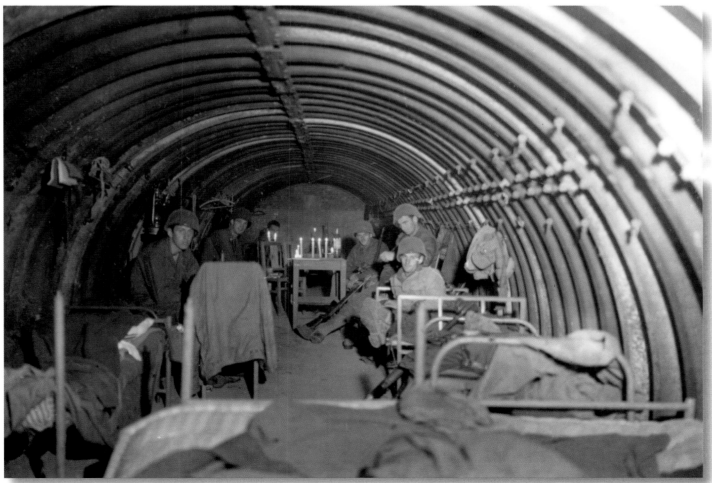

MAJOR GENERAL WALTER M. ROBERTSON

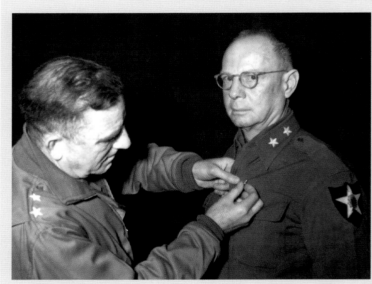

General "Robby" Robertson had attended West Point and was commissioned in the class of 1912. He first served in Hawaii, then during WW1 he helped train troops in the United States. In 1919 he arrived in France as the camp inspector for the Port of Brest. Rising through the ranks between the wars, he helped train the 2nd Division in the States and brought it overseas. His greatest moment is thought to be his defense of the Elsenborn Ridge during the Ardennes offensive. After the war he commanded the XVth Corps, and later served in the Philippines and the Sixth Army. He retired in 1950 and went on to be in charge of Civil Defense for the state of California.

General "Robby" Robertson of the 2nd Infantry Division is shown here in 1945 being presented with a Bronze Star by General Leonard Gerow. The medal was awarded for Robertson's defense against the Germans on the Elsenborn Ridge in Belgium.
(National Archives)

THE AIRCRAFT COLLISION

There is one incident which seems to have been remembered by most of the men who fought at Brest. On 5 Sept. there was a daylight bombing raid on the city. When such events occured soldiers on both sides tended to pause in their actions and look up at the show. This explains why so many soldiers were watching when a fighter, thought to be a P38, suddenly dove out of the clouds and cut a B-17 in half.

The tail sections fluttered to the ground and, as the story goes, German soldiers later claimed they had helped a very shaken, but alive, tail gunner out of the wreckage.

In the 2nd Division sector the bodies of two crewmen fell, penetrating a foot into the soft ground. The rest of the crew was found dead in the wreckage of the bomber, never having had a chance to jump free.

The most heavily mined area at Brest was the region just outside the city in the 2nd Division sector. A lack of mines caused the Germans to use whatever munitions were at hand. Here an artillery shell is wired to a fuse that will ignite if someone were to put pressure on the barbed wire, thus pulling on the wire attached to the fuse.
(National Archives)

1

2

3

THE INDIANHEADS VS. THE BLACK MARKET

One important item that had been growing short in supply during the battle was cigarettes. The black market was beginning to steal huge numbers of cigarettes, and other items, from the American quartermasters. In an unusual move, when the 2nd Division was sent from Brest to join the fighting in the east one battalion was held back. 2/38th was given the task of guarding American supply trains. The high command realized the most effective defense against the thefts: putting combat soldiers in charge of making sure their buddies on the front lines got their fair share.

Unlike the rear echelon quartermasters, the riflemen of 2/38th did not hesitate to shoot when black marketeers attempted to rob the trains. The word spread quickly that combat soldiers were guarding the supplies and they would not take bribes or look the other way. The soldiers knew all too well what it was like to be stuck in a foxhole with no food or tobacco and were not about to let someone rob their buddies. As an added unspoken incentive, if they did a good job they would not be sent back to the front lines; a reward more important than any bribe could ever be. With the combat soldiers protecting the supply trains thefts dropped dramatically. In November 1944 the 2nd Division railroad guards were finally sent back to the division, then serving in the Ardennes.

1, 2. The small size of the 57mm antitank gun meant that the crew could leave it in a position such as this. Then, when confronted by a German target in the next street, wheel it out, shoot, and pull it quickly back under cover. This could not be done with the larger and heavier 3" antitank gun. One drawback of the 57mm was that, unlike the smaller 37mm gun, there was no canister (shotgun) round issued for the 57. This would have been a useful type of ammunition for the gun crews to use against German infantry.

3. This French B1Bis or Somua tank turret (47mm gun) was turned into a strongpoint by the Germans.

4. Two M-18 tank destroyers wait to be called up in the eastern sector of Brest. The closest is marked to B/705th TD Bn. This photo shows that after all the bombs and shelling some sections of Brest remained relatively intact.

5. A 38th Infantry Regiment 57mm gun crew waits in a Brest street for the call to move forward. Although often thought of as being too small for antitank use, the 57 was a very powerful weapon when the gun crews were able to obtain a supply of the British Discarding Sabot (DS) ammunition. The DS ammunition used a disposable sleeve around a smaller projectile, thus doubling the velocity of the round. A 57mm DS round could penetrate up to six inches of armor at a 0 degree deflection angle.

6. Many American units picked up captured German vehicles in the break-out form Normandy. This amphibious German schwimmwagen is seen driven by Captain Jim Love of the 38th Infantry Regt. Antitank Company.

(All photos courtesy Jim Love)

"Street fighting is a misnomer as the street is the one place we can not go."
Infantryman at Brest

IN THE CITY

Chapter 13

Once the Americans got into the built-up areas of Brest, they started their first extended period of city fighting. Numerous reports and suggestions on city fighting were collected from the battle for Brest (primarily from the 2nd Division), which were compiled and distributed to the rest of the forces in Europe. These lessons would come in very handy when the Americans started fighting for the larger German cities.

This M1917A1 heavy machine gun crew has opened up the tripod to flatten the gun as close to the pavement as possible. When positioned along a street, one machine gun could control its entire length and prevent anyone from crossing it. The tube wrapped around the barrel is used to catch the steam created when the barrel heats up in extended firing. The metal can to the right of the gun would be used to catch the steam and allow it to condense back into water. *(National Archives)*

Some of the ideas would change as the Americans gained more experience fighting in cities, but the lessons learned at Brest were the foundation they built on.

What the Americans discovered was that, in the city, the center of the street formed the unit boundaries. Each block or building had to be assigned to a specific unit, so that it would not be accidentally by-passed before being cleared of Germans. Machine guns and heavy weapons were positioned to fire down the open streets, turning them into killing zones no one would venture into. Most movement was

The M1A1 flamethrower is seen here being tested by men from the 35th Engineer Combat Bn. in Brittany. This flamethrower was cumbersome, difficult to use, and not very rugged. Although they were only used a few times in Brittany the mere sight of flamethrowers in action convinced some Germans to surrender rather than risk being burnt. *(National Archives)*

by passing through holes blown in the walls of adjoining buildings (called "mouseholes").

The Germans had developed a great deal of experience fighting in cities on the Eastern front. They knew to place the majority of their men in the corner buildings, and not in the middle of a block where they would have poor fields of fire and could easily be surrounded. Each intersection was covered with machine gun fire, and snipers were positioned either in the upper stories or low in the basements. At times a machine gun would be positioned in a high structure so the bullets could ricochet down the street. All that was needed for a firing port was to remove a single brick from a wall, but at major intersections well-constructed pillboxes could ensure control of the area.

If the Germans thought they were going to lose a house they set it on fire, thus preventing the Americans from entering it and slowing the advance for a few hours. Once it had burnt there was a rubble filled pit, loaded with debris that a tank or TD could not pass over until it had been filled in. A burnt structure also needed at least a day or two to cool before men could comfortably pass through it.

Unlike the fighting in the country, city fighting demands more men per area, as the soldiers have to guard not only the width of their sector, but also the height. In the 2nd Division a rifle company was generally assigned a two block sector, with one platoon per block and a third in reserve.

The Americans quickly found that street crossings must occur in the middle of a block and under cover of smoke. Sometimes they just threw smoke grenades to try and get the German machine guns to open up. Once spotted they could be knocked out by heavier weapons. In street crossings the troops made sure they could get inside quickly by either shooting off the door locks, or simply blowing open the door with a bazooka or rifle grenade.

Opinions differed as to whether it was better to enter a house from the ground or top floors. Some men claimed it was better to enter from the ground floor; a few shots of armor piercing ammunition fired up would result in Germans coming down the stairs to surrender. Being on the ground floor also meant you could set fire to the house and drive off anyone upstairs. Other soldiers claimed it was better to start at the top of a building and work down, since you could roll grenades down the stairways to make sure your path was clear. It also allowed the Germans a way out so they would not feel trapped and fight to the last man. Scaling ladders were used to let men enter windows above ground level.

One American said, *"The German quits when we enter the building he is in. Of course he could hold out for a while, but he figures*

Right.
This remarkable still from a news-reel shows a tank destroyer firing near the gates of the hospital, just outside the eastern section of the city wall. More than likely it is firing past the hospital at a strong-point located on the wall. All known positions along the wall were targeted by direct fire weapons such as tank destroyers and self-propelled guns while the infantry attempted to find a way through the wall.
(National Archives)

Below.
Concrete shelters such as this were used by German soldiers during air raids. Sentries on duty could quickly get inside while the bombs and strafing took place, but be on hand to keep an eye on the surrounding area. When the Americans moved into the city these shelters became individual pillboxes for the more dedicated Germans.
(National Archives)

our men might not play Kamerad (take his surrender) *if he did. When he finds himself surrounded he gives up.*"

Once in a building the Americans left one man per floor as a guard to prevent any missed Germans from escaping. Shooting out locks while indoors was deafening, so axes were issued to break down doors. Flashlights were mandatory to check dark rooms. Advances needed to stop well before nightfall, as it took some time for the units to reorganize and make sure they had complete coverage of their front line before dark. It could take a company commander 3-4 hours to check all his positions for the night. Relief or reinforcements were not brought up at night since moving through the rubble in the dark was too difficult. The buildings provided adequate coverage during daylight hours.

During the daylight hours it was up to the squad leaders to perform. Communications were difficult and the small SCR 536 radio was worthless in the city. Maps were useless in the rubble. Aerial photos had to be updated each day because the terrain changed with each building destroyed or burnt. Any soldier who spoke German was valuable. They could often get the enemy to surrender without a fight. One sergeant took 120 POWs in 12 days only because he spoke German. It was strongly suggested that every GI be taught how to say a few words in German, such as "*Come out with your hands up.*"

Demolitions were used extensively in the city fighting. Both pole and satchel charges were constructed by the engineers and issued to the riflemen. One problem was that a too large explosion would not just blow a hole, but bring down the entire building. If there was not an engineer with the troops to match the charge to the target, the men would tend to withdraw a house or two before setting off the explosion. One solution to this problem was to place the charge in the fireplace so that the heavier side walls there would absorb the explosion and prevent a collapse. When engineers were not present, rifle platoons were assigned a man from the Ammunition and Pioneer platoon to handle the charges. There was always the danger of walls collapsing in the city. In one incident the 44th Engineer Bn. lost seven men killed and five injured when a wall collapsed on a

A German surrender party consisting of an army major, navy captain, and marine chief petty officer enter the 9th Infantry lines to negotiate the surrender of the eastern sector of Brest. They have been blindfolded to prevent them from seeing the locations of American positions and emplacements.
(National Archives)

1. Col. Erich Pietzonka, formerly commander of the 7th FJ Regt., was made overall commander of the eastern sector of Brest. He is seen here with his Knight's Cross and Oak Leaves discussing the surrender with American interpreters. The Oak Leaves to his Knight's Cross were awarded on 16 Sept. 1944 for his service during the siege of Brest. The American on the left wearing goggles on his helmet is Col. Hirschfelder of the 9th Infantry Regiment.

2. A group of Germans wait in Woodrow Wilson Place for the surrender ceremony. Col. Pietzonka can be seen here, with his back to the camera, talking to one of his officers. This paratrooper, with a cane, wears both the "Kreta" and "Afrikakorps" cuff titles on his left sleeve.

3. Major General Robertson, commander of the 2nd Infantry Division.

work party clearing a street. Walls were purposely blown down to fill antitank ditches and armored bulldozers were used to clear the streets to bring up tracked guns.

Due to the limited range in the city the heavy machine gun was of little use. Many of the heavy machine gun units traded in their bulky guns for the light .30 caliber machine gun. The troops were enthusiastic about the new bipod mounted M1919A6 light machine gun. The troops liked it because it was lighter, easier for one man to carry, and quicker to set up. Brest was used as a testing ground for an experimental M1 carbine that fired in full automatic mode. They were issued to the 2nd Division for a three week test, but the results were mixed. Some men liked them as they were lighter and more accurate than a submachine gun. Others felt it was too inaccurate and fired too small a round. To increase firepower the 702nd Ordnance Company converted 15 round standard carbine magazines to hold 30 rounds. They also built a compensator for the carbine to reduce its tendency to pull up when fired, but many soldiers still preferred the M1 Garand rifle.

Wheeled guns, such as the 57mm, were held in a ready position until needed then wheeled around a corner, fired, and withdrawn to cover. This limited mobility made tracked vehicles like tank destroyers and self-propelled howitzers invaluable. Both were used to blast pillboxes and stubborn German positions. The Americans frequently used the noise of a mortar barrage to cov-

er the sound of the approaching engines. The only drawbacks were that these weapons could not hit high targets and with their open tops were very susceptible to sniper fire from rooftops.

Artillery played a limited role in the city fighting. The shells came in at too low an angle to shoot over the heads of the Americans. The regular artillery units were used to blast the area in the inner city, far from the fighting, to reduce morale and interdict supply routes. The 4.2" chemical mortars were considered the most effective artillery support in cities. They had a very high trajectory that could shot over buildings and their accuracy allowed them to fire within 100 yards of the front line.

The M1A1 flamethrower was a fairly crude model, but the mere sight of it was effective at getting Germans to surrender. Fragmentation and white phosphorous grenades were heavily used to clear rooms, and the supplies at the front lines quickly ran out. The answer was to keep a good stock of grenades on hand in company supply dumps, roughly a block to the rear of the fighting.

The M-14 thermite grenades were found to be able to melt the metal locking mechanisms on pillbox doors and shutters. Many Germans were trapped inside their emplacements when a thermite grenade fused the doors shut.

Left.
In this still frame from a newsreel General Robertson can be seen offering a cigarette to Col Pietzonka. According to witnesses at the time, Pietzonka glanced to the cameramen nearby and told the American general that he appreciated the offer, but given the intense scrutiny of all the photographers could not accept.
(National Archives)

In the Old City

The most formidable defensive line the Germans had was the massive stone wall that surrounded the old city. The Germans had sealed up every entrance, cleared fields of fire up to 300 yards in front of the wall, and planted a large number of mines in front of it. The German garrison was safe from Allied air and artillery attack in deep concrete shelters. They had only to fire their machine guns while safe behind thick stone and concrete, to keep the Americans from scaling the wall.

The wall stopped where the Penfeld River flowed through the city. It continued on the other side to protect the western (Recouvrance) sector of Brest. The gap left by the river opening would eventually prove to be the weak link in the defensive line. Because the western flank of the old City of Brest was protected by the Penfeld River, the Germans had not defended the wall on the western side as heavily as they had to the north and east. The 29th Division did not have the difficulties in crossing the wall that the 2nd Division had.

The 29th Infantry Division in Brest

In the 29th sector the 175th Infantry attacked east towards the old city wall. At 1900 hrs. on 16 Sept. E/175th had scaled the wall and became the first American troops to enter into the actual city of Brest. They soon discovered a tunnel running underneath the wall and moved the rest of 2/175th inside the wall. By the night of 17 Sept. the 175th had cleared the area between the city wall and the Penfeld River of all German resistance and taken over 600 prisoners.

Steady progress continued on 17 Sept. with the rest of the 29th moving deep into Recouvrance. Part of the German defenses consisted of small steel pillboxes that were conical in shape. The steel was thick enough to resist a 57mm antitank gun and the curved surface made most shots ricochet off. The soldiers were forced to invent new combat methods to advance in this urban area, but combined efforts by infantry and engineer units kept the Americans moving.

It was discovered that the German pillboxes at Brest were more modern and stronger than those later found in the Siegfried line. The defenses on the German border had been constructed years earlier, but the emplacements at Brest were able to take advantage of the many years of German combat experience. The key to knocking out the German positions was found to be getting men behind them. Once the Germans realized the Americans were in the rear of their positions they frequently gave up.

The 175th was assigned to mop up the last defenders dug into the area around the city wall and clear the northern section of Recouvrance. The 115th and 116th, along with the 2nd Rangers, moved street by street through the city. The attached tank destroyers proved instrumental in firing at specific hard targets. By the night of 17 Sept. the 175th had their area clear of active German resistance, and the 116th was on the bluff overlooking the sub pens. The 115th had been slowed down by numerous fortified houses and not made as good progress.

F/116th was treated to a spectacular sight when at 1000 hrs. on 17 Sept. they agreed to accept the surrender of some German soldiers in a theater. 56 Germans had come out to surrender. A group of 110 French civilians then came out of a nearby church. The civilians had hidden in the church basement for 42 days. Quickly both the French and American flags were flown over the church entrance and someone began to play the Marseillaise, followed by the Star Spangled Banner, on the organ. As the French civilians stood with bared heads, the German POWs silently marched past them into captivity.

The end was in sight once the 115th broke through to just above the submarine pens. Looking over the pens from behind, they were faced with an area of level ground dotted with a number of pillboxes, some made from 14" thick steel. The pillbox garrisons lived underneath and were connected to the sub pens by underground tunnels. A self-propelled 155mm gun was brought up to place direct fire on these pillboxes, but the heavy shells just bounced off them. On the night of 17 Sept. the attached 5th Ranger Bn. developed a new technique for destroying German pillboxes, consisting of pouring thickened gasoline down the ventilators and detonating this with a shaped beehive charge. But before this method could be disseminated among the American units the German will to resist crumbled.

That night the 29th kept illumination flares over the Brest waterfront to prevent any Germans from slipping out of the city to the Crozon Peninsula. A doctor from the 29th Division ventured down into an underground German hospital to check on how the wounded were doing and found that the staff and patients had broken into the alcohol supply. He said, *"They were all drunk, patients and everybody else. They were wandering up and down the halls singing and having a swell time. It looked like a fraternity house party after a football game."*

The next morning, at 0745 hrs. on 18 Sept., a group of German officers approached the 2/115th lines under a white flag. The four German officers (Army, SS, Navy and Air Force) were disappointed to be able to talk to only a battalion commander; they desired a higher ranking officer. The clean and well groomed Germans requested that they be allowed to surrender in an orderly manner, and wanted assurances that their wounded would be taken care of. The Germans were sent back in a jeep to prepare the surrender of the area at 1100 hrs. All firing west of the Penfeld River was ordered to cease at 0900 hrs.

Right, below and opposite page.
1. 2. 3. 4. and 5.
Most of the inner ring of Brest fortifications were put down when the town was remodeled after the war. These photos could have been taken around Recouvrance or Fort Bouguen. Today it would be very difficult to pinpoint where these fortifications once stood.
(National Archives)

A section of the Brest city wall, showing how difficult it must have been to scale it under the eyes of German machine gunners. The official caption of this photo indicates that this was the location it was first scaled, however there is no confirming evidence.
(National Archives)

Meanwhile, in the 1/115th sector the attack continued until two German officers appeared with a white flag near the oil storage facilities. A direct telephone line was run to the German positions and surrender terms were conveyed to the Germans by field telephone.

At 1030 hrs. the Americans began to see the German garrison start to assemble under a white flag. Major Miller, the CO of 2/115, went out with a small staff to meet them. Expecting 2-300 Germans, Miller was amazed to find a few thousand coming forward. To the end the Germans were under strict discipline. The roll was called, the commander shook each man's hand, and they marched off into captivity.

The Americans then ventured forth into the underground chambers and were amazed to find how well the Germans had been living. They found soft beds, photographs, cases of cigars and alcohol, and a large underground mess hall. Major Miller made his way deep down to the commander's office where he accepted the final surrender of both the army commander and naval admiral in charge of the submarine pens.

Across the Penfeld River the 2nd Division was mopping up the city of Brest. Ramcke had already left for the Crozon Peninsula. A number of captured Americans were liberated from German hands and returned to their units. The men of the 29th engaged in a minor orgy of looting the German supplies until the division was pulled back to Le Conquet for a rest. Recouvrance and the sub pens were taken over by rear echelon units assigned to evaluate if the port was at all usable. For the very first time since D-day the 29th was allowed a decent rest. Except for one hour of calisthenics and drill each day the 29ers were allowed to sleep, see movies, lie on the beaches, and, at long last, get a shower and a fresh change of clothing.

Plans were underway to send 15% of the division on leave to England, but the needs of the Army prevented this since the entire unit was needed in Germany to attack the Siegfried line. During the month of September the 29th Division and Task Force Sugar had captured 27 major strongpoints and taken over 13,000 POWs. In return they

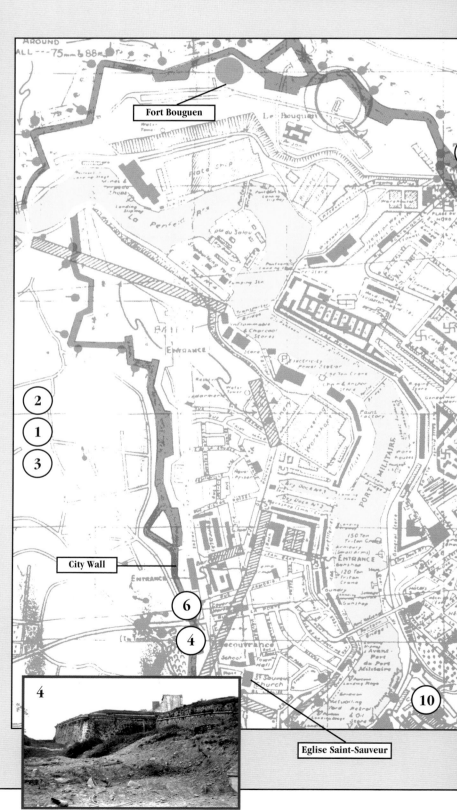

Fort Bouguen

City Wall

Eglise Saint-Sauveur

A view of where route N-12 enters Brest to the northeast of the city. The damage gives an idea of what the 2nd Division had to fight through to move up to the city walls. The man-made mound can be seen along the top right of the horizon. This shows what a wonderful observation point it was in the flat terrain. *(National Archives)*

The old city wall at the main entrance on the eastern side of the city *(National Archives)*

The western edge of the railroad yards where the tracks run into the base of the Citadel. This was almost as important a target as the submarine pens, because equipment (such as replacement torpedoes) was brought in along these tracks. Much of the basic fortifications around Brest were built in previous centuries by the French, but they still withstood the American shelling. *(National Archives)*

The Citadel at the mouth of the Penfeld River was spared much of the aerial bombardment due to the higher priority of the sub pens and railroad yard. By the time the ground fighting drew close to this area the Germans surrendered. The stone medieval style castle would have made a great defensive structure had the Germans decided to hold out top the last man. *(National Archives)*

had suffered 2,646 casualties. General Gerhardt later remarked that he felt the training his unit had received in attacking fortified positions had made all the difference. Without it he was not sure they would have ever been able to penetrate the German lines.

In the 2nd Division Sector

On 16 Sept. the 38th Infantry operating in the center sector got onto the wall about 1830 hrs. The Germans counterattacked and forced the Americans back. The next day B/9th actually scaled the wall. The 2nd platoon, under Lt. Lawrence S. Goldmeier, had crossed a ditch 30 feet deep and 20 feet wide. Goldmeier's platoon consisted of 19 men armed with rifles, three BARs, two Thompsons, and two attached machine guns. Lt. Goldmeier had joined the unit as a replacement officer on 15 Sept. He and ten of his men climbed the 35 foot high stone wall that rose at an angle of 65 degrees. At the top they came under fire from German machine guns protected behind thick concrete. By the time it was dark two of the men and Lt. Goldmeier were wounded and the platoon pulled back. The rest of his company had tried to enter the city through the gate on the Kerinou road, but were stopped by heavy machine gun and mortar fire.

On the same day a company of 159 Russians were disarmed by the Germans and sent out under a white flag to surrender to the Americans. They were taken prisoner by C/9th Infantry. The Germans distrusted them so much they wanted them out of the defensive lines. They feared the Russians would suddenly change sides and let the Americans pass the wall.

To the west the 9th Infantry had sent out patrols looking for a way through the wall. Patrols from companies K and I were ordered that if they found a way across to grab it, then quickly follow with the rest of the unit's platoon, and then the company. They were not to wait to for orders, but just get across the wall and grab a foothold at all costs.

Lt. Smith's and Lt. Berg's patrols were pinned down by heavy fire from the wall near Kergoat. Probing further to the west a patrol from the 1st platoon found a hole in the wall that appeared to have been made by artillery fire. At this point the wall was only eight feet high and a foot thick, so the patrol was unsure if this was in fact the actual city wall. Beyond the wall was a narrow canyon with a sheer cliff on the left, a small hill to the right, and the Penfeld River to the right of the hill.

Lt. Smith moved the 1st platoon through the wall and into the canyon, sending one squad left and another to the hill on the right. As they got to the hill the 17 Germans dug into it surrendered. They had been manning six machine guns. Had they opened fire they would have been able to prevent the Americans from entering the city.

The area then came under fire from a machine gun located in a tunnel on the other side of the Penfeld River. This was on the 29th Division's side of the river, but was placed so the 29ers could not get to it, and so the one gun could command the canyon the Americans were moving through. Private Nick Pappas twice fired a bazooka into the tunnel with no effect before running out of bazooka ammo. Lt. Smith called out to some 29th men across the river to be careful as they were going to blast the tunnel with rifle grenades. The Germans apparently understood and three came out to surrender. Sent back into the tunnel for their comrades, a total of 80 Germans surrendered from the one position. Company I continued to push through the hole in the wall and found that hundreds of German troops in tunnels were ready to surrender. The second platoon herded them together and took charge, allowing the first platoon to continue to press into the city. Lt. Ray said that, *"The Germans seemed dazed by the prolonged artillery fire and bombing to which they had been subjected."* By the end of the day the rest of the battalion had entered the city and the artillery bombardment was stopped.

With the 9th inside they were able to move in behind the other German positions on the city wall and help the 38th Infantry to also gain access. Both regiments swarmed into the center of Brest and by noon on 18 Sept. most of the firing in the city had stopped. Just after noon on that day a party of German officers appeared carrying a white flag. Major William F. Kernan, the commander of 3/9th Infantry, was led to the command post of the 7th Parachute Regt. inside a concrete building just off President Wilson Place. Here he met Colonel Erich Pietzonka and, with the assistance of interpreter Captain Vsenolod Podlesski, agreed to the following:

1. Both sides cease firing

2. French civilians to be barred from the City of Brest until the Germans are evacuated

3. German troops be adequately guarded against "terrorists."

4. All German able-bodied troops to leave their arms in their dugouts and assemble in President Wilson Place at 1500 hrs; when a formal surrender would be made.

Pietzonka had made it clear that he no longer had contact with all the troops under his command and warned of possible fighting by isolated units. He was specifically interested in obtaining an acknowledgment that his troops had fought honorably and according to the rules of war. At 1250 hrs. Americans accompanied German messengers under white flags to bring the surrender agreement to the German positions in Brest.

Message sent to all German positions:

"Sector East- 18.9.44 1400 hrs.

To all combat teams:

From Sector West came the suggestion for a truce. Americans penetrat-

143

ed into the heart of the city from west and north. CP completely surrounded. A truce affecting all units of Sector East is necessary at once. Am leaving final decision to the individual combat teams. We, at Wilson Place, are powerless. If the occasion necessitates it, destroy all weapons and assemble at Wilson Place at 1600 hrs. We have performed our duties to the last.

Hail Führer, People, and Fatherland

Signed: Pietzonka
Colonel and commanding officer Sector East "

German messengers were sent out to all sectors from the Elorn River to the Penfeld River, still in their hands. Colonel C.J. Hirschfelder, commander of the 9th Infantry, arrived at the German headquarters at 1420 hrs. to confirm the terms of surrender and prepare for it. An additional agreement allowed the German officers to keep their orderlies with them in captivity, with an additional understanding that all women who had worked for the Germans be given protection and evacuated by the U.S. Army. The Germans were obviously more afraid of being handed over to the local French population than of continuing the fight.

Major General Robertson arrived in President Wilson Place for the formal surrender at 1500 hrs. on 18 Sept. After arrangements were made to remove German casualties from the city, Robertson offered Pietzonka a cigarette. The German officer nodded to the group of cameramen and newsreel photographers watching him carefully and said, *"Tell the general I appreciate his kind offer, but with all this around I just can't do it. I am sure the general will understand."*

Later on, Colonel Pietzonka asked Captain Podlesski why the Americans did not attack harder in the last few days. He was told that they wanted to take their time and spare lives while still in the learning period of warfare. *"We are still learning,"* said the American, *"but I think we are learning very fast." "Yes, I think you are right"* Pietzonka replied. Pietzonka later remarked that his 1st Battalion had done well, but the 2nd Battalion had done worse than he had hoped, mainly because of the large number of untrained naval personnel that had been assigned to it.

When taken to the POW collecting point, Pietzonka asked how the Americans had entered the city. When shown how they had penetrated the wall by the river he remarked, *"Unbelievable!"* and asked his staff, *"Wasn't that place secured?"* When told that the men holding the position had surrendered Pietzonka continued, *"As late as 2300 last night I received a report from that same sector saying everything was quiet and under control".*

Those present at the surrender recall the most striking fact was that

the victors were all dirty, unshaven, and battered from combat, while the Germans for the most part were in clean uniforms, carrying suitcases, and ready for captivity. Of course these were the men who had been in the underground bunkers away from the fighting. The remnants of the German combat troops were just as dirty and tired as the Americans. They had been marched off earlier, without a chance to clean up first. From 17 to 18 Sept. the 2nd Division processed 3,307 POWs.

The final cost for the 2nd Division at Brest was 2,314 casualties. They had received 3,590 replacements during the campaign, and captured roughly 11,000 of the 37,362 POWs taken at Brest. The division had fired 1,758,000 small arms rounds and 218,000 shells. The eight mile advance into Brest had averaged only one mile every three days. The grand prize, General Ramcke, had eluded the Americans and left Brest to continue the fight from the Crozon. Even with the city of Brest in American hands the battle continued.

Above. **A seemingly endless stream of Germans march out of the city as prisoners. The actual number of prisoners stunned the Americans, who had not realized the true number of Germans in the city. Once outside the city the prisoners were put on trucks, then brought to a railway where they were moved by train to central Allied POW collection points.** *(National Archives)*

Right. **One of the few landmarks left standing in Brest was the 150 ton crane on the Penfeld River. Since smaller structures were demolished it remains a question as to why the largest crane was left intact by the Germans. Careful examination of the crane showed that this German naval mine had been used to prepare the crane for demolition, but for some reason the charge was never ignited.** *(National Archives)*

THE CROZON PENINSULA

Chapter 14

The Crozon Peninsula forms the southern edge of the Bay of Brest. It commands the southern approaches to the city, and had been heavily fortified since the 17th century. At the start of the campaign the 6th Armored Division had kept the Germans bottled up on the peninsula with light cavalry screening patrols. These were taken over by Task Force A when the 6th moved further south. On 27 Aug. the bulk of Task Force A was able to shift south from the Daoulas Peninsula to concentrate on the Crozon. Reports from the local FFI claimed that there were over 10,000 Germans in the various positions on the Crozon.

Once the Daoulas Peninsula was cleared of Germans, TFA was ordered to reconnoiter the defensive line on the base of the Crozon. The most important position on this line was a hill called Menez-Hom. Known to the Americans as Hill 330, Menez-Hom has a commanding view of the surrounding area. The main road leading into the peninsula circles part way around the hill about halfway up the slope. On 27 Aug. the cavalrymen quickly discovered that a large German force was dug into the hill.

Continued probing the next day brought in 32 prisoners. All of them were Russians who had volunteered to help the German Army fight communism in Russia, but had found themselves stuck far from home. An attack on both sides of the main road was stopped by heavy German machine gun and artillery fire. Even with heavy air support the cavalrymen of TFA were unable to penetrate the German lines. However, a weakness in the German Army soon became apparent as Russian soldiers began to trickle in all along the line. On 29 Aug. 50 Russians surrendered, followed by 106 the next day.

Many of the Russians claimed that their comrades wanted to sur-

render as well, but were prevented by the watchful eyes of the Germans. Reports came in of actual fighting between German and Russian troops on the slopes of Menez-Hom. On the evening of 30 Aug. TFA had advanced to near the crest of the hill. There a Russian officer and 35 of his men handed 20 German prisoners over to the Americans. The Russians claimed that if they surrendered at that moment the Germans would kill some of their fellow Russians still in German lines, so the Russian unit was allowed to return to the enemy lines. There they attacked another German unit and freed the rest of their own men.

Meanwhile C Troop of the 15th Cav. Squadron had sent out a dismounted patrol to check the top of Menez-Hom. There they were attacked by German defenders and Sgt. Robert Downing was struck in the back of the head by a bullet. The round penetrated the skin, but traveled around the skull and came out in front of his right ear. This lucky sergeant suffered only the two small holes and a bad headache from the injury. In the same action Pvt. Bodlak, the squadron interpreter, was captured. Bodlack spoke excellent French and German. While he was being marched away as a captive, he told his captors they would soon be overwhelmed by the Americans. Once the German officer left, Bodlak told the NCO in charge that, "*My outfit are tough old recon guys and we have lots of tanks and armored cars. They will chop you up.*" Bodlak and his excellent German did the trick and the German NCO turned the group about and marched into the American lines, after gathering up what is said to have been about 300 Germans. This opened up the defensive line and forced the Germans to withdraw that night. A Russian company failed to maintain their assigned holding position and the German withdrawal became disorganized. General Earnest requested a battalion of infantry to follow up on the breakthrough, but none were available. The Germans were able to reorganize and build up another line of defense on the Crozon. Three German companies had been left behind to delay an American advance. These units were mainly composed of Russians, Poles, and Luftwaffe noncombatant troops. They posed little resistance to the Americans and Menez-Hom was finally captured on the afternoon of 1 Sept.

Dr. Bill Parker poses in front of a German Flakpanzer 38 (t), [Panzerkampfwagen 38 (t) mit 2cm Kwk 38], a 20mm antiaircraft gun mounted on a Czech 38 (t) chassis. This vehicle was normally issued, from April 1944 on, to armored reconnaissance companies. The photo was taken by Dr. Parker's driver somewhere in the vicinity of the Crozon Peninsula.
(Courtesy Bill Parker)

Above and inset, right.
German fortifications on the Crozon Peninsula are subjected to Allied bombing attacks. Visible at the bottom of the photo is the defensive wall across a narrow stretch of the Crozon. This wall was the final defensive line of the Germans and once broken the remaining resistance quickly collapsed.
(National Archives)

German observation point and pillbox at Camaret on the Crozon. The southern tip of the Crozon was defended by men under command of the German 343rd Infantry Division.
(National Archives)

Task Force A once again moved forward, but quickly ran into the new German line. While probing the new German positions on 3 Sept., a platoon from A/17th Cavalry Squadron entered the town of Telgruc. Even though the Americans had their aerial recognition markers out they were bombed and strafed by American aircraft. One officer and six men were killed, three officers and 21 men were wounded, and approximately 50 French civilians were killed or injured in this attack.

General Earnest and Task Force A now found themselves up against an enemy very determined to hold their ground. The Germans had chosen to defend a line in terrain that was open to the north and wet and swampy to the south. With plenty of time to prepare the defenses they had built a number of camouflaged observation posts and cleared lanes of fire in front of their positions. High ground to the rear provided good observation for artillery and mortar fire. The line ran roughly from Saint-Efflez through Saint-Laurent and then south to Keradennec.

On the northern shore of the Crozon was the Lanvéoc airfield. This was defended by one 155mm, two 105mm, and two 75mm batteries. The center of the line was supported by the 804th AA Bn. with two batteries of 88mm flak, one 105mm, one 76mm, and one 75mm battery. In the south were one 105mm and four 47mm batteries. Taking all information into consideration, corps intelligence thought there were over a thousand Germans on the main defensive line and perhaps 2,500 on the peninsula total. General Middleton would later say of the Crozon, "*In all my military experience, I have never seen any-*

BREAKING THE GERMAN LINE AT SAINT-EFFLEZ

It was drizzling on the morning of 15 Sept. 1944. The 3rd Battalion/28th Infantry, under Major Ward, moved up to the front lines on the Crozon Peninsula. On the left was Company K under Captain Clarence Hollingsworth. On the right was Company L under 1st Lt. John O. Gawne. Both companies were understrength from the heavy fighting to the north of Brest. After a ten minute artillery barrage they moved out at 0800 hrs., initially meeting with only scattered small arms fire. About 0900 hrs. both companies were stalled against the German main line of defense just east of the small village of Saint-Efflez. To their front was an open field covered with German machine gun fire.

At roughly 1000 hrs. Lt. Gawne snapped. After fighting his way from Normandy, he was suddenly filled with an uncontrollable rage for all the young men on both sides that were being hurt and killed. Why didn't Ramcke just give up and spare them all this useless fighting? Jumping up from behind a small rise he madly charged the German machine gun that was holding them up, and promptly fell - his left side smashed by a few rounds.

After working his way back to a small dirt road on their left flank, Lt. Gawne held his bleeding side and told the men on the line, "*Be careful boys, look what they've done to me.*" He then staggered back down the road to a nearby farming village. Walking down this road he was exposed to German observation from the south and was shelled with small mortars. As he reached the cluster of stone houses known as Luguniat, a company medic, Pvt. Ira Bathurst, came out to help him to cover. Lt. Gawne waved him off saying it was no use both of them getting hit. Bathurst ventured out into the mortar fire anyway, and helped the lieutenant into a farmhouse and onto a bed. Gawne then tried to get the medic to bring his wrist watch back up to the company as it was the only one they had.

After giving Gawne a shot of morphine, the medic realized that unless he got this man back to the aid station soon, he was done for. When the medic left to get help, Lt. Gawne looked at his bloody hand and, in his last conscious moment in France, left an imprint of it on the stone wall. Meanwhile, Bathurst discovered that the men bringing up the telephone connection to the rear had come under German fire and dropped the reel out in a field. After they refused to venture back to get it, Bathurst dashed out into the open, grabbed the wire reel, and brought it back, saying "*Here's your phone, now get me an ambulance up here right away.*" After passing through the battalion aid station, and the 107th Evac. Hospital, Lt. Gawne was sent to Morlaix where he was flown to a hospital in England. After losing most

of the ribs on his left side, and over half his liver, he finally woke up many days later.

Back at Company L command had passed to 2nd Lt. Thomas K. Yelland. He would be wounded a few hours later, around 1500hrs, and command would be assumed by Technical Sgt. Charles E. Ballance. Ballance, the senior NCO left in Company L, reorganized the men and got them moving. Shortly after reorganizing the company Ballance was shot and killed. Captain Lowry was sent down from Bn. HQ to assume command. Over in Company K no less than four lieutenants were killed or wounded. Company I, in reserve, was committed to the left flank in an attempt to swing around the German defenses, but little progress was made.

The 3rd Battalion was finally able to break the German defenses at Saint-Efflez because of Captain Hollingsworth. He had noticed that a ravine ran down his left flank, right into the German lines. On the morning of the 15th it had been filled with fog and Hollingsworth hoped this would be the case on the next day as well. With his company at half strength, Hollingsworth reorganized his unit and put one full strength platoon under Lt L.H. Goal. This platoon was send into the ravine with orders to attack at dawn under cover of the fog. Aided by Sgts L. Stubblefield and Alfonse Schittaci, the attack down the foggy ravine succeeded. Goal's men were able to get into the enemy lines before the Germans knew what had happened. Attacking the Germans with grenades and bayonets at first, Lt. Goal added to the confusion by turning a German machine gun on the defenders. When the fight had ended the Germans had withdrawn from the position leaving 60 prisoners, 25 machine guns, and a knocked out assault gun. It was later discovered that in using the ravine the men had avoided an extensive antipersonnel minefield in front of the German lines. After the encounter Hollingsworth wrote, "*I always hated fog before, but now I love it, it's wonderful!*"

As an after note, medic Ira Bathurst made several trips up and down the dirt road from Lanvéoc to help evacuate casualties from the front line. It was not until a day or two later that he again passed by the area and found it marked off with engineer's tape. Inquiring why, he was told that the road was heavily mined. Telling the engineer that he didn't believe it as he had traveled that road a number of times, Bathurst was shown where an antipersonnel mine fuse protruded above ground. In one of those stranger than fiction stories, Bathurst learned he had walked right through a thick minefield many times without ever having realized it.

thing quite so good as the fortifications in the Crozon area. They are the most highly organized I have ever seen." This was quite a statement from a man who had witnessed the German trench systems of WW1.

There was no way the lightly armed cavalry units could capture these positions so TFA began screening patrols in front of the German positions. There were no roads running parallel to the German line so TFA formed about 350 men into dismounted patrols. They soon found their light carbines and submachine guns were no good for this sort of terrain and requested that M1 Garands be sent down to provide better range and firepower. Requests for more infantry were refused because all available men were involved with attacking Brest.

When reconnaissance detected a German position air strikes were called in. On 6 Sept. a limited attack was made, but it only managed to force the Germans to withdraw from a few of their outposts. At first no one thought the Germans had enough strength to mount an attack against TFA. However, French civilians reported that at night the Germans were shifting troops over from Brest. General Earnest began to worry about a possible German attack penetrating his thin line and moving north into the rear of the VIIIth Corps.

TFA continued to patrol the German lines, keeping a careful eye on them. Part of their job was to prevent the Germans from finding out just how few Americans were on the Crozon. The German positions were routinely struck by fighter-bombers and shelled by tank destroyers. On 12 Sept. Earnest told his men, "*We are sitting on a keg of dynamite here. This situation is just like a bottle of champagne.*

If we shake it too much, the cork will pop out. And we haven't the troops to hold them." Finally, on 13 Sept. the 8th Infantry Division began arriving with enough manpower to keep the Germans sealed in.

On the night of 13 Sept. the 2/28th Infantry arrived to form a reserve in case the Germans decided to attack. They were quickly followed by the remainder of the 8th Infantry Division. TFA was then assigned the mission of maintaining contact between the two infantry regiments which would attack down the Crozon, the 28th on the right and 121st on the left.

The 8th Division at Crozon

The next attack on the Crozon was focused on the two main ridges that run down the peninsula. A small stream runs between them. The 28th Infantry was assigned the north ridge and the 121st was given the southern one. Preliminary softening up of the German defenses was done by a bombardment from the 34th Artillery Brigade, assisted by the 174th Artillery Group on the Daoulas Peninsula. The Germans were able to observe some of the American artillery moving onto the Crozon and shelled their positions heavier than at any other time in Brittany. Clearly the Germans realized this was the time to use up all their available ammunition.

The 3/28th began the northern assault moving towards the Lanvéoc Airfield. At 0800 hrs. on 15 Sept. the 3rd Bn. jumped off. This followed a heavy German artillery barrage on the American assembly areas. 1/28th took 43 casualties before even moving from their assembly area. By midmorning the Americans were just in front of the German defenses at Saint-Efflez. Extremely strong German defenses pinned them down with extremely high casualties among officers and NCOs.

The next day, 16 Sept, 1/28th was committed to the right flank along the sea. They drove off a strong counterattack originating from the airfield about midnight. L/28th, having taken massive casualties, was moved to the battalion reserve. A group of German soldiers had dug into the sides of a hedgerow and let the initial American advance pass by. L/28th, well behind the main lines, found itself temporarily cut off when these Germans suddenly appeared behind them. The Germans were eliminated with the help of fire from the 45th Artillery Bn. This was one of the few times an artillery unit was ordered to fire at a target inside their own lines.

Pfc. Jacob Reif, a German speaking rifleman from A/28th, was pressed into service as a translator to help search some German POWs. On a German captain he discovered what appeared to be a recent field order. Although he was ordered to move back up to the lines, Reif refused until he could get the paperwork to an intelligence officer. There it was discovered the field order listed every major German position on the Crozon. This information allowed American artillery to smash every major German artillery unit, strongpoint, and supply position in the area.

On 17 Sept. 1&3/28th attacked again and finally took Lanvéoc Airfield. That night the 8th Recon Troop was sent up to reinforce

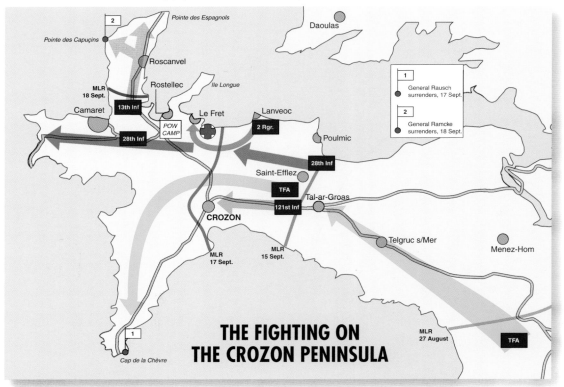

THE FIGHTING ON THE CROZON PENINSULA

them at Hill 73, and they all dug in for the night. On the morning of 18 Sept it was clear the German lines had been broken. Following close behind the 28th Infantry was the 13th Infantry Regiment, ready to take over and make the final assault at the defenses on the northern tip of the peninsula.

Back on the southern ridge, the 121st had also attacked on 15 Sept. They went up against heavy mortar and artillery fire and minefields. The advance was slow, but hearing from POWs that many Germans wanted to surrender G/121st sent an interpreter and two German POWs forward. The defending Germans refused to give up unless they were under fire, so Lt. Chauncey E. Barney rapidly fired his carbine into the air and the 43 Germans put their hands up. The rest of Lt. Barney's company swiftly moved into the vacated positions and caught the remaining Germans unaware. Thus 2/121st was able to push forward in advance of the rest of the regiment. Lt. Paul Boesch of H/121st found a map of the German defenses, which allowed his battalion to move against a lesser defended section of the line. Later in the day the 2/121st was able to enter Tal-ar-Groas. That night the American lines were heavily shelled by German artillery and light 20mm antiaircraft guns.

On the morning of 16 Sept. the southern attack resumed. 1/121st again ran into heavy resistance and made little progress. Not until late in the day was the area around Tal-ar Groas cleared, when a pillbox to the rear of the town was finally captured. This broke the main German defensive line on the Crozon and the Americans began to move forward. All the officers in E/121st became casualties, but the going became easier as more German noncombatants were captured. In the 121st sector two battalions were ordered to press ahead while the 3/121st moved behind to clean up any bypassed pockets of resistance. At 1700 hrs. the town of Crozon was captured and a small fortress nearby surrendered a few hours later.

Now the 8th Division moved the rested 13th Infantry up to capture the final positions. Stretching across a narrow section of the peninsula was a thick stone wall and a moat filled with water. The emplacement was heavily defended with barbed wire and minefields. The entrance through the wall had been bricked up. The position looked so impregnable that plans were made for the Rangers to conduct an amphibious assault around it.

General Ramcke had personally made an inspection of the Crozon defenses on that last day. He had ventured out of his bunker accompanied by his runner, Feldwebel Engler. There he had been attacked by fighter-bombers. Seeing the German ammunition

This sailor has been turned into an ammo bearer for a machine gun team in one of the many composite groups of army, navy and air Force personnel defending the city. No field gray uniforms were available for most of the sailors trapped in the city, so he wears the standard navy blue jacket with white herringbone twill work trousers. He has added a regulation nsavy dishcloth as a neck scarf. His primary job is to keep his machine gun crew supplied with ammunition, but he is armed with a 98K rifle and a stick grenade for when the Americans move up to his position.
(Reconstruction by Militaria Magazine)

This particular Fallschirmjäger helmet was found in 1984 near the town of Telgruc on the Crozon Peninsula. It is painted in a dark green color and still has the Luftwaffe eagle decal on the left side.

General Joseph Rauch, commander of the 343rd Infantry Division, surrenders to General Earnest of Task Force A. These color photographs were taken by Dr. Bill Parker during the surrender at Cap de la Chèvre. General Rauch and his staff are seen on the left, while General Earnest is clearly visible in his helmet with the single star of a brigadier general.
(Courtesy Bill Parker)

supply was running low and realizing the situation was hopeless, Ramcke returned to his bunker. He had prevented the capture of Brest as long as possible, but with no hope of evacuation he had no reason to continue the fight any longer. He ordered his men to destroy the code books and he began the surrender negotiations.

With 14 battalions of artillery in direct support, the 13th attacked the wall on the morning of 19 Sept. The infantry followed the massive barrage very closely and were able to scale the wall before the Germans had time to come out of their shelters. This appeared to be the end for the German garrison. Under a flag of truce Ramcke's adjutant delivered the following message to the Americans:

"To whom it may concern: I hereby request an immediate cease-fire through the bearer of this letter, 2nd Lt. Karl Wahl, accompanied by his interpreter, Sonderführer Dr. Gutkess, for this area. Cease-fire must include air attacks as well. Everybody concerned is requested to give my two parlementaries safe conduct and lead them to the competent American CO. They are, according to international agreements, to be given the opportunity to return to my GHQ. I am ready to receive and request the visit of an authorized American field officer representing Major General Troy H. Middleton, Commanding VIIIth Corps, U.S. Army."
Ramcke
General der Fallschirmtruppe und
Kommandant der Festung Brest,
Kommandeur der 2. Fallschirmjäger-Div

At 1700 hrs. on 19 Sept. 1st Lt. James M. Dunham, a platoon leader from I/13th Infantry, was shown where Ramcke's command post was. It was in a bunker 75 feet underground, part of a coastal artillery position at the Pointe des Capuçins. Dunham ventured down with a

few of his men to verify it was the correct location. According to the official records, later on at 1830 hrs. a second party consisting of Brigadier General Canham, (Assistant Division Commander), Colonel Robert A. Griffin (13th Infantry Commander), Lt. Colonel Earl L. Lerette (3/13th Commander), and Lt. Dunham was led down into the command bunker.

It has long been claimed that General Ramcke said to General Canham, "*I am to surrender to you. Let me see your credentials.*" To which Canham is reported to have gestured to some American riflemen nearby and replied, " *These are my credentials.*" This phrase became the motto of the 8th Infantry Division and a well known tale in the American Army.

Research by Greg Canellis, the son of a 13th Infantryman, indicates that soldiers present at the meeting recall such an exchange, but recall it was actually Lt. Dunham, and not Canham, who first uttered the famous quote. Canellis was able to confirm this with a statement from Lt. Johnie Hendrix of Company M, the only other officer present at the initial meeting. Hendrix was a heavy weapons company officer supporting Dunham's attack. It makes more sense for Ramcke to have questioned surrendering to a combat worn lieutenant than a one-star general. However, it may also be possible that similar statements were made by both men. Members of the Canham family recall that the general maintained it was he who spoke the famous words.

In attempting to wrestle facts from history there are times like these where a definitive answer will probably never be known. After more than 50 years memories have faded and most of the participants are no longer with us. In many respects it does not really matter who said what, but that the Germans had finally given up. 873 German POWs were taken on the northern tip of the Crozon

This group of FFI soldiers, on what appears to be a captured German wagon, was photographed on the Crozon Peninsula. The driver of the wagon might be an American as he wears U.S. fatigues and leggings, except for the fact that he is armed with a captured German Mauser.
(National Archives)

After the fighting had ended, 8th Division troops take a break on a Crozon beach. Just in front of the jeep is Ken Walb of 2/28th. Anti-invasion beach obstacles, constructed by the Germans, are still in position. Brittany was one of the locations the Germans thought the Allies might choose to invade France.

(Courtesy Frank Orville Gray)

and the rest of the German defenses on the Crozon began to crumble. Ramcke was taken prisoner along with Lt. Col. Moller, Capt. Dr. Hooven, Capt. Schmidt, a naval radio operator, and few orderlies.

He was brought to General Middleton's headquarters and, after eating breakfast with Middleton, was paraded before a group of press photographers. There he explained to Middleton that he had been promoted to General der Fallschirmtruppe during the siege. Gesturing to the photographers he said he felt like a film star.

Middleton replied that posing for the cameras was little enough to ask of Ramcke seeing as how he had finished his military duties. Middleton then went on to comment that his own military work, however, was not yet done. Ramcke then questioned Middleton what else he had done in the military.

Middleton replied that besides capturing Brest he had served for 34 years in the U.S. Army. To which Ramcke responded that he had him beat - he had served for 39 1/2 years! General Ramcke was then

evacuated to England as a VIP prisoner and eventually sent to a POW camp in the United States.

The Final Pockets of Resistance

The 2nd Ranger Bn. had been brought to the Crozon on 17 Sept. At that time they had been ordered to move forward along the northern coast and capture the area around Le Fret. Extreme caution had to be exercised on that operation as Le Fret was the hospital area and no artillery could be used for fear of hitting the patients (including some American POWs). After securing Le Fret, the Rangers were going to be used to capture any of the coastal strongpoints on the Crozon that refused to surrender. Plans were made for using rubber rafts in amphibious assault against them if need be, but the German garrisons quietly gave up.

Once the main German lines on the Crozon had broken, Task Force A was ordered to clear the southern section of the peninsula. This

included the last bastion of the German 343rd Infantry Division on Cap de la Chèvre. Assisted by the 83rd Armored FA Bn., two companies of the 35th Engineers, and a company of tank destroyers, the 15th Cavalry Group rapidly penetrated to the southern tip of the cape. Seeing their position was hopeless, the staff of the 343rd German Infantry Division made contact with the Americans and prepared to surrender. At 1800 hrs. a formal ceremony was held for the 343rd Division commander, General Joseph Rauch, to surrender to General Earnest. There was some scattered resistance as cut off German positions attempted to hold out, but for the most part the fighting was

over on the Crozon. The 121st Infantry was given the task of clearing these positions, which often were unaware of Ramcke's surrender.

With the Crozon Peninsula under control of the Americans, TFA was sent south to clear one final pocket of resistance on the Douarnenez Peninsula. Roughly 250 German marines were holding positions on this smaller peninsula. They had been ordered to evacuate that position at the beginning of September, but had been unable to find the boats sent for them. Moving onto the Douarnenez, the men of TFA at first saw no evidence of German defenders. Then a few Germans

Top.
**General Ramcke is led out of the VIIIth Corps HQ
to a waiting vehicle. His aide, seen a step behind
and to the right of the general, accompanies him.
The large number of MPs in the background
are to prevent a possible last minute rescue attempt
by some of Ramcke's men.**
(National Archives)

Above left.
**The first stop for General Ramcke after his surrender
was this photo taken with General Canham (far right)
of the 8th Infantry Division. The identity of the other
Americans remains unknown, although the master sergeant
at far left is probably an interpreter.**
(National Archives)

Above right.
**Major General Bernhard Ramcke wears his Knight's Cross
(earned at Crete), with Oak Leaves (North Africa).
Missing are the Swords and Diamonds awarded to him
via radio during the siege of Brest. The actual decorations
would be presented to him in a British POW camp
by a member of the Swiss Red Cross. Ramcke was promoted
to General der Falschirmtruppen (three-star general)
during his defense of Brest.**
(National Archives)

Right.
**General Canham (with glasses) then brought Ramcke
to the 8th Infantry Division HQ to meet
General Donald Stroh. Ramcke's dog was the subject
of much discussion among the news reporters.
The dog's name and ultimate fate remain unknown.**
(National Archives)

The last organized resistance in the Brest area was a small German naval garrison at Audierne, on the Douarnenez Peninsula just to the south of the Crozon. Here the troops of the Lezongar strongpoint surrendered on 29 September 1944. The German POWs wear the dark colored navy uniforms instead of army field gray.
(National Archives)

wandered into the column and told them that the rest of their comrades in the area were ready to surrender. Major Johnson from TFA met with the German commander to arrange the surrender. On 19 Sept. the Germans, for some reason, refused Earnest's offer to take them prisoner. General Earnest told them they had one last chance. He said that they must surrender by 0800 hrs. the next morning, 20 Sept., or his men would move in and destroy them.

The next morning a problem arose when the local FFI unit refused to cease firing on the German positions. This prevented the Germans from surrendering and forced TFA to take action. That afternoon they started working their way forward. When the Germans realized it was not the Americans who were firing at them, but the FFI, they began to give up.

Much to the Americans' great frustration the FFI continued to fire, sometimes shooting at the Americans by accident. When the Germans found out they could surrender to the Americans, and not be turned over to the FFI, they put down their arms. Task Force A, one of the first units assigned to fight in Brittany, was finally dissolved on 22 Sept. 1944. The components of the task force were then scattered throughout the army.

The battle for Brest was over.

Above
The address of Brigadier General Earnest on the Crozon Peninsula for the dissolution of Task Force A was heavily attended by the men who had served under him. Many of the elements of his command had never trained together before being sent on this mission along the north Brittany coast, far into enemy territory.
(National Archives)

Right.
Ambulances line up at the 107th Evacuation Hospital to pick up German casualties captured on the Crozon. Veterans of the 107th confirm that they did try to provide the same care and treatment to Germans as they did for Americans. This became difficult when large numbers of wounded were brought in, but the hospital staff did everything they could to care for all patients (even civilian).
(Courtesy Allen Walker)

THE FIGHTING IS OVER

Chapter 15

Top.
The return of the city by the U.S. Army to the citizens of Brest on 20 Sept. 1944. The ceremony was held at the Place Anatole France where Brest had been handed over to the Germans four years before. A few British soldiers can be seen in this photo. They are probably members of the port reconstruction unit sent to evaluate the condition of the Brest port facilities.
(National Archives)

Right.
Major general Troy Middleton shakes hands with Jules Lullien, Mayor of Brest. During the ceremony Middleton remarked on his two previous visits to Brest: once headed to fight in WW1, and the second headed home in 1919.
There are few civilians present, as they were prevented from entering the city until it was deemed safe by the military authorities.
(National Archives)

After the fighting had ended and the city was cleared of Germans, the combat troops were moved out for a brief rest. Rear echelon units moved into Brest to examine the dockyards and other facilities. Although placed at roughly 10,000 Americans killed or wounded, accurate casualty rates for the Brittany campaign are hard to determine. The campaign spanned such a large area, period of time, and both the Third and Ninth Armies. 38,000 German POWs were taken (of which 20,000 were combat troops), but Lorient and Saint-Nazaire would stay under German control until the end of the war. The Americans decided that the cost of capturing them was just too great, possibly due to the shortage of supplies and transportation that lasted well into 1945.

General Middleton officially handed the city back to the French mayor Jules Lullien on 20 Sept. 1944. During the ceremony Middleton commented on his time spent in Brest in WW1. There was not much of a city to hand back. The area inside the old city wall had been pulverized by the air and artillery bombardments. Almost every building was either gutted or severely damaged. The wharves, cranes, and dry docks were wrecked. Bridges had been demolished and used to block the Penfeld River. Ships had been scuttled in the harbor and the breakwaters ruined. The port rehabilitation units did a quick survey and decided that, because Brest was so distant from the front lines, their efforts would be better spent working on port facilities further to the east. It can only be assumed that had the Americans

wanted to, they could have rehabilitated the port facilities to some extent, as they had done at other cities.

The Americans had learned a great deal at Brest. They had tried out some experimental equipment with little fear of it being captured

by the Germans. They began to develop tactics and techniques for the assault of fortifications and cities, which they would need for the coming fight in Germany. They had also captured prodigious quantities of German materials for evaluation, including material related to the on-going German submarine program.

The main question asked whenever the Brittany campaign is mentioned is - was this fight really necessary? The popular feeling is that it was waste of time, effort, and manpower. This is generally decided without much thought or understanding of the facts. The Brittany campaign contained so many different aspects it would be impossible to try and second-guess the outcome. When questioning why choices were made one must always keep in mind that the Allied military leaders did not have all the information we have 50 years after the fact. They did not know the 319th Division would be left on the Channel Islands. They did not know if any German torpedo or U-boats were operating out of Brest. They did not know if a large contingent of noncombatant Germans would suddenly surrender and allow the city to fall, or if the die-hard paratroopers would hold out to the last man.

General Bradley is most often quoted on the subject when he says in his memoirs that Brest had to be taken because of General Ramcke's paratroopers. Bradley states that, "*Had Ramcke been ignored I have no doubt that he would have caused us no end of trouble. A limited offensive in Brittany was preferable to a long, vulnerable, possibly troublesome, defensive seal.*"

This statement is probably true. Ramcke's history of slipping back into German lines in Africa shows he did not give up easily. That his men raided outside Brest in August, most notably the Lepkowski raid, shows that his men were not only willing, but able to venture outside the city to continue the fight. Scattered in the records are indications that there were a number of raids made out of the city during August. The Americans had trained their own paratroopers to operate independently, and in small groups, to cause trouble behind enemy lines. This was probably what the Allied command expected of the German paratroopers. If even a small group of paratroops ventured out of the city, or out of Brittany (depending upon how they were sealed off), they could create a great deal of havoc with the vital supplies. In one incident in July 1944 a fire in the ammunition stockpiles in Normandy destroyed 1,500 tons of material before it could be stopped. It burned for four hours and was stopped just before it reached a stockpile of TNT. Although this fire was probably accidental, it shows what a determined saboteur might accomplish.

The Germans had been in France for years. They knew the terrain, as well as which Frenchmen would be willing to help them. Had Ramcke been left at Brest his men could have served as essentially a commando unit based in the Allied rear area, operating with the support of the German Navy on the Channel Islands. Had such a force struck during the Ardennes offensive they could have disrupted the main flow of supplies to the front.

General Patton, however, claims that Bradley told him that the real reason for attacking Brest was only to show that the Americans could finish anything they started. Had the Americans given up the fight they would certainly have suffered from some loss of morale. Yet this did not stop them from deciding that cities like Lorient or Saint-Nazaire should be surrounded, but not attacked. This is too glib an answer and one that does not give Bradley enough credit. American manpower, equipment, and supplies were in short enough supply in 1944. Bradley was too smart to throw them away on morale, not when he could have used them elsewhere.

Some historians have argued that the supplies and men used at Brest could have been better utilized on the main front. Possibly,

Above.
One of the large dry docks which made Brest a valuable port for the German Navy. A number of destroyed vehicles are scattered about the area, victims of either the aerial bombardment or the extensive artillery shelling. Across the Penfeld River is the shattered remains of the city of Brest.
(National Archives)

although the total amount of supplies used at Brest was not really enough to have made much of a difference. Some of the troops would have had to stay in the Brittany area anyway to guard Ramcke's men. If the rest were sent to the east their supply trucks would have added to the already congested roads, and they may well have been the straw that broke the quartermaster's back. General Lee stated at the time that he could not support one more armored division moving to the front. The supply trucks then would have to travel further to reach the units, thus consuming more gasoline. This would have meant that more space would have to be used to ship gasoline and less of something else, such as ammunition, would reach the front.

The supply roads leading to Brittany were different than those leading to the main bulk of the Allied Armies. The smaller ports in Brittany were used to bring in a modest amount of supplies that otherwise would not have landed in France. Using the Brittany railway - captured nearly intact due to the FFI, OSS, and SAS - to move material to Brest did not detract from moving supplies to the east. After the battle 11,000 tons of unused artillery ammunition were shipped east on the railways. This shows that, during a period of time when truck convoys were frantically trying to supply the rest of the Army on congested roads, the railways from Brittany were operating. Therefore, the distance of the Brittany ports was not a major factor if taking the railways into account.

That the assault on Brest took as long as it did was partially due to the initial shortage of artillery ammunition. Had Middleton been given the amount of ammunition requested he would not have delayed the attacks as long as he did. The delay, while adequate ammunition stocks were obtained, resulted in a steady stream of casualties by the daily attrition that always takes place when two armies are opposite

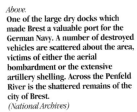

Left.
The truck on the left bears the markings of the 44th Engineer Battalion. Many of the walls remaining after the fighting passed were pulled down by the engineers so they would not collapse upon passers-by. Some American engineers were injured, and even killed, trying to make the streets safe for the return of the civilian population.
(National Archives)

lowing up on the Quiberon Bay plans. Had Quiberon been cleared of Germans it could have been used as a supply landing point, even without construction of an artificial harbor. Had the actual logistical needs of the Allies been followed more closely, knocking out the coastal guns at Brest could have been given a higher priority, and components of the artificial harbor towed to Quiberon. With that additional source of supply Eisenhower would have been able to pursue his "broad front" strategy (attacking all along the front, not just in the north).

As late as 13 Sept., when the Americans were at the edge of Brest, Eisenhower had said that no one knew for certain when, or if, the Channel ports would be taken and that he felt he still needed Brest to receive troops and equipment shipped from the states. He hoped it would not be needed, but he wanted the additional port as a back up, just in case. This is a curious statement to make, when it had been decided long before the invasion that Brest would never serve as a major port. It is even more odd when you consider that Eisenhower's own planners had already decided, on 3 Sept., to abandon the plans for Quiberon Bay, because they erroneously assumed the Channel ports would soon be in operation.

In truth, Brest should be considered a German victory. Ramcke held out for much longer than expected and in doing so caused the Allies to abandon their carefully thought out logistical plans. If there had been a fast boat available to evacuate him from the Crozon, chances are he would have returned to Germany as a major hero. The flip side for the Germans is that had they evacuated Brittany promptly, there would have been more men and equipment available to use in the defense of the German borders.

Many aspects of the fight for Brittany and Brest will always remain controversial. The hypothetical questions of "what if" can never be answered for certain. Historians will always have their favorite generals, and tend to see only the facts that put their favorites in the best light. What is certain, however, was that the fighting in Brittany was according to one participant, "damn bloody hard." It is important to remember that the soldiers on both sides participated in combat that rivaled what went on in the rest of the ETO.

each other. The logistical failure to provide the necessary supplies for the VIIIth Corps resulted in a longer battle, with more casualties, than necessary.

It is too easy to say in hindsight that attacking Brest was an error. Likewise, one should not conclude that the Brest campaign was a vital component of the war in Europe. It was, however, probably the right thing to do at the time - given all the information available to the commanders in the field. The error that did occur was not fol-

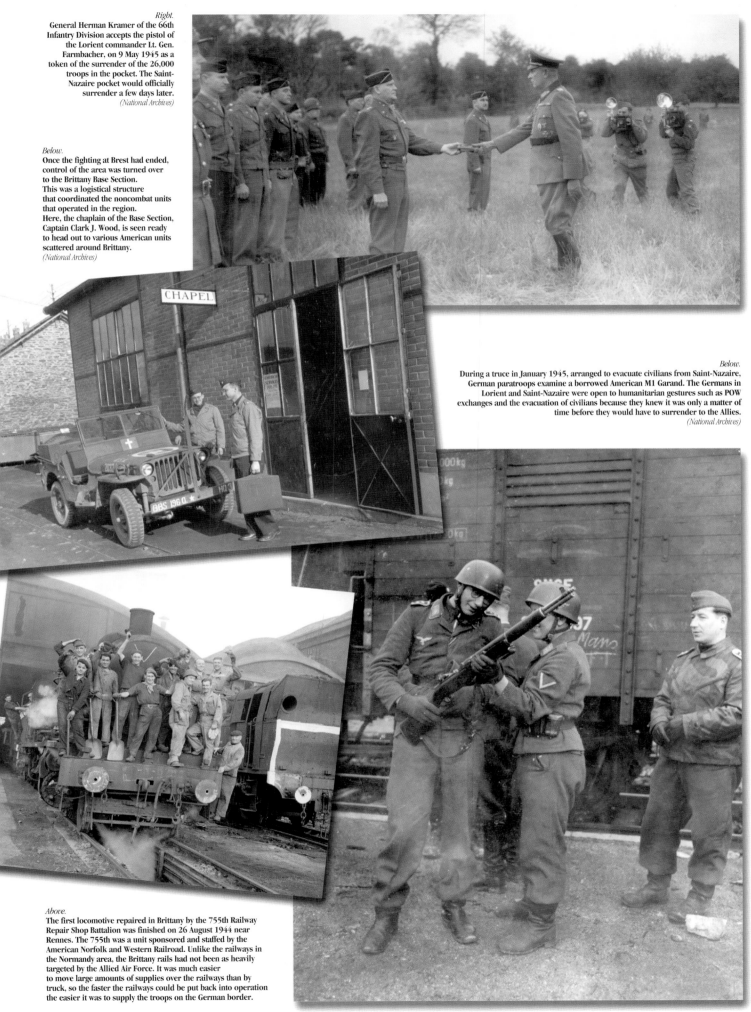

Right.
General Herman Kramer of the 66th Infantry Division accepts the pistol of the Lorient commander Lt. Gen. Farmbacher, on 9 May 1945 as a token of the surrender of the 26,000 troops in the pocket. The Saint-Nazaire pocket would officially surrender a few days later.
(National Archives)

Below.
Once the fighting at Brest had ended, control of the area was turned over to the Brittany Base Section.
This was a logistical structure that coordinated the noncombat units that operated in the region.
Here, the chaplain of the Base Section, Captain Clark J. Wood, is seen ready to head out to various American units scattered around Brittany.
(National Archives)

Below.
During a truce in January 1945, arranged to evacuate civilians from Saint-Nazaire, German paratroops examine a borrowed American M1 Garand. The Germans in Lorient and Saint-Nazaire were open to humanitarian gestures such as POW exchanges and the evacuation of civilians because they knew it was only a matter of time before they would have to surrender to the Allies.
(National Archives)

Above.
The first locomotive repaired in Brittany by the 755th Railway Repair Shop Battalion was finished on 26 August 1944 near Rennes. The 755th was a unit sponsored and staffed by the American Norfolk and Western Railroad. Unlike the railways in the Normandy area, the Brittany rails had not been as heavily targeted by the Allied Air Force. It was much easier to move large amounts of supplies over the railways than by truck, so the faster the railways could be put back into operation the easier it was to supply the troops on the German border.

During a visit to Brittany 40 years later, former Lt. John O. Gawne is shown with his son, the author.
They stand in front of the field on the Crozon Peninsula where Lt. Gawne was wounded on 15 September 1944
while commanding Company L, 28th Infantry Regiment.

ACKNOWLEDGEMENTS

This book was researched over the course of many years. I've talked to so many people it was impossible to keep track of everyone.
This short list mentions some of the more helpful individuals, but is by no means complete.
I am indebted to everyone that took the time to answer my sometimes unanswerable questions.

VETERANS

Irving Altman, 107th Evac. Hospital
Lew Atkinson, 56th FA Bn.
Ira Bathurst, 28th Inf. Regt.
Alvin Berg, 644th TD Bn.
Nels Bloch, 687th FA Bn.
Norvall Cummings, 35th Eng. C. Bn.
Charles Curley, 38th Inf. Regt.
Bob Dwan, 15th Cav.
Mike Eliasof, 28th Inf. Regt.
Bob Edlin, 2nd Rangers
William Ford, 107th Evac. Hospital
Bill Given, 6th Arm. Div. HQ
Bill Legard, 13th Inf. Regt.
Horace Lennon, 25th Arm. Eng. Bn.
Jim Love, 38th Inf. Regt.
George Martin, 603rd Engineer Camouflage Bn.
John McBurney, 13th Inf. Regt.

Dan McGuirl, 168th Eng. C. Bn.
Jim Moncrief, 6th Arm. Div.
Joe Newcomb, 56th FA Bn.
Oscar Olson, 28th Inf. Regt.
Dr. William Parker, Task Force A
Arthur Plaut, 115th Inf. Regt.
Ekkehard Priller, 2 F.J. Div.
John Raaen, 5th Ranger Bn.
Brad Rice, 45th FA Bn.
Bob Riding, 28th Inf. Regt.
Don Van Roosen, 115th Inf. Regt.
Rick Rosania, 511th Eng. Co.
Russ Ruch, 159 Eng. C. Bn.
Cliff Simenson, 23rd Special Troops
Angus MacLean Thuermer, U.S. Navy
Charles Tisdale, 28th Inf. Regt.
Bruno Stadnicki, 557th FA Bn. (SP)
Paul Warp, 68th Tank Bn.

Allen Walker, 107th Evac. Hospital
John Walker, 23rd Special Troops
Bill Walker, 644th TD Bn.
John Watts, 513th Eng. (Light Pontoon) Co.
Lloyd Wideman, 28th Inf. Regt.
Jack Wilhm, 28th Inf. Regt.
Henry Wilkins, 28th Inf. Regt.
Jim Wooley, 8th Div. Arty.

I was also assisted by many families
of Brittany veterans. Special thanks to the families
of General Troy Middleton,
General Hermann Ramcke,
and General Donald Stroh. Others include
Eric Olson and family, Greg Canellis,
Dave Canham, John Chapla,
Frank Tompkins, Bruce Frederick, Jackie Koon,
and the Orville Gray Family

I am deeply indebted to Yannick Creac'h who was my eyes and ears on the battlefield itself. Also assisting were Paul Gaujac, Benoît Senne, Eric Pilon, Nicolas Guiffant, Jean-Yves Nasse, Alain Leberre, Bernard Cabioch, Steve West, Lawrence Patterson, Erich Craciun, Rudolf Muller; not to mention Philippe Charbonnier and the entire staff of *Histoire & Collections*, as well as the following French models and collectors: Franck Bachmann, Nicolas Beaujan, Jean-Michel Besson, Vincent Brasart, Bertrand Cornette de Saint-Cyr, Gilles Goria, François Kovats, Thierry Paradis, Claude Peltret, François Philippe, Patrice Roger, Franck Viltart and Benoît Weiss. Special thanks to my wife Deirdre for her infinite patience and assistance.

The majority of information in this book comes from unit records held in the American National Archives, as well as interviews with the above-mentioned veterans.
"These are my credentials" information in chapter 14 taken from a letter written by Johnnie Hendrix to Greg Canellis dated 2 July 1999.

Supervision: Philippe Charbonnier.
Lay-out by Jean-Marie Mongin. Maps by Denis Gillé, Magali Masselin and Jean-Marie Mongin.

ISBN: 2-913903-21-5

Publisher's number: 2-913903

© Histoire & Collections 2002

SA au capital de 182 938,82 €

5, avenue de la République
F-75541 Paris Cédex 11 - FRANCE
Telephone: (33-1) 40 21 18 20
Fax: (33-1) 47 00 51 11

This book has been designed, typed, laid out and processed by *Histoire & Collections*, fully on integrated computer equipment

Printed by
KSG-Elkar/KSG-Danona
in May 2002
European Union